Faded dreams

Faded dreams

The politics and economics of race in America

MARTIN CARNOY

CAMBRIDGE
UNIVERSITY PRESS

Published by the Press Syndicate of the University of Cambridge
The Pitt Building, Trumpington Street, Cambridge CB2 1RP
40 West 20th Street, New York, NY 10011-4211, USA
10 Stamford Road, Oakleigh, Melbourne 3166, Australia

First published 1994

Printed in the United States of America

Library of Congress Cataloging-in-Publication Data

Carnoy, Martin.

Faded dreams : the politics and economics of race in America / Martin Carnoy.

p. cm.

Includes index.

ISBN 0-521-47062-5

1. Afro-Americans – Economic conditions. 2. Afro-Americans – Politics and government. 3. United States – Race relations. 4. Racism – United States. I. Title.

E185.8.C365 1994
330.973′089′96073 – dc20 94-6767
CIP

A catalog record for this book is available from the British Library.

ISBN 0-521-47062-5 Hardback

To Jean and Juliet

Contents

Preface

When I was in high school, my father developed the first integrated housing project in New York State. It was in north White Plains, in an area called Hillside Ridge, and I remember it well because I worked as a day laborer on that project in the summer between my junior and senior years. The houses were upper middle class, but the fact that black and white families of any class would buy in the same housing development was a big deal in 1954. My father was an idealist entrepreneur – an immigrant from Nazi-decimated Poland who was scandalized by racial prejudice because he had seen its results in Europe. He used home ownership successfully as a tool to change the racial composition of a north White Plains school and then built the integrated development where I worked. He did not wait for racial integration to be "stylish"; he did what he thought was right, even when it seemed to almost everyone else that he was committing economic suicide.

My experiences in those far-off 1950s were an important part of my writing this difficult book. So my greatest debt of gratitude is to my father, who taught me not only to be scandalized by racial prejudice, but to try to do something about it. I only hope that numbers and reasoning are as effective as homes.

I also owe a great deal to those who, many years later, were so helpful to me in my research for the book. Hugh Daley, a doctoral candidate at Stanford University, did much of the census data processing that forms the foundation of the empirical work. He was also a frequent critic of the data and helped remedy many potential misinterpretations. Hugh and Raul Hinojosa worked with me on an earlier project on Latino inequality the results of which made an important contribution to this study. Frank Bonilla, the dynamic force behind the Inter-University Project at Hunter College, City University of New York, continues to inspire all of us working on ethnic inequality. Two seminars on racial discrimination held at the Institute of Policy Studies in Washington and two seminars hosted by the IUP and the Hispanic Agenda on Capitol Hill were crucial in shaping the study. My colleagues at Stanford who read early versions of my chapters – John Baugh, Nate Gage, Henry M. Levin, Ray McDermott, and Michael Wald – made the resulting manuscript infinitely better, as did others who read and critiqued with kindness – Marcus Raskin, Manuel Castells, and the reviewers for Cambridge, John Donohue III and Michael Reich. Their interest is deeply appreciated. Of course, I owe a special debt to my editor at Cambridge, Scott Parris.

Writing about racial inequality in America is a different project for a white person than for a black. Whites are part and parcel of racial inequality, but we do not feel the results of it in our everyday lives. This is not a question of insensitivity. It is simply that we can walk away from the material and social reality of racial inequality and blacks cannot. Racial inequality for a black writer is a personal experience. Writing about it must, by definition, be a presentation of that experience, even when it is done through the cold filter of empirical data, and even when it means arguing positions with which most blacks do not agree.

For a white writer, such a project is not about the experience of inequality; it is about understanding inequality from a more distant perspective. Most white social scientists who analyze racial inequality do so because it is an important issue and there is great controversy surrounding it. They can use their skills to make a point or support a particular explanation. I have a different objective: I believe that whites have just as great a stake in reducing inequality as blacks, even though the short-run costs for blacks are much higher. Like pollution and stress, racial inequality creates subtle, hidden costs – both physical and economic – that affect almost everyone. As a white person committed to the American dream not just for my children, but for all of our children, I see racial inequality dragging our future down, morally, intellectually, and materially. I do not experience racial inequality directly and I can walk away from its material impact, on me, today. But I cannot walk away from its meaning for our future, especially now that this meaning is taking on a special urgency.

1

Introduction

As someone who came of political age in the 1960s, I never cease to marvel at how great an impact my generation had on technological change and how minimal an effect on our social problems. Given our passions and ideals at the time, I thought things would be very different. Who would have dreamed that we would rise to the challenge of a changing global economy with new technology and new ways to organize business, but not purge our companies' racially biased hiring and promotion policies? That with our intense antiwar and civil rights movements, we would end up building the most technologically sophisticated military machine in history, but fail to bring inner-city black youth into America's mainstream? That we would launch the information revolution, but not undo the inequality between blacks and whites?

This combination of technological success and social failure poses a major question – one that many of us feel compelled to unravel. Why, with my generation's once ardent commitment to building a just nation and our talent for making such significant changes in other aspects of life, were we not able to overcome our racial problem?

For the past half century, the most important symbol of the problem has been *economic* inequality. This is not the only way the race issue manifests itself. Yet our society puts so much emphasis on income and wealth as a gauge of a person's worth that wage discrimination against African-Americans and their disproportionate poverty have been the main measures of their unequal roles in society.

Racial economic inequality is often confused with ethnic diversity. It should not be. Diversity is at least partly a matter of personal choice. It is not unusual or of social concern that young people from different ethnic groups associate with friends from the same group. Nor is it a social problem that as they grow older they may choose to maintain traditional ethnic values that distinguish them from other Americans. But economic inequality is not chosen, at least not by those toward the bottom of the ladder. Systemic inequality – especially wage and income inequality in a nation that places primary value on economic performance – is imposed, either directly or indirectly, by courts and hiring practices that are racially and ethnically biased. Ours is a nation of great diversity. It has used diversity to generate economic power and a social ideal of individual mobility and progress. Yet it is also a nation of racial (and ethnic) inequalities that – far from generating economic power – drain our national energy.

We know now that no matter how optimistic we were in the 1960s, racial inequality will not go away easily. Among whites, the most popular interpretation of that intransigence, fueled by the revival of laissez-faire economic and social policy, is that racial inequality is imbedded in deep-seated differences between blacks and whites. This leads to a politics of dancing around the issue – of explaining it away on broader, race-neutral policies – and avoiding attacking it head-on.

I believe that this interpretation misreads the changes in racial inequality that have occurred and why they have occurred. A generation ago, we as a society *did* achieve large reductions in racial economic inequality. Blacks emerged from the shadows of the rural South and urban ghettos during and after World War II to demand and get better education, better jobs, and more equitable treatment on the job. Many more were included, and to a greater extent, in the American mainstream. Anyone who participated in the civil rights movement knows that changes in inequality were *made* to occur. Today, despite a generation of apparent inertia, black men and women lead many major institutions and are role models for both blacks and whites, not just because they are leaders of black causes, but because they are genuinely admired for their skills and character as men and women who happen to be black. Such people as Marian Wright Edelman, Anita Hill, Magic Johnson, and Colin Powell are *national* figures identified with much more than civil rights. This was not the case a generation ago.

Yet there has also been enormous resistance in businesses, political organizations, and communities to reducing racial inequality. Here we are, fifty years after Gunnar Myrdal's *An American Dilemma* brought racism out of the closet in 1944, and thirty years after the Civil Rights Act was passed in order to end racial discrimination in 1964, and it is still very tough to be black in the United States. Even more frustrating, the economic gains seem to have ended, even receded, for those families that moved up in the past. And an appallingly large group of black Americans remains lodged in the increasing social chaos of urban ghettos.

One of two black children now grows up in poverty, a much higher fraction than twenty years ago. One of two young black males has a criminal record, and half of the total prison population is black. One of two black children is born out of wedlock. Again, that number is up over the past two decades. Residential segregation, though informal, defines neighborhoods by race and ethnic group only slightly less today than in the 1950s and 1960s. As blacks have moved out of cities into the suburbs, segregated housing has moved with them. Almost all black children grow up in such informally segregated neighborhoods, North and South, most with low-quality services and low-quality schools. Many black communities – the poorest half – are worse off today than a generation ago, in both relative and absolute terms. Drug crime and violence are now typical of minority ghettos. The biggest single killer of young minority males is gunshot wounds. That violence still extends to the very justice system allegedly responsible for controlling it: in 1992, an all-white jury in a Los Angeles suburb was capable of acquitting four policemen videotaped beating a helpless black man. And despite escalating violence and worsening economic conditions in inner cities, national and state politics seems to have turned away from minority concerns.

These facts are discouraging for all of us who thought that we had laid the groundwork for a new and better America, and also for our children, who thought they would inherit it. But beyond any political discouragement, we and all Americans are paying a high economic price for our failure (or unwillingness) to do what is necessary to bring black and other marginalized Americans into the mainstream. As business becomes ever more global and competition increases, the negative effects of racial inequality are shackling our economic and social energy just when we need it most.

This does not have to be so. Despite the prevailing wisdom, there is nothing inherent in blacks themselves, in the way people get employed in the new global information economy, or in our national values that would put greater racial equality beyond our intellectual and economic capacity. Although the race problem is complex, there are no insurmountable barriers to solving it and no real shortages of ideas, money, or experience. Many of the actions that government can take to equalize economic opportunities for blacks do not require major federal spending. Others do, but the amount of money needed is small compared with the cost of weapons systems, the subsidies we are willing to give farmers, or the amount our nation spends on prisons every year. Large, rapid gains by blacks and other minorities in the past show what is possible and what future strategies can work.

To understand how to remedy our social problems we have to understand what makes them so difficult to solve. Some people think that if African-Americans tried harder to succeed, they would do better. Some believe that our institutions are profoundly racist and continue to keep blacks down. Others believe that the changing world economy, with its more sophisticated skill requirements, has made it much harder for both blacks and whites who are less educated to do well.

In this book, I examine these explanations for racial inequality and find them seriously flawed. Though each is persuasive in its own way, none is able to show why racial inequality declined in certain periods during the past fifty years but did not change or even increased in others.

The book paints a new picture of why racial inequality changes in America – one that puts politics at center stage. I argue that blacks caught up with whites mainly when government policy makers, usually under political pressure by blacks and backed by an important segment of the white community, pushed for greater economic and social equality. Similarly, the greatest obstacles to black gains in other periods have been government policies. Policy makers usually assumed away the race problem or used it against blacks and whites for political purposes, legitimating existing inequality and often making it worse.

My argument has some unpopular implications: it implies that reducing economic differences between blacks and whites still depends on national politics. This does not mean that government can make blacks and whites ignore each other's skin color, intermarry, or live in the same neighborhood. But government can gradually and systematically eliminate wage and job discrimination, improve the education and living conditions of disadvantaged black children, equalize the treatment of blacks by the police and courts, and develop the inner cities where so many poor blacks are caught in permanent disadvantage.

The other side of this coin is also controversial. I argue that black inequality will not be solved by the free market, as many free-market proponents claim, or by blacks' adopting a different "attitude" and acting just like whites. The fact that government got off employers' backs on the affirmative action issue in the 1980s did not produce greater income equality – far from it. And it doesn't work for blacks to assume white behavior either: for example, wage differences between young black and white male college graduates – who would seem to be very similar in their behavior patterns – may be even higher now than among black and white male high school graduates, where behavioral dissimilarities are greater.

We Americans do not like to hear that equal individual efforts in the marketplace do not produce equal results. We do not like the idea that government – which we tend to mistrust – is needed to set things right. But in this case, the argument is logical: economic possibilities for African-Americans have always been set in the context of politics and government intervention, from the days of slavery to Emancipation to Reconstruction to disenfranchisement at the end of the past century to the civil rights movement to the recent days of white backlash.[1]

So it is in the 1990s. If government does not take the lead or is not willing to respond to policial demands by minorities, blacks – and not just poor blacks – will have a very difficult time catching up.

EXPLAINING RACIAL INEQUALITY

Why can't our technologically dynamic, democratic society sustain the drive to bring African-Americans fully into the fold of its amazing technological and political achievements? The answer to this agonizing question varies enormously. Opinions on race and racial inequality are an integral part of every American's upbringing. Everyone has an explanation for why the economic performance of African-Americans is poorer than that of whites and why blacks tend to be marginalized from mainstream institutions. Race is a widely discussed and highly visible political issue, as it has been throughout U.S. history.[2] The explanations are as charged with emotion and ideology as is the question.

Still, at any historical moment, certain groups of explanations are more important than others. They represent the range of politically "legitimate" views of the world at that particular moment, and each implies a different political solution to the race problem. We are inundated by these views in our daily lives, often without being aware of it.

So it is today. Three dominant "legitimate" explanations define the race issue. They are the ones politicians and the media present to the public. Each has its followers who claim that it is correct. But each tells only a piece of the story, and each has its own ideological bias. Each helps us understand something about why racial inequality prevails, but at the same time keeps us from seeing a larger, more complete picture – one that might help us as a nation develop a sustained process of incorporation and inclusion. I call these three explanations "individual responsibility," "pervasive racism," and "economic restructuring."

Individual responsibility means that individuals have the power to control their own lives and, by their choices, to control their destiny. The individual-responsibility argument lays the blame for racial inequality on blacks who do not respond to economic opportunities and on white liberals who tried in the past to use government intervention to make things better but only made them worse. Those who push the individual-responsibility argument hardest are free-market fundamentalists. But even less rabid fans of the market are drawn to laying responsibility on blacks for their own problems. Among them are a small group who have long believed that blacks are simply genetically inferior.

Individual responsibility has tremendous appeal in a society that has so much faith in the individual and in individual achievement as a source of social mobility. And individual responsibility is a difficult argument to counter when some minorities of color, such as Asian-Americans, have surpassed whites in median family income by taking full advantage of public education.

Those who think pervasive racism is to blame for the lack of black progress in the past twenty years also have a fundamentalist ideology: our national institutions – including politics and the economy – are so steeped in historical racism that they cannot get out from under it. They are on a racially biased "automatic pilot." In the past decade, the argument goes, with greater social tension and ideological shifts in the Supreme Court, pervasive racism has become more legitimate – it has been allowed to seep out of its container – and it will take some profound transformation of America's thinking before racial inequality will again decline.

This argument's appeal is also obvious. For the blacks and other minorities who encounter discrimination directly and consistently throughout their lives, racism is a profound reality, full of humiliation and anger. They see individual-responsibility arguments as theoretical constructs that only rationalize inequality rather than explain it, just as the proponents of individual responsibility see the pervasive-racism argument as a rationale for blacks' failure to take individual responsibility for their own difficulties.

The most recently popularized explanation for the standstill in black progress is that businesses are now producing more sophisticated, high-tech products and services. Since they require highly educated workers, blacks are at an increasing disadvantage. The problem here is not racial inequality, but growing *class* inequalities that result from this economic structural change. Blacks are unable to make progress because they constitute such a large fraction of the less-educated population – the hard to employ in the new high-tech economy. They share their difficulty with others who are not black but who are also less educated and in the same declining job market. The proponents of this explanation argue for more government intervention – yet on the basis of class rather than race, and on the side of human capital investment and a full-employment policy rather than on racially tagged antipoverty programs.

All these explanations are partly correct and persuasive enough to appeal to those who want to believe them. They are coherent, but limited by their particular assumptions about how U.S. institutions have been put together historically. To one degree or another, each can be supported with empirical studies. In statistics-hooked America, numbers flourish like poppies on a California hillside. But each has a major drawback. It doesn't hold up when examined over a longer period of time, with changing historical conditions.

The reason for this fatal flaw is subtle. In their own way – consciously or unconsciously – the proponents of each explanation try to "depoliticize" racial economic inequality. Why do they take political conflict over the race issue out of economic differences? Because in their own way they believe that the market is overwhelmingly powerful in defining inequality, and it is in the market – as a just or unjust institution, depending on the view – that racial inequality can or cannot be changed. Because the proponents of all three explanations understand that politics was important to race relations *in the past,* they need to make their market case by assuming an actual relation between markets and politics that downplays the impact of changes in the politics of race. In doing that, they will greatly reduce the possibility that changing current political conditions could also be a major factor in understanding racial inequality.

In the individual-responsibility argument, the driving force behind economic and social change is the free market. The market is controlled by an "invisible hand" – an unseen, rational, and "perfect" mechanism that rewards motivated individuals (the more productive) and punishes the lazy (the less productive). It is also blind to color, class, and gender.[3]

If inequality changes, it is *necessarily* because productivity-enhancing characteristics that can be acquired by both blacks and whites, such as education and job experience, change. So the individual-responsibility argument attributes all reductions in racial inequality to decisions by blacks, *as individuals,* to do better in school, attend more effective schools, acquire more education, take jobs with more training, or work harder in their jobs. Politics and government action can only interfere with this process – the perfect market cannot be improved upon in terms of allocating workers with the "right" characteristics to the most appropriate jobs. Any government attempt to impose "artificial" (non-market) values – such as affirmative action – on the characteristics of black workers cannot reduce inequality, because whatever inequality exists is rational and justified from the market's point of view. Racial inequality, in this explanation, is *immune* to politics.

Pervasive racism is the mirror image of the individual-responsibility explanation. Instead of depoliticizing racial inequality as individual responsibility does by assuming that it does not exist or is "rational" in market terms, it goes to the other extreme, considering all institutions, including the labor market, racist. Institutional racism is a set of materially based arrangements – the distribution of wealth, residential patterns, language dialects – that are consequential for intergenerational inequality. But as in the individual-responsibility argument, this also makes the market immune to political change, for a very different reason. Here, immunity occurs because market relations *dominate* political relations. Whether consciously or not, society necessarily functions to reinforce and reproduce racial inequality through these materially based arrangements, just as it reinforces and reproduces capitalism and capitalist class relations, and gender inequality.

The economic-restructuring argument rejects institutional racism and free-market explanations, but makes its own attempt to depoliticize race. First, it pushes the politics of race into the past: whatever role racial politics played in U.S. history, it ended with the Civil Rights Act of 1964 and subsequent actions by the Supreme Court and the Equal Employment Opportunity Commission. The only vestige of "historical racism" is a race-based division of labor, with most blacks at the bottom of the occupational and educational ladders. Second, it attempts to depoliticize race by attributing post-1973 changes in racial inequality to the world economic structure's transformation from nationally based industrialism to internationally based postindustrialism – out of the control of politics.

The superimposition of this new global postindustrial structure on the leftovers of past racism translates into racial decline even when racism itself has been purged from the system. The shift from national industrialism to global postindustrialism created a situation where less educated men and women, regardless of race, lost economic value relative to those more educated. This explanation again takes politics out of race – racial inequality is repositioned into the *class* structure of occupational skills and global economic change. The race issue is "above" national politics, which can react only in terms of reducing unemployment and redistributing skills among the social classes as global markets change outside the national government's control.

Despite their shortcomings, these depoliticized explanations are what most Americans, from voters to academics to government policy makers, use to justify the lack of political action on racial inequality. After all, the explanations allow for changes in individual and even government action, but not for political change that makes things better specifically for blacks. They seem so openly geared to turn off the heat we generated in the 1960s around the race issue that we have to wonder why they became so popular and created so much hopelessness across the political spectrum. Where did these explanations come from and how are they sustained intellectually? More important, do they make sense in the face of what we know about historical changes in racial inequality?

POLITICS AND THE CHANGING SHAPE OF INEQUALITY

The answer to both these questions lies in the changing politics of race. Explanations for racial inequality are deeply rooted in the context of their political times and their political philosophy. But this means that, intentionally or not, they usually miss the powerful role of politics. When we look at changes in racial inequality over time, the one variable that seems to have changed as much as any in the past fifty years is the way politics deals with race. The racial inequality of the 1970s was different from the inequality of the 1930s and 1940s mainly because of political changes. Political shifts on race have taken place within institutions and have changed institutions. It is such changes that unify the 1940s with the 1960s and the 1950s with the 1980s. But it is also those changes that make each period unique. Racially depoliticized explanations such as individual responsibility, pervasive racism, and economic restructuring fail to explain this periodicity of change, because they underestimate the role that the politics of race plays in changing economic inequality. These political changes are just as fundamental as markets or individual efforts to understanding racial inequality. Indeed, it is in the interrelationship between politics, markets, and individual responsibility that an understanding of the ups and downs of racial inequality is likely to be found.

Most writing in the 1990s about racial inequality has focused on why economic and social conditions stopped getting better for blacks in the two preceding decades. This book is no different. It looks at the past mainly to explain why gains for blacks ground to a halt in the late 1970s and 1980s. After going through the individual-responsibility, economic-restructuring, and pervasive-racism explanations of the slowdown, I come to a different conclusion. We cannot understand the continuing difficulties of blacks in the labor market without also observing that government in the past two decades has found it politically convenient to let those difficulties continue and even worsen. Politics was crucial in reinforcing the economic and social conditions that were to blame for the stagnation of black progress.

Racial politics helped sell old 1920s policies of holding wages down and raising short-term profits as the solution to very new economic problems – problems set in the context of a high-tech, information- and telecommunications-based global economy. Such antiworker economic policies succeeded, at least in the short run, in making the economy function moderately well, even if for the benefit of the few. But the policies are anachronistic and so is the divide-and-rule politics behind it. They are also extremely costly: they have left a legacy of tremendous social conflict, productivity that is only slowly rising (if at all), and an economic demoralization that may take years to overcome.

One political party has successfully used race as a political tool to gain national and local office. It has manipulated racial divisions to make more palatable to white workers a general antilabor wage policy and subsidies to the rich. The other party has been ambivalent and defensive about resisting economic and social policies that have badly hurt blacks and other low-income groups. Is this because racism among voters has increased, or rather because leadership has found that racial divisions can work for its own political purposes? The race issue has not been swept under the rug, as many claim. On the contrary, it pervaded the political economy of the 1970s and 1980s in a startlingly overt and negative way.

One of the main reasons for the turn that national race politics took was the gradual disintegration of the civil rights coalition. Politics can change the nature of racial inequality, and it does. But the American people, including black Americans, have largely given up on the race issue, because they have given up on politics. And in giving up on politics, they have run away from confronting the crucial role that politics plays in defining how society deals with racial differences.

There is another side to this argument. Black Americans, much more than other groups, including white women, have had their social role defined by national politics. When the Constitution maintained slavery, blacks were economically and politically separated from whites. Civil War and post–Civil War legislation changed the conditions of black participation – again at the behest of national politics. Even in the 1960s, 1970s, and 1980s, national politics set the tone for black progress – or lack of it.

This connection between blacks and politics is not only a case of legal history. When more commercially skilled groups, such as the Jews, Chinese, and Japanese, came to the United States, they were able to develop an economic base within ethnic enclaves. They moved up economically despite discrimination, because they were able to distance themselves somewhat from dominant white economic and political structures. Blacks lacked these commercial skills and had to earn their living by working the land or working for white employers. Their relationship to the land and to their employers depended on politics.

A political explanation for changes in black progress is not a replacement for all other explanations. Rather, it makes otherwise rigid, depoliticized explanations rooted in racism, changing economic structures, and even individual responsibility more dynamic and coherent. A political explanation also suggests more hope for future improvement. How politics frames racial issues and how government policies treat these issues can be changed and changed more quickly than ingrained individual fears about race or long-established business practices. Politics is only partly hidden in the far reaches of the human mind and only partly etched in the stone of the market's so-called profit-maximizing behavior. Even those far reaches of the mind and market "laws" can be confronted and changed. In democratic societies, political practice cannot be rationalized easily in terms of objective laws, such as supply and demand. Politics is shaped by normative rules – how things *should* be, not how they are. Normative rules can, by their very nature, be shifted, and fairly quickly.

THE BOOK AND ITS STRUCTURE

This book tells a story not only about race, but also about the meaning of politics and government in American society. Government in this story is neither the blundering, invasive bureaucracy of the fundamentalist free-marketeers nor the racist arbiter of economic relations in a racist society nor a group of relatively helpless national politicians trying to count the effects of a global economy run by omnipotent multinational corporations. Instead, government is an arena for conflict among competing groups with competing political power and visions for the nation within the context of a complex capitalist economy and socially stratified society. Even if that competition is constrained by vast differences in the groups' economic power, government is inherently different from the economy. Government is influenced by social and political ideals, as well as by social and political corruption and degradation. And when a particular vision falters, politics can begin marching to the tune of a different social view.

The book is divided into two major sections. Chapters 2 through 6 describe the economic changes for blacks and whites over the past half century, from the beginning of World War II and the end of the Great Depression to the Reagan–Bush era (Chapter 2), and examine the three main explanations for those changes. Chapter 3 presents the three explanations–individual responsibility, pervasive racism, and economic restructuring – and the theories of politics underlying them. Chapter 4 examines the case for the individual-responsibility explanation; Chapter 5, the case for the economic-restructuring explanation; and Chapter 6, for the pervasive-racism explanation.

The second part of the book argues the logic of the political argument. This argument is divided into four chapters, corresponding to the four most important ways that politics can affect racial inequality. Chapter 7 analyzes the role of politics in black education; Chapter 8, the role of macroeconomic policies and infrastructure investment in the employment of blacks and their wages; Chapter 9, the influence of legislation and the courts on the relative income of blacks; and Chapter 10, the effect of national ideological leadership on all these government policies. Chapter 11 looks at the chances for black mobility in the 1990s and suggests a strategy for putting it back on the political agenda.

2

The ups and downs of African-American fortunes

Depending how you look at it, African-Americans' glass in the 1990s is half-full or half-empty. On the positive side, African-American life is vastly different from what it was at the end of the Depression in 1940. Blacks' civil rights have been transformed, even if not equalized in practice. Their voting rights have brought them fuller political participation, even if not a full measure of political power. And their economic rights – their access to decent jobs and wages – have also taken a giant step, even if they remain a far cry from equal opportunity. Blacks are included in the economic mainstream today in ways unheard of fifty years ago. They work at much more challenging jobs than those they held then, and they earn much higher incomes, both in absolute terms and compared with those earned by whites.

On the negative side, many blacks still live in poverty, in slums, and face a much greater threat of physical violence than they did back in the 1940s in the rural South or Harlem – a violence that now comes almost entirely from blacks themselves. These conditions are at least partly, and maybe mainly, the outcome of our national development in the past twenty years. Gains in economic and social inclusion for blacks have all but come to an end, and have done so a long way from the equal treatments in schools and workplaces that seemed so achievable a generation ago. If the economic progress that blacks made between 1940 and the mid-1970s had continued into the 1980s and the early years of this decade, our society would be very different today. Instead, lower-income blacks fell even farther into poverty in the 1980s. Those who had attained middle-class status became more separated economically from the black working (and not working) poor. But the black middle class also barely grew in the 1980s. And black families – with one-half headed by doubly-discriminated-against black women – continued to be at a great disadvantage compared with the average white family.

Before going on to an explanation of how and why all this happened – how and why African-Americans were able to do so much better economically and then stopped doing better – we need to know precisely *what* happened. The past half century tells a story of African-Americans' incomes beginning to catch up to whites' and then leveling off far short of equality, leaving many blacks still in poverty and most frozen economically. It is a story of great change and great disillusionment in just fifty years. Parts of two generations of blacks moved up socially – much of one generation into the industrial and service working class and many of their children into the middle class and higher. If both upward movements had continued for another generation, blacks might have been distributed across income groups not much differently than whites. But since both the upward mobility into the industrial working class and the movement into the middle class ended in the 1970s, a large group of unincorporated working-class blacks was suspended in increasing poverty, violence, and social alienation. Another, less publicized "middle-class" group had emerged from poverty in the 1950s and 1960s and had expected its fortunes and those of its children to keep expanding. It was also suspended – not in poverty but still distant from the American dream.

THE GREAT ADVANCE

Almost all the gains for African-Americans came in the thirty years after 1939, during the long New Deal expansion initiated by the beginning of World War II. Between 1939 and the early 1970s, a black male worker pushed his average earnings from 42 to 67 percent of a white male worker's earnings (Figure 2.1).[1] Black women did even better, almost reaching parity with white women by the end of the 1970s (Figure 2.2), despite the fact that black women on average were still more poorly educated than white women.

Yet this long period of black progress was very uneven. Blacks' incomes relative to whites' leveled off for a crucial decade during the Eisenhower 1950s. This was true for both men and women. The slowdown in the 1950s was important for three reasons. First, it signaled the end of very rapid gains in the 1940s – gains that came from a major incorpora-

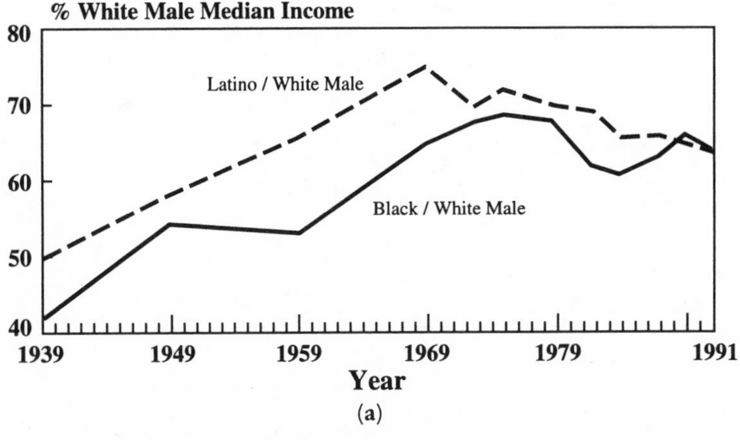

(a)

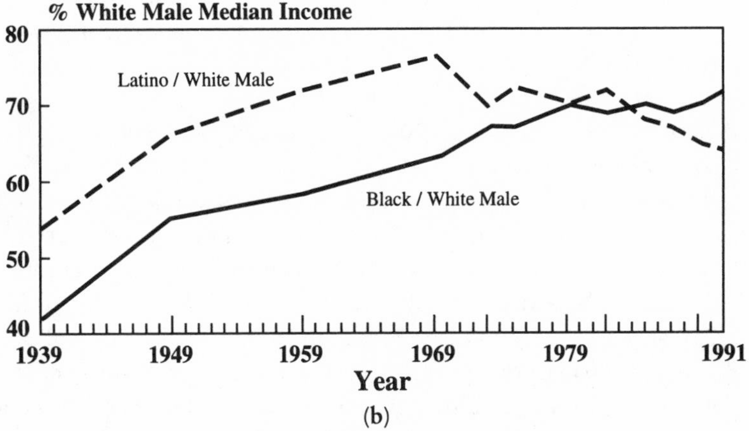

(b)

Figure 2.1. Minority–white male median income ratios, by race and ethnicity, 1939–91, for (a) all income earners and (b) full-time workers. From U.S. Census Bureau, Public Use Sample, 1940, 1950, 1960, 1970, and 1980, and Current Population Survey, March Survey, various years: (a) all-income-earner sample; (b) full-time-worker sample.

tion of blacks into the industrial working class. Second, it represented the politically pregnant pause that preceded the next round of gains in the late 1960s and 1970s – gains that came mainly from black access to white universities and partial incorporation into white-collar professions. Third, it helps us understand why black incomes went up – it tells us that, far from being "evolutionary," blacks' relative economic improvement was concentrated in special political periods: the 1940s and the dozen

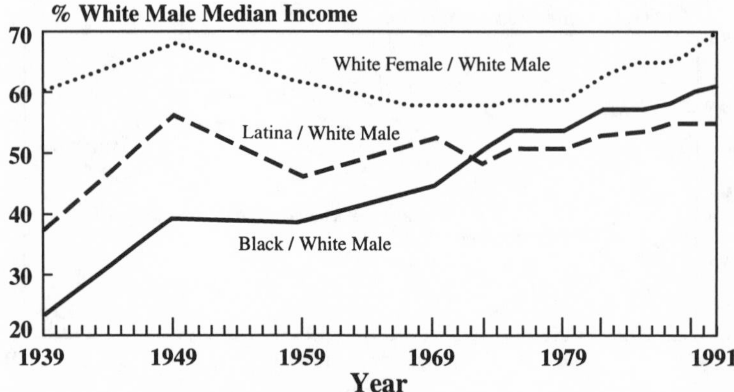

Figure 2.2. Female–white male median income ratios, by race and ethnicity, full-time workers, 1939–91. From U.S. Census Bureau, Public Use Sample, 1940, 1950, 1960, 1970, and 1980, and Current Population Survey, March Survey, various years, full-time-worker sample.

years between the early 1960s and 1975. And once those gains were won, they could be taken back.[2]

The gains made in these two periods reflected a major upgrade in the kinds of work blacks did and the increased wages they got in every kind of work. Black men moved from agricultural to higher-paying, higher-skilled factory jobs and, eventually, office jobs. Black women shifted from domestic service and low-paying factory jobs into retail sales and office work. Blacks also continued to move north and west into the cities, a migration that had begun during World War I. The fact that black men *and* women were getting more pay helped change the position of the black family. Two-parent black families earned 60 percent of what white, two-parent families were making in 1959, a figure that leaped to 80 percent by 1979 – a period of only two decades.

The gains were made in an era when absolute incomes were rising quickly. A black family in 1969 had about three and a half times the purchasing power that it had in 1939. Poverty rates for blacks plummeted, from 55 percent in 1959 (the first year these statistics were kept) to 29 percent in 1974, a short fifteen years later.

By any measure, these were significant advances. As part of a larger movement for minority political and economic rights, they transformed the lives of blacks, especially in the segregated South. In both North and South, they pushed an increasing number of blacks into the middle class

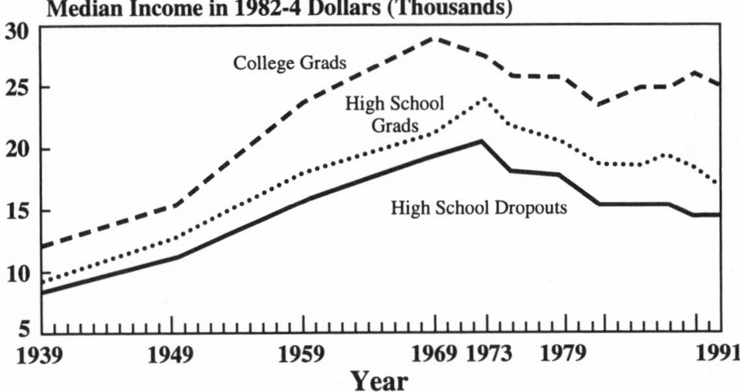

Figure 2.3. Real median income, full-time-employed white males 25 to 34 years old, by educational level, 1939–91. From U.S. Census Bureau, Public Use Sample, 1940, 1950, 1960, 1970, and 1980, and Current Population Survey, March Survey, various years, full-time-worker sample.

for the first time, extending to them white America's idealized consumerist self-image. Today, almost one in three black households earns income above the white family median and participates in the American mainstream, although being in the middle class is not altogether the same for blacks as for whites. Blacks still tend to have to work more hours to earn the same income and have many more demands on their paychecks from low-income relatives.[3] Even so, the past fifty years have brought those higher-income black families and individuals out of economic marginality and into consumer America.

THE GREAT RETRENCHMENT

The uneven but seemingly inexorable drive to higher black incomes was hit hard by two powerful changes after 1975. The first resulted from what happened to U.S. workers as a whole. The "great U-turn," as economists Bennett Harrison and Barry Bluestone call it,[4] ate away at the 60 percent rise in the average worker's real weekly earnings from 1947 to 1973. After 1973, with the onset of increased global competition and economic and political retrenchment, business and government attitudes toward labor hardened. The average white male's real earnings declined in the rest of the 1970s and 1980s (Figure 2.3). This meant that for the typical male-headed family to keep up its purchasing power and consump-

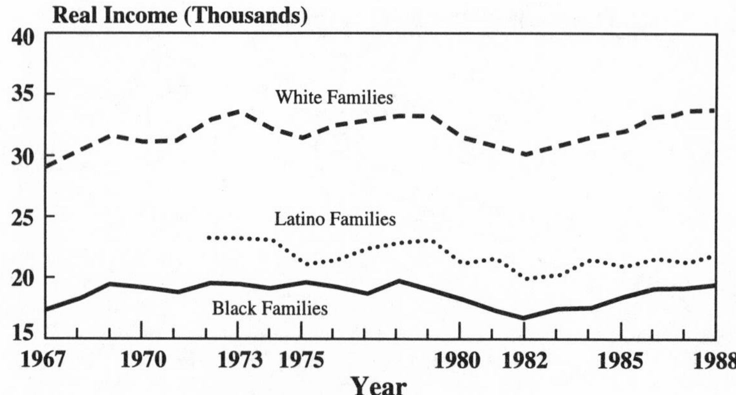

Figure 2.4. Real family income, by race and ethnicity, 1967–88. From U.S. Census Bureau, Current Population Report P-60, no. 166.

tion level, its members had to work more weeks and hours every year, regardless of race or ethnicity. The family accomplished this by having wives and mothers move from part-time to full-time jobs. Women were propelled to work in the 1980s for another reason: women's wages began to rise relative to males'. Even with male median income declining about 8 percent between the early 1970s and the end of the 1980s, rising wages and longer hours for women helped keep median family income fairly constant (Figure 2.4).

The second reversal hit blacks in 1979. Suddenly, they were caught up in the U-turn every bit as much as whites, and more. Black male workers who had full-time jobs stayed more or less "even" with (declining) white incomes after 1973, but the incomes of black men who were less than fully employed fell compared even with declining white incomes in the early 1980s. It was only in the last years of the decade that relative incomes began to catch up again, thanks to the continued economic expansion. Yet black men made no gains compared with whites during the decade. Since black males had already entered the 1980s at a distinct disadvantage, the retrenchment of those ten years made their economic difficulties seem that much more permanent.

What about black women? Could they have picked up the slack of declining male real wages? In part they did. Black women gained relative to white men and in absolute terms. In the 1980s, their gains fell behind those of white women, but the average black two-parent family at least

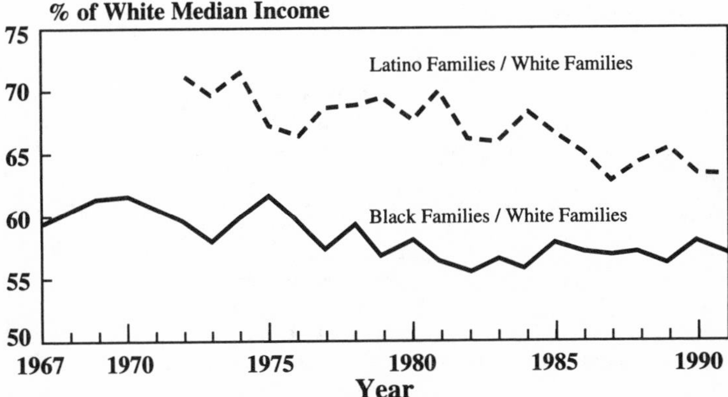

Figure 2.5. Family median income ratios, by race and ethnicity, 1967–91. From U.S. Census Bureau, Current Population Report, *Money Income of Households, 1991.*

did not lose purchasing power. The real problem lay elsewhere. Because black women, like white women, earn so little in absolute terms, when they are raising a family without a husband present they and their children have a one in two chance of being below the poverty line. Even if black women's median real earnings stayed steady after 1973, they also stayed low, at about $15,000 (in 1986 dollars) for those employed full time and lower for the average female-headed household (about $11,000 in 1988). The poverty rate in those female-headed minority families remained at a high 50 percent.

Important as low female incomes are in explaining black poverty, they are only part of the problem for minority family incomes. When white women raise families by themselves, they also suffer high rates of poverty – on average, 30 percent. But the proportion of African-American families headed by women alone has been growing steadily since the 1950s and has reached extraordinarily high levels. Today, almost one out of two black families does not have a husband present, compared with one in six white families, and, for example, one in seven families of Mexican origin.

The higher incidence of single-parent black families plus stagnation in the relative incomes of individual male and female blacks has meant steadily declining black family income relative to whites. Figure 2.5 shows how black (and Latino) families did economically compared with

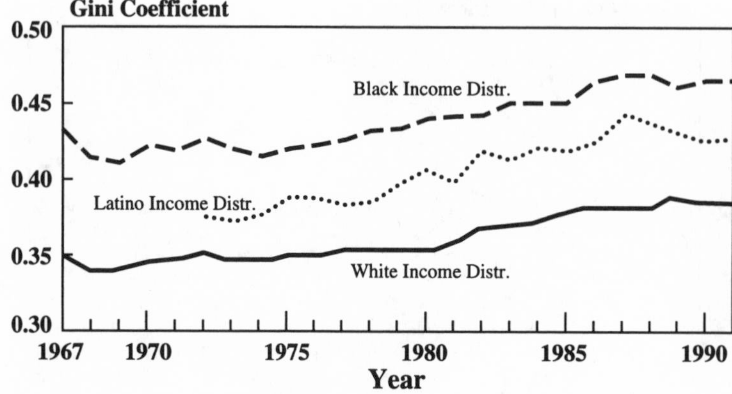

Figure 2.6. Family income distribution, by race and ethnicity, 1967–91. From U.S. Census Bureau, Current Population Report P-60, no. 180.

whites from 1967 to 1991. There was a fall in the ratio from 60 to 57 percent during this period, all during the late 1970s.

Although the black population is not increasing as rapidly as that of Latinos or Asians, the downturn in black incomes poses a growing problem for the nation's future. Blacks are still the largest minority group and are gradually becoming an even larger fraction of the labor force and the young population. Black men and women together increased their share of the labor force slightly, from 9.9 percent in 1980 to 10.6 percent in 1989, but the black share of the population under 15 years of age (the potential labor force) is higher and also rose, from 14.9 percent in 1980 to 15.5 percent in 1989.

ECONOMIC CHANGE AND INCOME DISTRIBUTION

Overall family income distribution did not change much in the United States in the generation after World War II. But the turbulent economics and politics beginning in the mid-1960s transformed the situation, first equalizing incomes and then, beginning in the mid-1970s, distributing them less equally. The most important feature of the new income inequality was that inequality *between* race and ethnic groups changed little. The much larger impact on overall U.S. income inequality came from increasing disparity *within* groups, as measured by the increasing variance in each group's family income (Figure 2.6).[5]

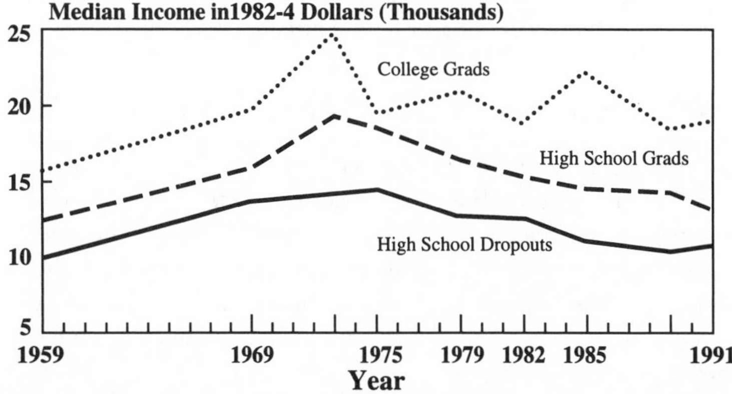

Figure 2.7. Median income, full-time-employed black males 25 to 34 years old, by educational level, 1959–91. From U.S. Census Bureau, Public Use Sample, 1940, 1950, 1960, 1970, and 1980, and Current Population Survey, March Survey, various years, full-time-worker sample.

This happened in two very different stages. During the first stage, beginning in 1973–5, rapid inflation, a changing labor market, demographics, and a restrictive wage policy produced rapidly falling real (adjusted for inflation) male wages, especially for those with lower levels of schooling. The growth in inequality reflects the sharp drop in the incomes of the poorly educated in the late 1970s and early 1980s (as shown in Figure 2.3 for young whites and Figure 2.7 for young blacks). Because of this unusual falling away of the bottom, blacks' and Latinos' incomes – which were distributed less equally to start with – became more dispersed than whites' for both men and women, so minority family incomes also became much more dispersed.

The second stage of increasing inequality took place after 1980. The enormous growth of high incomes in the 1980s, when the top 1 percent saw their incomes rise by more than 70 percent, had a greater impact on overall inequality for white families than for minority families.[6]

The widening disparity between black and white incomes, especially in the 1970s, was accompanied by a severe decline in black male labor force participation. The labor force participation rate among young males (16 to 19 years old) fell for blacks to below the white rate in the early 1960s and has continued downhill ever since. In 1969 there were 7 percentage points' difference between young whites and blacks (50 percent vs. 57 percent), by 1979, 20 points' difference, and in the late 1980s, 15 points' difference, as white participation rates fell again. Very few of these increasing differences were due to school attendance differences.

WHICH HOUSEHOLD INCOMES FELL AND WHICH ROSE?

The fall in black fortunes after the mid-1970s, and especially after 1979, was tied mainly to a decline in the incomes of *low-income* black households, where, almost by definition, part-time work was the rule rather than the exception. The black middle class expanded slightly in the 1980s and their average income continued to increase. They, like their white counterparts, became ever more separated economically and socially from the poor.

"Middle class" is such a general term that most Americans, from fairly low income families to rather wealthy ones, claim to be middle class. In terms of consumption, anyone who owns a house or apartment, two cars, and the typical electronic household goods could be called middle class. A more restrictive definition – the percentage of black households with income higher than the white median household income but who earned less than $100,000 – gives a somewhat more meaningful sense of what happened to the black middle class. In the 1980s, the white median household income in 1989 dollars was about $30,000, before taxes.

The proportion of black households with higher than white median income but less than $100,000 increased rapidly in the 1960s, at a slower pace in the 1970s, and barely rose in the 1980s (Table 2.1). The black middle class, even defined in this restricted way, therefore continued to grow in relative terms during the entire thirty-year period but at an ever slower rate. Since white median income grew steadily until the early 1970s and then stayed essentially constant until 1989, black households were moving up rapidly in absolute income terms – much more rapidly than whites – in the 1960s, continued to move up somewhat relative to the white middle class in the 1970s, and moved up only slightly both relative to the white middle class and in absolute terms in the 1980s.

There is another way to look at what happened to this "upper middle class" of black households. Although their relative numbers hardly grew in the 1980s, those who were in that group did very well. Their real average income went up more in the 1980s than in the 1970s, increasing from $44,000 in 1969 to $46,000 in 1979 to $49,000 in 1989 and keeping pace with the rising incomes of the corresponding top 30 percent of white households.

Table 2.1. *Proportion of black households by income group, 1959–89 (percent)*

Year	Proportion with >white median but <$100,000	Proportion with <white median but >$15,000	Proportion below $15,000
1959	18.6	—	—
1969	25.0	31.4	43.4
1973	26.1	30.2	43.3
1979	28.1	26.8	44.8
1985	28.7	24.7	46.0
1989	29.0	27.0	43.2

Note: Income based on 1989 dollars.
Source: Current Population Survey, *Household Incomes*, 1991, Table 2.

And just as in the case of whites, the very richest blacks also flourished in the 1980s expansion. The black elite $100,000 club (in 1989 dollars) had stayed constant at a minuscule 0.3 percent of all black households from the 1960s to 1984, but then shot up to 0.6 percent in 1985 and to about 1 percent in 1987–9.

In contrast, after doing much better in the 1960s and early 1970s, low-income black households, already poor in 1969–73, stagnated economically in the next seventeen years. There was no systematic reduction in the percentage of blacks living in poverty since the mid-1970s and a sharp four-year rise in poverty from 1980 to 1983 before some decline later in the decade. The poverty rate for blacks living in families was 30 percent in 1975 and 31 percent in 1989. Because women's incomes continued to rise in the 1980s, female-headed household poverty rates, which had dropped from 71 percent in 1959 to 54 percent in 1975, fell again slightly in the 1980s expansion to 51 percent.

However, these numbers represent the percentage of families below the poverty line – they don't describe what happened to the economic situation of those who were poor. The mean income of black-headed household families in the bottom 40 percent of black family incomes dropped from $9,300 to $9,030 (in 1991 dollars) between 1970 and 1980, and to $8,520 by 1990. This poorest and almost majority portion of the black community became steadily poorer relative to the white median in the 1980s and poorer relative to the top 30 percent of black households.

During the 1980s, then, income patterns in the black community followed patterns in the white community. Things got generally worse for the poor regardless of color and relatively better for those families with already higher incomes. The problem for blacks was that so many of them were still in the poor or nearly poor category in the mid-1970s and they had little if any upward mobility in the 1980s. Part of their difficulty had to do with the constitution of black households – almost half of them headed by a woman, and often by a woman with below-average education. Thus, although women's incomes continued to rise in the 1980s, they rose relatively slowly for high-school-educated women, and even slower for black high-school-educated women. Nor were black women (or men) graduating from college in increasing numbers. All of these conditions were hardly the makings of rising black incomes.

THE CHANGING ECONOMIC POSITION OF BLACK MEN

Black men stopped gaining on white men in the 1980s, but did the slowdown hit all groups of black men equally? Most analysts argue that as blacks were incorporated into the industrial labor force in the 1940s, 1950s, and 1960s, the incomes of black men at all educational levels caught up rapidly to white incomes. But the trend we saw in the aggregate figures is even clearer when black men are categorized by education group. The age group we have chosen consists of relatively young men, 25 to 34 years old – the relative incomes of younger men indicate how newer entrants to the labor market are doing and provide a better picture of changing labor market practices than do incomes of older workers. Older workers' incomes are confounded by earlier job access and experience.

Young blacks did worse across the board than whites in the 1950s, losing some of the big gains they made in the 1940s. Then in the 1960s, they regained these losses. In the 1970s, despite industrial restructuring, high school completers who did not go on to college and those blacks who completed college continued to improve their incomes relative to whites, but in the 1980s, most young black men again suffered losses compared with their white counterparts – sharper than in the 1950s (Figure 2.8). Surprisingly, the losses on a relative level were greatest for male college graduates. By the end of the decade, black men were only somewhat better off relative to whites than they were in 1969, and this mainly at the high school and college completion levels – because of the big gains these groups made in the 1970s.

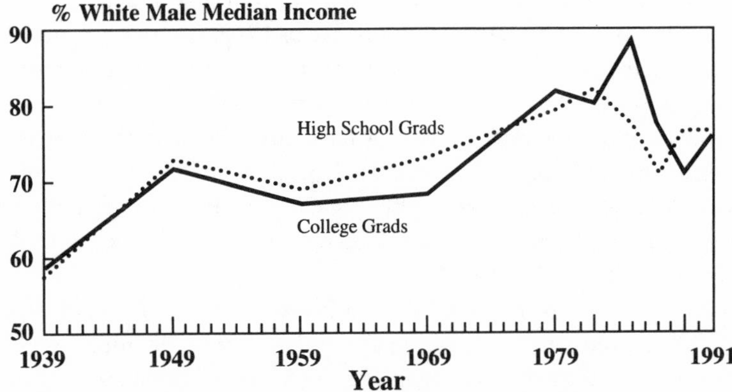

Figure 2.8. Black–white median income ratio, full-time-employed males 25 to 34 years old, 1939–91. From U.S. Census Bureau, Public Use Sample, 1940, 1950, 1960, 1970, and 1980, and Current Population Survey, March Survey, various years, full-time-worker sample.

Although the incomes of older, college-educated black men rose in the 1980s compared with whites', the decline in young males' relative income is an important measure of how the labor market was treating new entrants – hence, how well blacks will do in the future. Older, full-time-employed black college graduates did better in the 1980s largely because of the good jobs they had in the late 1960s and the 1970s. Younger black graduates were apparently not incorporated into the market in the same way.

The roller coaster aspect of black male gains is one of the features of racial inequality we have to explain in this book. Why did young black men do so well in the 1940s, fall back in the 1950s, increase in the 1960s and 1970s, and fall back again in the 1980s? Why did the relative incomes of black college graduates take so many years to begin going up, then rise so rapidly in the 1970s, and fall so suddenly in the 1980s? Was there some feature of black investment in education or in their movement from farms to cities that affected blacks' incomes compared with whites'? Or was the change related to some other feature of these different time periods?

The declining incomes of younger higher-educated black men compared with white incomes seems to contradict the slight improvement in the top tier of black family incomes. Of course, younger black men, even if they are college graduates, do not figure heavily in higher family incomes. But the incomes of 35- to 44-year-old college-graduate black men compared with those of whites rose between 1979 and 1989, from 71 to 76 percent, and so did the incomes of 45- to 54-year-old college-graduate black men, from 70 to 80 percent of white male incomes. Another clue to why black family incomes might not have gone down further lies in the continued strength of college-educated black women's incomes in the 1980s. Even so, the drop in highly educated younger black males' incomes began to pull down the top 5 percent and top 20 percent of black family incomes in 1988–9.[7]

More important is the signal that these lower incomes for young black male college graduates are sending about the future. The improving economic situation for prime-working-age college-educated black men in the 1980s was mainly the result of the opening of the job market to young blacks in the late 1960s and early 1970s. Once in these better jobs, they continued to ride the crest into a decade that gradually made things tougher for the younger cohort behind them. But that also means trouble ahead for today's young black college graduates as they reach prime working age. History suggests that they will continue to be caught in a trough – their incomes will remain low compared with those of whites. The trough will also affect future black middle-class family incomes. Unless black women with higher levels of education make up the difference, lower relative incomes for young black men could gradually produce lower black family incomes in the next decade.

THE CHANGING ECONOMIC POSITION OF BLACK WOMEN

Women have always earned less than men, and before World War II minority women were at a severe disadvantage in the labor market compared with white women. The second of these relationships has changed radically in the past five decades, to the point where in the 1970s full-time-employed black and Latina women with the same education as white women earned essentially the same incomes as white women. In the 1980s, however, minority women again fell behind their white counterparts, doing better income-wise absolutely and relatively over the decade than minority men but not as well as white women, except at the lowest and highest levels of schooling. By 1989, full-time-employed young white female high school graduates, 25 to 34 years old, earned 90 percent of black male income, and young white female college graduates earned 8 percent more than young black male college graduates. Young black

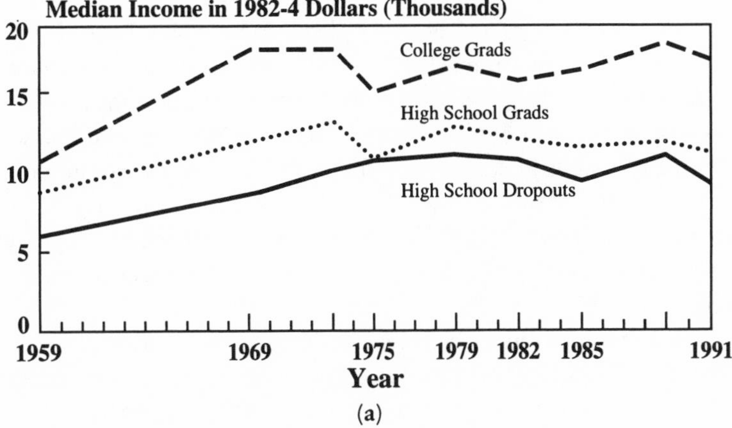

(a)

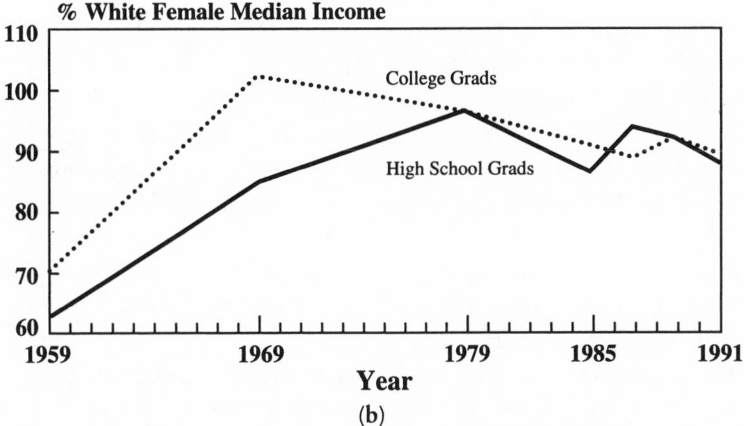

(b)

Figure 2.9. (a) Median income, full-time-employed black women 25 to 34 years old, by education level, 1959–91. (b) Black–white median income ratio, full-time-employed women 25 to 34 years old, 1959–91. From U.S. Census Bureau, Public Use Sample, 1940, 1950, 1960, 1970, and 1980, and Current Population Survey, March Survey, various years, full-time-worker sample.

women who graduated from college earned only slightly less than young black men (see Figures 2.7 and 2.9a).

Gender wage inequality – like race discrimination – is driven by relationships inside *and* outside the labor market that get translated into economic power and the shaping of work roles. Either because men prefer it that way or by women's choice, women are the principal raisers of children. No matter why they assume the role, the male-dominated production system punishes women economically for doing so by awarding them lower wages in the workplace. Economists have developed many arguments for the market rationality of lower wages for women, including the unwillingness of firms to invest in the training of those who are not dedicated to a lifetime in the labor force, self-imposed limitations for women on overtime, women's choice of less time-demanding professional jobs (the "mommy track"), and so forth. But the empirical tests attempting to support even the most carefully constructed of these rationales show a significant degree of occupational segregation and gender discrimination.[8]

The income differences between working men and women are large: white women working full time had a median income that was 66 percent of the full-time white male median income in 1989, up from the low of 56 to 57 percent that had prevailed from the 1950s to the end of the 1970s, and even above the level of the late 1940s (see Figure 2.2). One of the reasons that white female incomes were as high as they were in the late 1940s was the educational advantage that women in the labor force had over men at that time. The women who worked were a much more select group of individuals. As lower-educated, married, and "returning" (after child rearing) women came to full-time work in the labor force, they earned less than men. And in the 1980s, as white women were increasingly educated, more career-oriented, and (perhaps as a result of greater career orientation) subject to steadily, if not rapidly, declining discrimination, their wages rose relative to men's.

The treatment of African-American women in the labor market differed substantially from that of white women or the women of other minority groups.[9] Black women had to catch up educationally *and* in terms of the pay they received for their equivalent skills. They were discriminated against not just as women, but as black women. Figure 2.9b shows that black women were considerably worse off than whites at all education levels as late as the 1960s, even when they worked full time.

This does not mean that black women reached parity with whites in the 1960s and 1970s. Like black men, they still had less education and tended to work in lower-status, lower-paying jobs. Many continued to be occupationally separated into "black female jobs," not just into female jobs. One study shows that, even in the early 1980s, 40 percent of black women in service occupations worked as chambermaids, welfare service aides, cleaners, and nurse's aides.[10] But it is also true that during the 1960s the percentage of black women working in domestic and other low-wage services dropped from 57 to 43 percent and that the figure continued to drop to 31 percent in the 1970s. And the pay associated with such jobs for women was not significantly different from the pay in other women's jobs for those with similar education and age.

As white women gradually began to receive higher wages in the labor market, black women fell behind again. In the 1980s, all but the least-educated black women saw their incomes increase at a slower rate than white women's. The saving grace – at least for college-educated black women – was that white women's real median incomes rose so much during the decade that, even with blacks' slower increase, the real incomes of these highly educated black women went up. In 1979, a black female high school graduate earned $15,550 in 1989 dollars; ten years later, she earned $14,450. But college-graduate black women went from a median $20,200 in 1979 to $22,000 in 1989, adjusted for inflation. This difference between what happened to college-educated black women and to black men made it possible for upper-income black families to keep from losing ground to whites until the very end of the 1980s.

BLACK WOMEN AND THE BLACK FAMILY

Economic differentiation among women occurred and still occurs through marriage. Because society chooses to pay women less for their work, their economic well-being depends much more on other income earners and sources of wealth than does men's. It is here that white women gain much of their advantage over their minority counterparts. They marry higher-earning men than do minority women. They tend to have children later in life, giving themselves time to invest in education, to develop labor market skills, and to earn income. And when they do have children, they are much more likely than black women to be married and living in a household with a man present.

The logic and justification of a work system in which women are systematically paid lower wages than men lie in a "traditional" definition of the family. Historically, the family-based division of labor was able, in theory, to provide for the needs of parents and children because both parents were present and at least one of the parents could spend a significant part of her time caring for children. Industrialization posed a real threat to the traditional family. But once industrialization took place in Europe, the United States, and Japan, the successful fight for the "family wage," where the male worker earned enough so that his wife could stay at home, gave the family a century-long respite and a solid place in industrial ideology.

Not all groups got this respite, and eventually, under the stresses of urban poverty, male unemployment, and wage discrimination, marital dissolution and out-of-wedlock births began to grow in the black community. In 1960, 22 percent of blacks lived in female-headed households with no husband present, and the proportion rose rapidly in the 1960s and 1970s. By the late 1980s, the figure had doubled. Even though similar effects on family structure began to be felt among whites by the late 1970s, the proportion of black (and Puerto Rican) families headed by women remained more than three times the white rate.

Under such a family wage system, growing up in a female-head-of-household family more than likely means being poor. Thirty percent of whites classified below the poverty level live in single, female-headed families. The figure for the total of Latinos is slightly higher, at 38 percent.[11] For blacks, 60 percent of the poor live in female-headed families with no husband present – twice the percentage for whites.[12]

The main reason for the significantly higher proportion of black poor living in black female-headed households is not only that black families are much more likely to be headed by women, but that these women tend to be far younger and less educated than white women in the same category. On average, black women are also more likely never to have been married and to have had their children out of wedlock. The "typical" black female-headed family is formed when the woman is a teenager, has an "illegitimate" child, and continues to live at home with her mother (and grandmother) without a husband present. But at the other end of the spectrum, middle-age black women are also more likely than whites to be widowed female heads of household.

Research suggests that both male and female teenage blacks have a different attitude than whites toward having children out of wedlock, and that this attitude is rooted in their reality of joblessness and lack of career opportunities.[13] To these young blacks the cost of having a child early in life seems low, because they perceive the economic opportunities forgone as minimal, especially in the context of public assistance programs for dependent children. At the same time, to many poor, young women, having a child represents the one thing they feel they can do well.

The combination of youthful family formation, the absence of male income earners, and wage discrimination makes the black family triply disadvantaged. If the higher-wage-earning male is the single provider, his

Table 2.2. *Median female incomes by family status, race, and ethnicity, 1988 (dollars)*

	Race/ethnicity		
Family status	White	Black	Latino
Married-couple families	36,883 (59)	30,424 (35)	25,769 (57)
Female head of household, no husband present	18,658 (9)	10,995 (30)	11,321 (19)
Female, no family, living alone	13,548 (15)	7,107 (14)	7,495 (7)

Note: Numbers in parentheses are percentages of income units; they represent the proportion of *all* income units (including single males and male heads of household), so do not add up to 100.
Source: Bureau of the Census, *Money Income and Poverty Status in the United States: 1988, Current Population Reports,* Series P-60, no. 166, Table 4.

lower than white income usually leaves the family with significantly fewer resources than a single-earner, male-headed white family. If the minority spouse in a male-headed household chooses to work – and she is more likely to because of the male's lower income – she also has a lower income, on average, than her white counterpart (as opposed to fifteen years ago). And last, but far from least, black women are much more likely to be single heads of households than white women. This disadvantage is the most onerous, because the single income earned by minority women is low on three counts: minority women are less educated than white women and so get lower-paying work; because they are less educated, they are less likely to get full-time work; and minority women receive, on average, a 35 to 40 percent wage penalty even with the same education as white men.

The differences are summarized in Table 2.2. Black women who live in married-couple families earn lower incomes than white women, but do even worse when they are female single heads of household. Black heads of household are younger and less educated than their white counterparts, and are less likely, as single heads of households, to work full time, so they earn much less. But the worst of it is, black women are much more likely to fall into this low-income category and to raise children in what are almost *necessarily* conditions of poverty. A inordinately high fraction of this category of families is below the poverty level (52 percent of blacks compared with a "relatively low" 29 percent of whites).

The end result of the much lower proportion of blacks in married-couple families (83 percent of white families are married-couple families compared with 50 percent of blacks)[14] is the low median income of the average black family – this despite the relatively high average income of married-couple black families.

THE LOST GENERATION

Lower real median family income in 1989 than in 1973 and increased income inequality translated into continuing high levels of black (and white) poverty rates. Those Americans who were already poor became poorer in absolute purchasing power even as the economy grew. And so a generation after the Civil Rights Act and the Great Society, the American landscape in the 1990s is still marked by most of the problems those efforts were meant to solve.

Is this a problem of the black poor, unwilling to take advantage of opportunities to improve their lot, unwilling to work hard, and unwilling to develop a two-parent family life capable of supporting healthy, high-achieving children? The increasing gap between rich and poor black households does suggest that it is not "mainstream" blacks who are falling behind, but those who are not using the "traditional" channels to secure a better life.

Is this a problem of an economy going through a structural change that increasingly rewards the higher educated and increasingly punishes the less educated regardless of race or ethnicity? The rising incomes of higher-educated black middle-class families and the decline of already low incomes of less-educated poor black families in the 1980s are consistent with such an explanation. Like white families, black families were hurt economically in the late 1970s and 1980s mainly if they were poor and family members were less educated. The incomes of those black households above the white median rose along with higher white incomes. But the sharp decline in incomes of young black male college graduates compared with whites' incomes in the 1980s is inconsistent with the explanation. Highly educated black women may have made the real difference in higher black family incomes even if they lost ground relative to white women.

Is this a problem of pervasive racism, directed at all blacks but focusing particularly on poor blacks, who are least powerful and least able to manage economically in a racist society? The continued relatively large income gap between black and white men and the increasing gap between black and white women in the 1980s support this argument, as does the drop in the incomes of higher-educated black men compared with whites'. But other evidence suggests that racism may be decreasing even as these income gaps between blacks and whites increase.

Or does an important part of the explanation lie elsewhere, in the changing politics surrounding race (and class) in the 1980s? The rest of the book tries to solve this enormously complex puzzle. Let us begin by taking a close look at the different explanations for the standstill in black economic progress in the 1980s. Then we shall see how each explanation holds up against what has happened to blacks educationally, economically, and socially over the past fifty years.

3

The politics of explaining racial inequality

The past twenty years have produced a great letdown for African-Americans and, with it, a host of explanations for what went wrong. The great gains of the late 1960s and early 1970s ground to a crawl almost as quickly as they had begun. With economic crisis and white backlash, the 1970s produced a "new conservative" political victory in 1980, including a new economic program and the total domination of the national ideological debate by views considered extreme just five years before. By the early 1980s, explanations of racial inequality based on the rational workings of the free market had come to enjoy an official acceptance that had not existed since the 1920s – at least not in intellectual circles. Although there were responses to the market arguments, and good ones, from the black community, they were all set in the context of the political and economic power shift to the right.

This immersion in a dominant white conservative ideology brought legitimacy to the voices of conservative intellectuals, some old and most new, in the black community itself. For the first time since the days of Booker T. Washington, blacks closely linked to white conservative politics – such as Tom Sowell, Shelby Steele, and Clarence Thomas – were being taken seriously by a broad range of political analysts as representative of an important segment of black thinking.

Black voices on the other side of the ideological fence expressed increasing anger about the worsening conditions in inner cities, the decimation of the young black male population by gang warfare and drugs, the terrible plight of black (and Latino) children, and the use of racist images to win political power. The 1991 Clarence Thomas hearings raised another specter: the complex use of race not only in defining the nature of racial inequality, but in struggles over gender inequality and ideological interpretations of privacy.

The discussion of why the economic improvement of blacks came to an end in the early 1970s has taken place in the emotional crosswinds of this setting. Middle-class blacks moving to the suburbs and becoming more separate economically from the black urban poor have played a role, but not a major one, in the discussion. Middle-class blacks have not jumped on the conservative bandwagon, even if they are more likely than the poor to accept market arguments for black success and failure. The swing in white ideology has been the dominant influence, and it was only at the beginning of the 1990s, when the ideological pendulum began to swing back, that nonmarket explanations also began returning in full force.

As mentioned in the Introduction, three main explanations have emerged from the fray, each representing a different ideological position and each taking a different slant on essentially the same basic data: individual responsibility, economic restructuring, and pervasive racism.[1] These three explanations are key to understanding how different groups think about the race problem in the United States and what they think should be done about it.

INDIVIDUAL RESPONSIBILITY

"Individual responsibility" refers to the argument that individuals are the principal shapers of their economic and social destiny. Individual-responsibility explanations lay the blame for minorities' continued poverty on inappropriate choices made by two principal social actors: minorities themselves and white liberals trying to solve the poverty problem. They are the dynamic duo of maintained failure. Minorities – the argument goes – have chosen to maintain "victim" status long after the real conditions of victimization have disappeared; white liberals have continued to apply solutions to minority poverty that assume "victimization" and therefore lock minorities into continued, dependent poverty.

Linking these two groups are liberal antipoverty programs and general intervention, by which the government has attempted to "fix" economic markets. When then-Vice-President Dan Quayle blamed the 1992 Los Angeles riots on 1960s liberal programs,[2] he was laying the responsibility for poverty on years of government interference in the free market. The Quayle message hardly focused on causes of poverty or urban blight. Like all individual-responsibility explanations, it was a thinly veiled attack on the concepts of active government and social engineering.

The reverse side of this coin in a society that believes in social mobility is that only individual blacks themselves can be the authors of their economic success and inclusion in the mainstream. They must (and can) seize existing educational and job opportunities rather than wait for society to hand them a fairer deal.

Although individual-responsibility arguments are often confused with earlier claims that black failure is rooted in genetic inferiority,[3] they come from a different tradition. In that tradition, market evaluations of individuals' work are related as much to effort and perseverance as to ability. Ability is only one of the factors that determines an individual's success in the marketplace. Among the others are investment in education and training. Thus, individual responsibility places as much emphasis on individuals' overcoming adversity as on natural ability.

Conservative economists such as Thomas Sowell were early, avid proponents of the notion that blacks are responsible for their own condition.[4] Their criticism of government antipoverty programs is not so much that they affect blacks negatively as that they are futile. They insist on the power of markets to eliminate black poverty if blacks would simply invest in themselves and take initiatives similar to those of other immigrant groups. They are not necessarily opposed to efficient government education and training programs designed to increase opportunities for the poor – it's just that they doubt such programs will work if managed by government agencies.[5]

They also argue that the market functions just as fairly for minorities as for everyone else and that direct government intervention through civil rights legislation and affirmative action has little if any impact on minority gains. As the economy changes, it generates signals that, when followed, produce success for the largest number of people. Lack of success or economic decline for minorities only means that they are not responding to success-producing signals, such as the current high payoffs of a college education. And government intervention in labor markets does not and *cannot* do what it is supposed to do, because these free-market forces will only react to produce the inevitable market result.

This "economic" individual-responsibility explanation focuses on rational minority responses to economic incentives. Historically, as blacks went farther in school, attended better schools, and were thus able to move from rural to urban jobs, they began to catch up with whites.

Educational improvement and the resultant rural–urban shift were the primary sources of minority gains in the past, and the slowdown in educational progress and poor academic achievement are the main source of stagnation in the present.[6] In keeping with the concept of public education as a social investment, expanded and improved schooling for minorities can work to better their economic chances, *as long as minorities are willing to take advantage of it and as long as public schools are well run.* This "human-capital" model of change assumes that minorities do well economically when they take advantage of educational opportunities and that educational opportunities have improved significantly since the 1940s.[7] The model also argues that it may be economically rational to pay blacks less than whites *even when they have the same amount of schooling,* because blacks do not do as well in school as whites (blacks score lower on postschooling ability tests) and are therefore less productive.[8] Income inequality may arise from unequal access to schooling or differences in ability, but the market will "typically reward people according to their merits and not according to social or racial status."[9]

But the more popular analysis in the anti–social spending, anti–affirmative action climate of the 1980s was Charles Murray's. A decade ago, he made the case that the poverty programs of the 1960s had precisely the opposite effect they were intended to have. The argument was not entirely new. Others, including Sowell[10] and then–presidential adviser, now senator, Daniel Patrick Moynihan, who was himself heavily involved in writing much of the legislation but hardly an advocate of the individual-responsibility view, had long criticized poverty programs.[11] Unlike Sowell (and later Murray), however, Moynihan argued that the main obstacle to black progress was the weak structure of the black family, the result of slavery and, later, the rapid shift into urban areas. The 1960s concept of welfare programs, he claimed, exacerbated family deterioration. What was needed was a strong federal family policy.[12]

Murray melded these disparate critiques into a popular case for eliminating welfare and allowing market forces to make blacks better off. By providing welfare to families with dependent children, he argued, government contributed forcefully to a sense of dependency among blacks and to the deterioration of black families. Black male labor force participation rates fell, and black women were more likely to head families without a husband present. He purposely ignored Moynihan's call for a new kind of government antipoverty policy that would contribute to stronger families. For Murray, government intervention *necessarily* interfered with market forces that would produce less poverty through higher labor force participation and a greater proportion of two-parent families.[13]

More recently, Murray has joined Sowell in expanding his condemnation of government interference to affirmative action programs. These, they claim, hurt the very people they are intended to help. According to Murray, affirmative action creates psychological doubts among blacks and Latinos about their competence to compete on equal terms. It also increases racism and racial tension in colleges and the job market because of the disdain that white students feel for "unjustly" favored minorities. On both counts, for Murray, minorities are ultimately worse off than they would be if there were no affirmative action.

Black writer Shelby Steele has also built a popular following (especially among white intellectuals) by expanding this concept:

> The civil rights movement and the more radical splinter groups of the late sixties were all dedicated to ending racial victimization, and the form of black identity that emerged to facilitate this goal made blackness and victimization virtually synonymous. . . . Though changes in American society have made it an anachronism, the monolithic form of racial identification that came out of the sixties is still very much with us. . . . The victim-focused black identity encourages the individual to feel that his advancement depends almost entirely on that of the group. Thus he loses sight not only of his own possibilities but of the inexorable connection between individual effort and individual advancement. This is a profound encumbrance today, when there is more opportunity for blacks than ever before, for it reimposes limitations that can have the same oppressive effect as those the society has only recently begun to remove.[14]

Steele's account of his inner conflict between a chosen identity with white middle-class values of "hard work, education, individual initiative, stable family life and property ownership" and a forced identity with lower-class black victimization and poverty speaks to a widespread feeling among many Americans that blacks and other "oppressed" minorities drape themselves in this outmoded historical image to justify their unwillingness to make the sacrifices necessary for social mobility.

The Murray–Steele version of individual responsibility characterizes white liberals as instrumental in this process. Steele explains the failure of liberal programs in terms of white guilt: "I think the reason there has been more entitlement than development is (along with black power) the unacknowledged white need for redemption – not true redemption, which would have focused policy on black development, but the appearance of redemption which requires only that society, in the name of development, seem to be paying back its former victims with preferences."[15]

The underlying theme of choice and equal treatment in a free-market system that is neither race nor class conscious is a mystically powerful one. It has enormous appeal in a society that glorifies individual effort and the Horatio Alger rags-to-riches fable. To anyone who buys that fable, individuals who use race or class criteria to improve their gains are akin to Don Quixote doing battle against windmills. It makes no sense, at best makes no difference, and probably only makes things worse. Outside interventions that try to alter market rules interfere with more rational and efficient mechanisms that will, in the long run, leave all the players best off.

However, assuming away historical consciousness and the intimate ties between politics and markets does not work. Even in the idealized market model, individual freedom of choice is highly restricted by market rules and by economic conditions. The market is a harshly judgmental and unforgiving structure whose rules are set not in heaven but by those who have the economic and political power to use them to self-advantage. True, there is much to be said for the role of high expectations, aspirations, and willingness to work hard as components of individual success within a market structure. But the very structure of the market requires that there be winners and losers, and there are many factors besides native intelligence that determine who wins and loses, the number of people who can win and lose in any generation, and the economic distance between them.

Yet individual responsibility's alleged belief in race-free and class-free markets assumes another set of beliefs that ironically have more merit than the market myth. Individual-responsibility arguments appeal to the accurate view that the winners in the market are *better players* than the losers and that particular cultural conditions associated with the poor in general or especially unsuccessful segments of the minority population make it hard for them to take advantage of economic opportunity. The idea that these conditions may be perpetuated by the behavior of those who are poor and by some government programs has to be taken seriously. "Self-victimization" and welfare may, indeed, be partially to blame.[16] Even so, the proponents of individual responsibility have a difficult time explaining why blacks who succeed economically still tend to receive lower rewards than successful whites.

PERVASIVE RACISM

At the other end of the spectrum, most blacks and other "disadvantaged" minority groups see differential economic performance and social inclusion as the result of pervasive racism and racial discrimination. There are two versions of this explanation. The first locates racism at the level of the individual or an identifiable collection of individuals. Gunnar Myrdal's case for the unequal status of blacks hinged on racial discrimination resulting from individual and collective white prejudice. White prejudice produces black disadvantage and poverty, further feeding prejudice by confirming whites' opinion of blacks.[17] After the 1960s urban riots, the Kerner Commission Report also blamed individual white racism for the black condition.[18] Neoclassical economist Gary Becker explained discrimination in labor markets by individual employer, worker, and consumer "taste" for discrimination. Employers who had an aversion to hiring blacks were willing to pay (in the form of higher wages for white labor and reduced profits) to satisfy their aversion. White employees, through white unions, increased the cost to businesses of hiring blacks, and hence kept white wages high and black wages low. Economically more powerful white consumers preferred to deal with white employees (and were willing to pay higher prices to do so), but simultaneously kept black employees from getting jobs involving contact with whites. As a result of these individual tastes for discrimination, black worker employment was limited and blacks tended to receive lower wages than whites.[19] According to Becker's explanation, employers lose because of racism – without racism, they would have access to a larger labor pool and average wages for the average worker would be lower, even though black wages would rise.

Others argue that white racism and racial discrimination are hardly against employer interests, and therefore have not been opposed by business as Becker's analysis would predict. The racist "tastes" of white workers allow employers to make whites "pay" for segregation by paying them *lower* wages than they would receive otherwise. Black workers still get paid less than whites, so all labor is worse off. According to economist Michael Reich, the logic of this argument is borne out by the empirical evidence: the greater the segregation in the labor force, the lower are white as well as black wages – a result that is opposite to what would occur were Becker's model valid (white wages would be higher, the greater the degree of segregation). Reich argues that racial divisions among workers sap their bargaining power, keeping white wages *and* black wages down and raising profits.[20]

Reich's claim that business has an economic interest in supporting racial segregation and worker racism is part of a broader explanation of racial inequality. This broader version contends that racism is part of the *very structure* of society. Racism is not just the pejorative attitude that one individual or group has toward another of a different race. Rather, it is "much more complex than either the conscious conspiracy of a power elite or the simple delusion of a few ignorant bigots. It is part of our common historical experience and, therefore, a part of our culture. It arises from the assumptions we have learned to make about the world, ourselves, and others as well as from the patterns of our fundamental social activities."[21] In Reich's view, racism's continued strength derives from its positive link to business profits through labor division. But others argue that this pervasive, institutional brand of racism would keep economic and social equalization from occurring even under the most altruistic of schemes, even if individual racism diminished, and even if the business class lost its dominance over individual relations. Either society's institutions would reflexively "force" a reinstitution of inequality, or the main benefits of such schemes would revert to dominant white groups.[22]

Why would social institutions continue to revert to racial inequality? One claim is that it would help business make more money, and business is business. A more institutional argument, articulated by those such as Andrew Hacker, is that the system has functioned so long in a racist framework that it does not know how to do otherwise: "Ideas about equality and inferiority and superiority are not simply figments in people's minds. Such sentiments have an impact on how institutions operate, and opinions tend to be self-fulfilling. If members of a minority race are believed to be deficient in character or capacities, the larger society will consign them to subordinate positions."[23]

In such a model of American society, racism is outside of any individual's control, stuck on automatic pilot. Individuals and groups react, unthinkingly, to each other's race in a programmed fashion. Their reactions form a culture that inherently reproduces inequality and prejudice.

Just as the individual-responsibility explanation assumes an idealized social construction – the free market – that will make blacks the best off possible if allowed to function on its own, the pervasive-racism model assumes an "idealized" construction of a society that treats blacks unfairly and is highly resistant to changing the way it functions. In this case, historical ties between politics and markets are not assumed away, but rather are institutionally rigid and inherently racist, giving in only to intense social pressure by minority groups and then tending to bounce back when the pressure eases or is met by counterpressures from the dominant white community.[24] Even so, the historical record shows *perma-*

nent changes in the way the political system has dealt with the race issue. Not only has the government been willing to push economic and social institutions to change their behavior during certain periods, it has played a secular role in breaking discriminatory barriers through its own employment practices for at least fifty years.

Yet the pervasive-racism claim that political and economic *institutions* are far more important in perpetuating racial inequality than are individual attitudes and that these institutions have become more racist in recent years is convincing, especially to blacks and other ethnic minorities who lived through the 1980s. The Reagan administration hardly seemed a friend to blacks, and the Bush campaign in 1988, consciously using the image of a black rapist to turn voters against liberal social policies, showed that national candidates were not above old-time racist politics – and they still worked. Whether this means that racial inequality and discrimination actually increased in the 1980s, however, is open to question.

ECONOMIC RESTRUCTURING

The economic-restructuring argument as developed by sociologist William J. Wilson accepts the historically racist structure of U.S. institutions, but argues that the Civil Rights Act and other post-1965 legal changes transformed that structure. "Race relations in America have undergone fundamental changes in recent years, so much so that now the life chances of individual blacks have more to do with their economic class position than with their day-to-day encounters with whites."[25] For Wilson, the historical legacy of racism has been converted into a class problem, where poor blacks join poor whites and poor Latinos in an increasingly degradated underclass. The instrument of degradation in this case is not historical racism, but the changing economic structure.

This explanation for minority stagnation (and earlier gains) is that changing economic conditions brought a halt to black social mobility, particularly of those blacks left behind in urban ghettos with poor education even after the gains of the 1960s.[26] Minorities stayed poor in the 1970s and 1980s not primarily because they were locked into victimization (because of their race), but because centuries of discrimination had created a racial division of labor with an inordinate proportion of minorities at the bottom rungs. They, *along with lower-class whites,* were hit particularly hard by the economic changes after 1973.

Such economic changes are analyzed in the "deindustrialization" thesis developed by economists Barry Bluestone and Bennett Harrison, according to which manufacturing jobs left the northern inner cities of the United States for the sunnier shores of Japan, Taiwan, Korea, and Mexico and were replaced by service-sector jobs located in suburbs far from inner cities and requiring much higher levels of education.[27] Better-educated blacks left the inner city for the suburbs. Those who remained, along with Latinos and less-educated whites, were not qualified for these new jobs. They were left out in the cold by new, global competition and the economic restructuring that took place in response to it. And to boot, their better-educated brethren, who in the past had served as role models, were gone to greener pastures.

Robert Reich's version of this same explanation rests on the changing demand for different kinds of labor in the changing world economy. In Reich's words:

> All Americans used to be in roughly the same economic boat. Most rose or fell together, as the corporations in which they were employed, the industries comprising such corporations, and the national economy as a whole became more productive – or languished. But national borders no longer define our economic fates. We are now in different boats, one sinking rapidly, one sinking more slowly, and the third rising steadily. The boat containing routine producers is sinking rapidly. . . . The second of the three boats, carrying in-person servers, is sinking as well, but somewhat more slowly and unevenly . . . the vessel containing America's symbolic analysts is rising.[28]

Most blacks, because they finish only high school and a poor high school at that, fall into the first two categories. Relatively few are symbolic analysts – the people who use and create information – and are thus falling behind.

Like the individual-responsibility argument, this one sees some blacks as highly successful. But here past government action has played a *positive* role in that success. Government can and did intervene successfully to improve minorities' economic position, by making access to higher education easier and more affordable and by creating employment opportunities through direct federal and state programs. According to Wilson, this very success and changing economic conditions made earlier programs obsolete and halted social mobility. In effect, the racially based programs of the 1960s, such as affirmative action and the War on Poverty, helped the most capable and least poor blacks to move into the middle class of an expanding, restructuring economy. But the programs were not able to reach the minority group that was "truly disadvantaged," because they did not attack the underlying conditions of its poverty and its inability to succeed at schooling; nor were affirmative action and limited public employment efforts (such as the War on Poverty) able to counteract the more powerful negative impact on the poor of the economic slowdown and restructuring after 1973. Ultimately, the very growth of a black and Latino middle class, and their shift from urban to suburban living, separated successful role models from the ghetto residents left behind, which made the social conditions in poor urban areas even worse than they had been before.

"Race-based" government action therefore no longer works, because everybody who is able to take advantage of such programs already has. Poverty today is fundamentally a class issue. Only a macrosocial policy designed to offset the high unemployment and dislocation caused by changes in economic structure can improve minorities' (and poor whites') conditions.

Wilson argues that

> just as advocates for minority rights have been slow to comprehend that many of the current problems of race, particularly those that plague the minority poor, derived from the broader processes of societal organization and therefore may have no direct or indirect connection with race, so too, have the architects of the War on Poverty failed to emphasize the relationship between poverty and the broader processes of American economic organization. . . . Comprehensive economic policies aimed at the general population but that would also enhance employment opportunities among the truly disadvantaged – both men and women – are needed.[29]

Wilson's (and, implicitly, Robert Reich's) explanation for continued minority poverty deemphasizes race and affirms government's ability to intervene constructively to change economic opportunities for the poor. Wilson agrees with the individual-responsibility view that conditions of poverty create a culture of poverty, which tends to be perpetuated from generation to generation. This makes it much more difficult than the liberals of the early 1960s thought to change the behavior of the poor. But Wilson explicitly denies Murray's and Steele's contention that liberal government intervention was responsible for reinforcing the culture of poverty; on the contrary, Wilson argues that government programs had a limited effect on the underlying conditions of ghetto life. True, government bureaucracy often bungles because it does not understand the fundamental social problems it is confronting, but it has been successful in correcting the worst excesses of the market economy. It was *changing economic conditions* after 1973 that perpetuated poverty: "Indeed, it has been argued that many people slipped into poverty because of the economic downturn and were lifted out by the broadening of welfare benefits. Moreover the increase in unemployment that accompanied the economic downturn and the lack of growth of real wages in the 1970s, although they had risen steadily from 1950 to about 1970, have had a pronounced effect on low-income groups (especially black males)."[30]

The explanation rests, then, on two pillars: (1) structural changes in the economy are responsible for the increased marginalization of the poorly educated, inner-city members of the work force; and (2) the government failed to help the black poor in the 1970s and 1980s by allowing higher unemployment rates across the board – more an anti-working-class political response to the new international economic conditions than a policy omitting blacks per se.[31] Only by historical circumstances were blacks caught in their particularly vulnerable working-class position.

But the two arguments make sense only if we disregard the context in which Wilson's "class politics" responded to changes in economic structure. First, even those blacks who moved out of the ghetto into the middle class averaged lower incomes than whites of the same age and education. In absolute terms, they were much better off than those they left behind, but relative to those they were competing with for jobs, they were still much worse off. Second, class politics in the United States has never been separate from race and ethnic politics – one major reason that workers as a group never came to be as powerful politically in this country as in Europe, for example, was racial division in the labor force. Employers and government could always weaken white unions with the threat of black labor, and white unions allowed this to be the case by excluding blacks. In the 1970s, white working- and middle-class backlash against the black power movement and against black economic gains became a major political factor that shaped government action. Ronald Reagan's election would not have been possible without it – neither probably would have been the high-unemployment/low-wage economic strategy pursued by both Carter and Reagan. Most members of the white working class who voted for a conservative approach to economic growth – Reagan Democrats and blue-collar southern Republicans – did so because they blamed economic problems on government antipoverty and other social programs inextricably identified with inner-city blacks.

To recover its legitimacy with the white working class, government had to separate itself from the strong identification it had developed with black equality during the 1960s. Democrats were unable to do that (although many were willing to try), and Republicans were. Republicans sold their supply-side package to working-class voters on the basis of tax cuts, nationalism, and cuts in spending on the poor (read blacks). It was not until the Bush recession in 1990–1 that the white working class gave up on the low-wage policy, and even then, candidate Clinton had to reassure white working-class voters that his administration would not focus on blacks.

Nevertheless, economic conditions did change in the 1970s. The argument that they diminished the possibilites for incorporating poorly educated, inner-city blacks into the mainstream working class is persuasive. Undoubtedly, increased competition in the world economy and the new work organizations and technology that emerged hindered black job mobility and were more favorable to white skills and work styles. Equalization would, under these circumstances, be more difficult to achieve even if government were willing to make the effort. Even so, race cannot be ignored. Racial inequality exists beyond class inequality, and racial politics is part and parcel of class politics.

RACE AND CLASS

The relation between race and class in the United States is one key to understanding why racial inequality has changed. It is no accident that that relation is a dominant theme in all of these arguments. But the way the arguments deal with it helps explain why each on its own does not work.

Individual responsibility argues that race and class issues are unimportant in a free-market, democratic society. People are defined by their marketable skills, and marketable skills can be acquired equally by children of blacks and whites and by those of working- and middle-class origins – that is, if the free market is allowed to work. The pervasive-racism explanation rests on the premise that race is crucial in society independent of class (or gender) issues and that its importance increased in the 1980s. The economic-restructuring explanation argues that in the wake of the civil rights movement the race issue has become much less important than the class issue.

In objective terms, none of these assumed relationships is correct. Race and class affect the amount of education children acquire, the kinds of jobs they get, and what they earn as adults, even when they have the same amount of education and perform about the same on tests. There are also

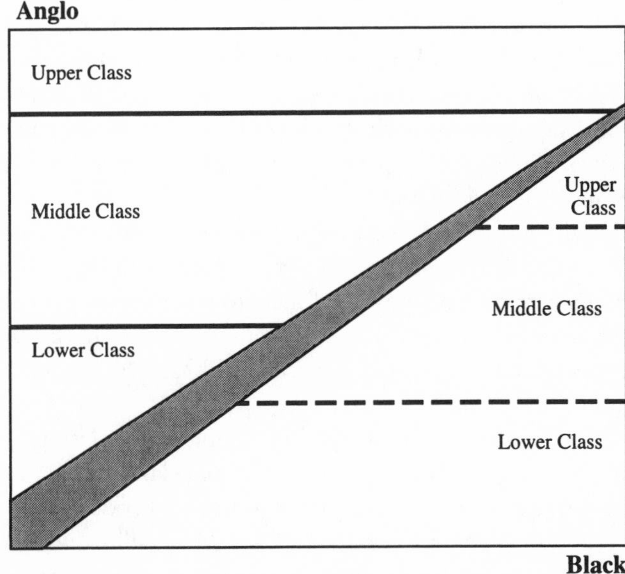

Figure 3.1. Model of class within caste. From H. Edward Ransford, *Race and Class in American Society* (Cambridge, Mass.: Schenkman, 1977), Figure 4-2, p. 52.

class distinctions among whites and blacks. The differences in wage outcomes are not small. A black male college graduate earns about 20 to 25 percent less than a white of the same age, but a third more than a black male high school graduate, even when both work full time. When years of education and ability are accounted for, higher-social-class white males earned about 30 percent more than lower-social-class males in the 1970s.[32] Race and class are also intertwined, with whites holding a disproportionate share of wealth and earning a disproportionate share of high incomes, and blacks forming an inordinately high percentage of the working-age poor.

One way to characterize this objective relationship is the "class within caste" model of what is called "competitive race relations."[33] A caste is a group that receives special social treatment because society has defined its members as somehow different and separate. The caste–class model has social classes among both blacks and whites, but the races are separated by caste barriers (see Figure 3.1). In competitive race relations, the caste barrier is "sloped," so that the higher social classes of blacks are higher than the lowest social classes of whites. It may also be broader at the lower end than at the higher, representing greater job and social access barriers between working-class whites and blacks than between white-collar workers and professionals. Both the pervasive-racism and economic-restructuring explanations can accommodate this model, but disagree about both the slope of the caste line and its width. In its most articulate form, pervasive racism argues that wage differences among black and white workers of all occupational levels inside and outside the workplace "constitute sources of employer power over individual and collective action by employees"[34] and are crucial to higher profits, providing a powerful incentive within the economic system for maintaining caste relations. Economic restructuring claims that the line is becoming increasingly vertical and has become highly permeable, especially at the middle and higher end.

The picture is further complicated by "subjective" class positions in each caste and subjective caste positions in each class.[35] These subjective positions emerge from conceptions of objective reality as conditioned by ideology, especially that promoted by politics. Most whites, whether members of the working class, fairly low income earners, or professionals earning high incomes, consider themselves middle class. They also generally believe in the social mobility myth of the American dream, at least as a theoretical construct. Blacks may consider themselves members of the working or even lower class, but they blame it on racism, not class. Their conception of working class takes on nationalistic, racial overtones which produce a working-class black culture that develops independently of white working-class culture. The subjective class notion of the two groups of workers can point blacks away from white middle-class values and draw whites toward identifying with the white dominant class. Thus, whether white workers earn relatively high incomes or not, they may view themselves as an "aristocracy" of the working class and separate from blacks (and Latinos) in objectively similar class conditions.

Both objective and subjective class positions change historically as the economy develops and social movements attempt to redefine the role that groups play in the society. Politics is fundamental to these changes, and William Wilson is correct in saying that class politics has always been the crucial feature of U.S. political history. But part of class politics has been the subjective separation of working-class whites, blacks, Latinos, and other groups. Because the United States was an immigrant society where new ethnic groups were constantly competing with earlier ethnic arrivals, and where African-American immigrants arrived as slaves, ethnicity and race always overlay class. Politics played off different ethnic groups against one another for its own purposes, and racial politics was an especially important form of this phenomenon. In this way, politics always played an important role in defining which groups of workers were higher on the social totem pole than others. Their values, family structure, and behavioral patterns were subjectively defined as "better" and "more American" than those of other groups, irrespective of their similar objective class position – this usually along ethnic and racial lines.

The notion of class and race is therefore heavily influenced by politics. The simultaneous struggle over class relations and race relations affects subjective class and race conceptions, and it is these subjective conceptions that define how the political struggle is played out. When blacks enter the political arena more as blacks than as members of particular social classes, it suggests that caste is important in defining subjective class and political roles. And when the white working class gives up much of its political class identity to side with business-dominated economic policies, it also suggests that caste allows political ideology to shape whites' subjective class position.

POLITICS, MARKETS, AND RACE

The second key to formulating a coherent explanation of changing racial inequality is a coherent formulation of U.S. politics. Politics cannot be avoided in a discussion of race because race is inherently imbedded in politics. The very discussion of racial inequality is political, drawing deep into our individual and collective political souls to elicit emotionally charged opinions about fundamental aspects of human relations and morality. A differing underlying view of politics and government is the implicit bedrock of each of the three dominant explanations of racial inequality we have been analyzing. Cutting through these political views helps us see why, no matter how superficially persuasive these explanations are, they lead us to an incomplete understanding of racial inequality.

Individual responsibility separates the marketplace individual from the political individual, with politics and government needed only to regulate markets minimally, invest in infrastructure when the market will not, and defend society from external and internal threat. Implicitly, the free market is an almost perfect mechanism that would best work on its own were it not for the sometimes imperfect humans who operate within it. Government, though necessary, is inherently imperfect, since it has no automatic forces that maximize the general good.

The seventeenth- and eighteenth-century philosophers who originated these ideas struggled mightily with the difficulties underlying such a separation between "passions and interests."[36] But the individual-responsibility argument ignores all this agonizing and justifies racial inequality as a product of rational market forces. It claims that somewhere in the past, politics may have interfered in markets, maintaining slavery even when it was not economically efficient and later perhaps allowing economic discrimination because of white worker "tastes" for racial separation, but that time is long past. Today, the argument goes, if blacks as individuals would get with the program and respond to market incentives – working hard, studying hard, creating decent families – their lot would be like that of whites. Politics and government have little to do with this process beyond continuing to provide equal (but not compensating) opportunities to those blacks willing to play by the rules.

But is it possible to talk about the shape of market or even human relations without talking politics – gender politics, boss–employee politics, race politics, school politics? And do not these politics enter into the legal, legislative, and ideological arena, shaping everyone's lives as much as the national market and global economy?

Politics is inherent in the structure of the economy and its growth rate. Both depend considerably on government investment and economic management, which the free-market model implicitly eschews. Politics is an inherent factor in determining how much government invests in schooling and who benefits from that investment. Politics is an inherent factor in determining the value the market places on personal attributes that cannot be changed, such as gender and race. The earnings of talented, intelligent, and highly educated women remain low even when they work full time. The economic distance between those who have "negative" personal attributes (female, working-class parents, black) and higher-social-class white males is affected, even in a free-market system, by the political power of these groups.[37]

David Gordon, Richard Edwards, and Michael Reich have argued that the complex set of relationships between capitalist markets and government policy varies greatly among the advanced industrialized capitalist nations and makes a big difference in income inequality, largely because of the way that employer–labor power relations have been resolved historically in each society.[38] Although their notion of how this institutional environment develops is a narrow one, limiting the definition of politics to the class conflict between employers and labor, their main point makes sense: the way social conflicts are resolved politically affects the economic value of different kinds of work. When the ratio of U.S. corporate executives' compensation compared with that of average workers increased from 43:1 in 1960 to 120:1 in the 1990s, and the same phenomenon did not occur in Europe or Japan (top compensation/average wages narrowed somewhat in Japan in the 1980s), you can be sure that the politics of deciding what ratios were socially allowable had as much to do with whether the ratio changed as market forces.[39]

Beyond class conflict, race and gender are crucial to the relation between politics and markets. In forming a strange alliance with white-male-dominated management, the white male working class has played a crucial political role in keeping the wages of black men and of black and white women lower than theirs, even if as a result white male workers have sacrificed bargaining power over their own wages. The politics of "family values" (a woman's place is in the home) and a not so subtle emphasis on greater "merit" and individual effort as distinguishing white workers from black has affected relative wages by deprecating women's and blacks' efforts to equalize them. This is not a new phenomenon: in the United States both women and blacks have fought to overthrow their politically defined roles for more than a century. In turn, their struggles have served as political issues for the (economically and socially dominant) white male groups that opposed economic equalization.

All this makes the *political* factor in earnings differences much more important than the proponents of individual responsibility would have us believe. Even when the schooling is the same for individuals of different gender and race, how do employers and society measure and interpret performance in a whole range of jobs? How much do employers pay different kinds of people for similar performances? What does society allow in terms of differential labor market treatment? Should government pay scales reflect private-sector treatment of women and blacks even when the public sector may "disagree" with private-sector behavior? Economists who believe that all-powerful free-market forces can settle the wage issue rationally and fairly assume these questions away.

They also assume that there is some real-life situation in which a democratic government would stay out of markets. This is a mystification of reality. Politics is in markets to stay. The issue is not *whether* politics is related to market outcomes, but *what* that relation is and *how,* in each of the views discussed here, politics influences racial inequality. This boils down to a discussion of political power and how and where it is expressed in democratic society. Individual responsibility argues that the good of all is served if no one intervenes on behalf of the poor. There is greater economic and social efficiency when those who do better in the market receive greater benefit from the government–private-sector partnership. Plain and simple, individual responsibility means that those who have accumulated wealth from previous or present market success (including family success) have a greater claim on government benefits than those who have not.

The pervasive-racism explanation goes to a different corner. It assumes that markets are imperfect, "bending" their rules to allow for individual racism. Government can and should correct such bias through its regulatory powers. Government's role is therefore far from negative – it is needed to correct racial inequalities within the market itself. That it does not easily do so leads some proponents of the pervasive-racism explanation to argue that both market and government are subject to racist behavior, either because market-based groups have inordinate political power (capitalists and managers) and racial inequality serves their interests, or because racism is institutionalized throughout society, both in markets and in politics.

There is a difference between the two versions: contending that business interests find racial inequality profitable (even though employers may not be the direct agents of racial discrimination) and can lean on government not to interfere in discriminatory labor markets assumes a political system that is racist because it will not confront powerful market interests and may intervene on their behalf even when this means supporting blatant inequality. This version of the pervasive-racism argument sees government as activist but deriving its power and legitimacy directly from market interests. Government in that view reinforces market-generated inequalities because private business finds equalizing interventions against its larger interests.

The second version claims that both market and political institutions are historically racist and jointly perpetuate racial inequality, even if only half-consciously. Government helps perpetuate racism not because market interests want it to but because it shares a common history with markets that make them react the same way on race. This means that government and business may seem to act more favorably toward blacks now, after civil rights, but always treat them as less equal than whites.

The essence of racial politics is impervious to change in this particular construction of the relation between market and democratic state because it still forms an integral part of the otherwise rational, modern capitalist soul.

Similar arguments are made about gender, ethnicity, and religion – all holdovers from the "past" and conceivably "outside" the process of change inherent in democratic, capitalist institutions that run modern society. According to Robert Reich, we can now add "nationalism" to these holdovers from the past.[40] While the economy becomes global and the wealth of nations increasingly resides in highly mobile symbolic analysts, nationalism lingers on, deeply imbedded in the structure of American thinking.

The fundamental error in this way of characterizing the relation between race and politics is that it underestimates the degree and impact of changes that have occurred in race relations and race discrimination – mainly through the *very political process itself.* Political institutions may be racially biased, but they are subject to constant change. Indeed, contrary to both the individual-responsibility and pervasive-racism conceptions of politics and government, it is at the level of democratic politics that the changes occur first and, through them, in the rest of society.

The economic-restructuring explanation recognizes this process of change, but falls back onto a flawed conception of politics in the United States. For Wilson, the race factor has disappeared and government has reverted to its underlying class politics. Here, politics is at the service of markets. Unequal, class-based economic power drives unequal, class-based government policies. The conflict between rich and poor, not black and white, is at the heart of those policies: a black yuppie is first and foremost a yuppie, not black. It is those policies, even devoid of racial bias, that have necessarily served only blacks of higher social class and failed to address the growing inequality in markets caused by structural changes in the economy.

The flaw in Wilson's political formulation is subtle and can be divided into two parts. First, the deindustrialization or global-economy argument alone does not explain why real wages fell so much in the United States during the late 1970s and early 1980s and why they stagnated during the rest of the 1980s. In this same period, Western Europe and Japan also greatly reduced the proportion of their labor force in manufacturing. But in those countries workers' real wages grew and urban poverty declined. In

Japan, growth rates were high and labor markets relatively tight, but not in Europe. The main difference is the role of government. In Europe, government labor regulations and the power of labor unions force employers to retrain workers and invest in raising productivity rather than seeking lower wage locations or wage givebacks. Although in recent years this "welfare state" policy seems to have also contributed to rates of unemployment higher than in the United States, it has also reduced poverty, even among the unemployed. In Japan, a tight business–government–labor relationship regarding economic policy means that everyone participates in economic growth, just as during the era of New Deal expansion in the United States (1940–73).

Robert Reich would argue that the Japanese and Europeans were much more successful than Americans in educating their populations to participate in symbolic analysis. But much more was involved, especially in Japan. There, a highly coordinated macroeconomic and macrosocial policy made participation one of its centerpieces. In the United States, in contrast, government support for business efforts to drive down wages after 1973 was crucial to the actual decline in real wages, especially for middle- and lower-skilled workers.[41] Government, even under President Carter, put pressure on unions to keep nominal wage demands down as a means of fighting inflation, but allowed profits to rise.

Second, Wilson's so-called class politics in the 1970s and 1980s was closely entwined with racial politics. Race was the foundation for bringing the working class into the Republican Party. In winning political power, certain political groups benefit from, even depend on, racial divisions and may want to perpetuate or exacerbate them. Just as in some periods there is a decline in institutionalized racism, in other periods subtle attempts are made to relegitimize it in new forms. In the United States, a political party need only win a majority of electoral votes. As the Republicans learned three decades ago, a racially divided and more populous South, many of whose working-class whites are vehemently anti–civil rights, could be combined with traditional conservative suburbanites to produce that majority. Although race was only one of the issues in this winning combination, the economic problems of the 1970s brought race as an issue sharply into the foreground. Wilson's analysis misses this underlying political relation between race and class. It is easier to imagine a raceless class politics in the 1990s than in the 1950s, but very difficult to imagine how a class politics – either for labor or for business, for the rich or for the poor – could be successfully formulated without implicitly taking some stand on the question of race. The same can be said for gender. When large groups of voters such as blacks and women play significantly different roles in the economy and society than white males – roles that are contested – how can class politics avoid dealing with race and gender?

AN ALTERNATIVE VIEW OF RACE AND POLITICS

Analyzing the underlying assumptions about the relation between the economy and politics in each of the explanations suggests why none of them captures what has happened to blacks in the past twenty years. Politics is not separate from markets, nor is it merely in the hands of special powerful interests. In a democracy, politics is the arena where social groups contest the vision and direction of the economy, including the distribution of income, wage policy, social investment, legitimate attitudes toward racial and gender differences, the treatment of poverty, and even notions such as property rights. All these issues are wrapped in a contested ideological view of the very relation between politics and markets. Race and poverty are also ideological issues, just as subject to change as others and highly contested in the political arena. Politics itself therefore plays a crucial role in shaping civil society's attitude toward markets and their effect on people. It shapes how people view the race issue and how they view economic rights.

Objective realities are still important. When the economy seems to be doing well, it is difficult to convince voters that the relation between politics and markets should change or that racial divisions are a problem. When a high percentage of voters consider themselves well off, income transfer, antipoverty, and other programs that deal with changing economic rights are a difficult sell. And when social movements such as the civil rights movement or labor unions are disorganized, their ability to influence political strategy is reduced.

Such a formulation suggests another explanation for earlier black gains, for continued black poverty, and for the recent slowdown in black income increases relative to those of whites.[42] Politics in the 1940s, 1950s, and 1960s gradually redefined the race issue in a way that was highly favorable to minority mobility. After the 1960s, the situation changed, and the change was based at least partly on the ability of politicians to mobilize whites again around negative minority images. As a result, what Wilson, Bluestone and Harrison, and others characterize as a change in *class* politics appears to have also required a change in *racial* politics. It reaccentuated race, built a consensus against helping the poor because the public was given to believe that they were predominantly minorities, helped produce stagnation in minority education, and reduced relative minority incomes even in the middle class.

Unlike individual responsibility's "inept politics," pervasive racism's "institutionalized race politics," and economic restructuring's "class politics," American politics in the second half of the twentieth century should be seen as "ideological power politics." In ideological power politics, competing visions of economic and social development are projected onto the national political stage as a way of gaining and reproducing political power. The visions define party political projects around fundamental party ideology. They are geared to organize base constituencies and win potential converts. They differ between parties and at different points in time. None of the visions connected with the major political parties has ever questioned the primacy of free markets and private control of capital. But there has been a great deal of variation in the vision of government's role in those markets. Because race has such an important place in the heart of American ideology, it has also always played a role in the vision, but one that has changed in each party in the past fifty years.

Why are political visions so important for political power? If there were no underlying social conflict in market economies, as the individual-responsibility argument claims, there would be no real need for politics or political visions. If everyone accepted that the free market by itself always produces the "best" economic results, there would also be little need for politics – foreign policy would be the only important political issue. But neither of these characterizations of politics is correct. There is widespread social conflict and great uncertainty regarding the effectiveness of unregulated markets. Visions – even by those who profess to believe in the "inept government" argument – define how government proposes to arbitrate such conflict and uncertainty. The conflict is not only between labor and management, but between different groups of workers historically pitted against each other. Nor does social conflict originate only in labor markets. It also occurs in the family, in schools, and in other important "sites" of society.[43] All of these conflicts end up being played out and shaped in the larger political system.

According to this political explanation, government – which is the expression of that system – necessarily arbitrates and influences how the conflicts are resolved in these sites. Government's employment and wage practices can help break or reinforce racial, ethnic, and gender stereotypes in the economy as a whole. The implementation or disregard for antidiscrimination and affirmative action programs sets the tone for hiring minority men and both white and minority women in the private sector and can initiate significant changes in hiring patterns for various types of jobs – especially professional jobs. Educational policies may not be able to change the structure of work and wages,[44] but they can have a crucial impact on the amount and quality of schooling that minorities get – and hence the choices available to them in a highly education-structured labor market. Government's civil rights policies also set the tone for social relations among ethnic groups at the street level. Since politics here is central to race, taking the high road to reducing social conflict necessarily reduces the legitimacy and impact of racial discrimination. Playing backlash politics necessarily affirms ethnic stereotypes and affects social mobility.

Competing political visions are represented in everyday life by such competing concepts of how to deal with social problems, including racial inequality. Although fundamentally ideological, these visions have important material consequences for different groups. Which vision wins political power makes a difference not only for social relations but for living standards, income distribution, and the way families organize their work lives.

This view of politics is very different from the one spelled out in the three arguments that dominated the debate on racial inequality during the 1980s. It is a view that predicts the possibility of change in the vision of race policy and claims that the way the vision constructs the relation between race and class is crucial to the change (or lack of it) in blacks' absolute economic position and their position relative to whites.

Showing that politics is the key to explaining changing racial inequality, and that an "ideological power" view of politics underlies that explanation, is not an easy task. Before turning to it, we must review the evidence for each of the three arguments.

4

Are blacks to blame?

In the land of opportunity, those who consistently fall behind are immediately suspect. So it is with African-Americans. Suspicion is especially widespread in the 1990s because, unlike a generation ago, today most white Americans are convinced that blacks have been given every chance to succeed, and have even been pushed ahead of whites by affirmative action and government subsidies. Despite this help, they seem to fail at the economic game. Is it not logical that there is something wrong with them, not the system?

The image of failure is not just assigned to poor urban blacks. Many whites feel that the children of black working- and middle-class families are also not doing as well in school as whites, are dropping out of college with much greater frequency than whites, and are not working as hard or keeping to the same family values as other ethnic groups.[1] The implicit message is that there is something about African-Americans' values and motivations that keeps them from taking advantage of educational and economic opportunities. Were those values to change, so would black fortunes.

This is an appealing image for whites and for many successful blacks. It fits with the standard evaluation of their own individual success stories, and it corresponds to a more recent, frequently invoked "model minority" – Asian-Americans.[2] But is the image correct? If blacks had just focused on doing better rather than on past oppression and the system's need to make amends, could they have made much larger gains, as the individual-responsibility argument claims?

DID BLACKS TAKE ADVANTAGE OF EDUCATIONAL OPPORTUNITIES?

If there is an answer to this question, it should lie in blacks' response over the years to educational possibilities. Education is American democracy's ideological answer to its inherently unequal labor market. Public schools have long symbolized the social mobility of our immigrant dream society. Like everyone else, minority leaders have taken this symbol seriously. Even a century ago, on the occasion of the 1895 Atlanta Exposition, the most famous and well-connected African-American of his time, Booker T. Washington, declared that Negroes should take their place as equals among whites only when they had educated themselves to a level commensurate with such equality.[3] Washington's posture at Atlanta was designed to accommodate whites and to gain "social peace" in an era of intensified, government-sanctioned racial segregation, and that is what the speech is remembered for. But it also reflected his and other Negro leaders' deep and abiding belief that education was a key to blacks' progress. It is that aspect of Atlanta's legacy that had the greatest impact on their political action and that of other minorities in subsequent generations.

Whatever the educational strategy – and Washington and his contemporaries differed widely on what kind of education was most valuable – the belief in schooling as a passport to the middle class seemed to make good sense. Minorities were systematically kept out of schools and universities, so catching up educationally appeared crucial. Whether it was Washington's "practical," job-oriented, industrial and craft schooling that was the hallmark of his Tuskegee Institute or W. E. B. Du Bois's liberal arts college education to produce a "talented tenth" as "leaders of thought and missionaries of culture among the people,"[4] African-Americans – and, later, the Mexicanos who came streaming into the Southwest during and after World War I and the Asians who had been in California since the nineteenth century – desperately wanted more education and struggled to get it throughout the twentieth century.

Considering the status of minority education in 1940, efforts to upgrade education for minorities have been amazingly successful. Black schools in the South and Mexicano schools in Texas and California began seeing significant improvements in teachers' salaries and teacher–pupil ratios in the 1940s. School and university integration began in the 1950s, often with intervention by federal troops, and public funds allocated to predominantly black and Latino schools increasingly approached the amount spent on white schools. The Warren court's decision on *Brown v. Board of Education* was a political turning point for the civil rights movement, as was an earlier decision in California – *Mendez v. Westminister* (1946) – which mandated equal treatment for Latino, Asian, and black children in that state's schools. And as part of the wave generated by *Brown v. Board of Education,* Mexicanos in Texas waged a successful campaign to end overt discrimination in Texas schools.

But, as I argue later, blacks and Latinos had to fight for access to high-quality public schools, and this meant convincing state and national governments to provide more equal education for minorities. It was not that blacks were less likely than whites to give their children high-quality education; they could not get it even when they wanted it. The first step was to gain more equal treatment in the public system, which required strong and sustained political and legal action. This point bears emphasis. The individual-responsibility argument stresses the failure of blacks to respond to opportunity. But the data suggest that for a century government had to intervene in their favor before blacks could take advantage of educational "opportunities." That is still true: impressive differences continue to exist between learning conditions accorded urban black and suburban white children.[5]

The quantitative gains in education attained by blacks and other minorities during this process were large. And in terms of rate of change, blacks did as well as anyone else – at least until recently. In 1940, only about 12 percent of 25- to 29-year-old blacks and 6 percent of Latinos (primarily of Mexican origin) had completed twelve or more years of schooling. This compared with about 40 percent of young whites who had attained that level. In 1965, 65 percent of whites, 50 percent of blacks, and 52 percent of Latinos in this group had graduated from high school. By 1987, 86 percent of whites, 83 percent of blacks, and 60 percent of Latinos had completed high school or more.[6]

The data for Latinos suggest that they did not catch up as much as blacks, but this was mainly because most younger Latinos in the new wave of post-1965 immigration had low levels of schooling to begin with or stayed in U.S. schools for only a few years, until they were old enough to work. When Latinos born in the United States are separated out, the educational picture changes. For example, the percentage of 25- to 34-year-old Mexican-Americans in the census sample who had completed high school or went on to college increased more rapidly than that of

Table 4.1. *Native-born Mexican-origin and black labor force, 25- to 34-year-old males, by level of education, 1960, 1970, 1980 (percent)*

Level of schooling	Mexican-origin			Black		
	1960	1970	1980	1960	1970	1980
<12 years	78.1	45.8	31.0	68.8	47.4	23.4
High school complete	12.8	35.2	33.8	19.2	37.9	39.2
Some college	3.8	12.3	22.9	7.0	9.7	24.3
College complete	2.8	2.5	5.8	3.2	3.0	8.1
Graduate school	2.4	4.2	6.4	1.9	2.3	4.9

Source: Department of Commerce, Bureau of the Census, U.S. Public Use Census Samples, 1960, 1970, and 1980.

blacks from 1960 to 1970 (the 1950s school generation of Mexicano-Latinos), but then, with civil rights in the 1960s, the black percentage took off in the 1970s (see Table 4.1).

BLACKS AND UNIVERSITY EDUCATION: HAVE BLACKS STOPPED TRYING?

In the same way, it took decades of civil rights struggles to open white universities to black high school graduates. The new entrants swelled the ranks of what had been a small group of distinguished older black intellectuals. At the end of the nineteenth century, blacks had established their own system of black colleges fostered by white philanthropists. Even in the 1960s, most blacks graduated from black, not white, universities.[7] And by the end of the 1960s, with access to white universities won, blacks entered and graduated from the mainstream system in increasing numbers.

In 1976, the percentage of all high school graduates 18 to 24 years old who were enrolled in college was about the same for blacks, Latinos, and whites, at 33 percent.[8] A year later, the percentage of recently graduated high school seniors also reached parity among blacks, Latinos, and whites, at about 50 percent.[9]

Yet this was the historical high point for the proportion of minorities entering college. The proportion of both young blacks and Latinos en-

Table 4.2. *Enrollment rates of 18- to 24-year-old high school graduates and recent graduates in institutions of higher education, 1965–91*

Year	18- to 24-year-olds as a percentage of high school graduates			Enrollment as a percentage of recent high school graduates		
	Whites	Blacks	Latinos	Whites	Blacks	Latinos
1965	—	—	—	51.7	—	—
1966	—	—	—	51.7	—	—
1967	34.5	23.3	—	53.0	—	—
1968	34.9	25.2	—	56.6	—	—
1969	35.6	27.2	—	55.2	—	—
1970	33.2	26.0	—	52.0	—	—
1971	33.5	29.2	—	54.0	—	—
1972	32.3	27.1	25.8	49.4	—	—
1973	30.2	24.0	29.1	48.1	—	—
1974	30.5	26.6	32.3	47.1	—	—
1975	32.3	31.5	35.5	51.2	—	—
1976	32.8	33.4	35.9	48.9	41.9	52.6
1977	32.3	31.3	31.5	50.7	49.6	51.3
1978	31.3	29.6	27.2	50.1	45.7	42.9
1979	31.3	29.4	30.2	49.6	45.4	44.8
1980	32.1	27.6	29.9	49.9	41.8	52.7
1981	32.7	28.1	29.9	54.6	42.9	52.1
1982	33.3	28.0	29.2	52.0	36.5	43.1
1983	33.0	27.0	31.5	55.0	38.5	54.3
1984	34.0	27.2	29.9	57.9	40.2	44.3
1985	34.9	26.0	26.8	59.4	42.3	51.1
1986	34.5	28.6	29.4	56.0	36.5	44.4
1987	37.5	30.0	28.6	56.6	51.9	33.5
1988	38.6	28.0	30.9	60.7	45.0	57.0
1989	39.8	30.8	28.6	60.4	52.8	55.4
1990	39.2	30.4	26.8	61.5	46.3	47.3
1991	41.0	28.2	31.4	64.6	45.6	57.1

Source: U.S. Department of Education, National Center for Educational Statistics, *The Digest of Educational Statistics,* 1991, Tables 171 and 174; 1990–1 data: NCES, *Digest of Educational Statistics,* 1992, Tables 170 and 173.

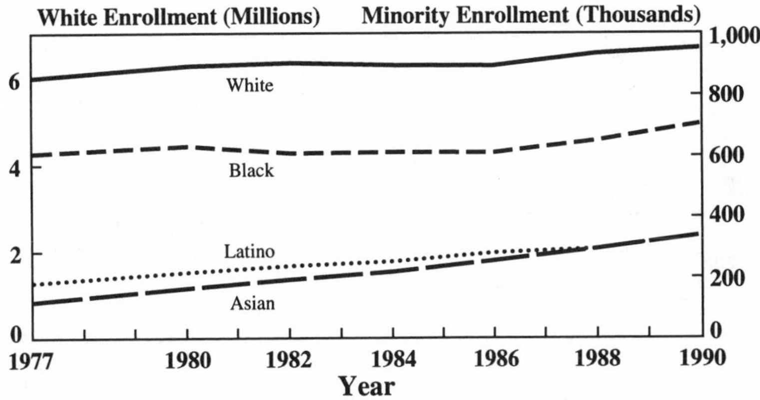

Figure 4.1. Total enrollment, four-year colleges, by race and ethnicity, 1976–90. From National Center for Educational Statistics, *Digest of Educational Statistics, 1993,* Table 201.

rolled in college fell in the late 1970s, as it did for whites. But white enrollment rates recovered in the 1980s, and black and Latino rates did not. Whites' rates are now far above those of the mid-1970s, whereas minorities' rates at best have stayed level. If there was any catching up, it was only in the last three years of the 1980s (Table 4.2). Even more telling is the slow growth of blacks enrolled in four-year colleges between 1980 and 1990, and all of that in the last two years of the decade (Figure 4.1) – this *despite* an increase in the absolute number of black high school graduates. There was an increase in the number of Latinos enrolled in college, although enrollment declined as a percentage of the total population of high school graduates among Latino 18- to 24-year-olds. A much higher fraction of Latinos (about 55 percent in 1976–88) also continued to attend two-year institutions than blacks (43 percent) or whites (35 percent).

No growth in black college enrollment rates until 1988 also meant no growth in the percentage of the young minority labor force with four-year college degrees. After rapid increases in the 1970s in the proportion of minorities who completed sixteen or more years of school, the completion rate slowed in the 1980s for blacks, and probably for native-born Latinos. The most disturbing statistic is the decline in the absolute number of bachelor's degrees awarded to blacks in the 1980s and the slow growth in the number awarded to Latinos even as their population grew rapidly (Figure 4.2).[10] Not only were young blacks and Latinos less likely

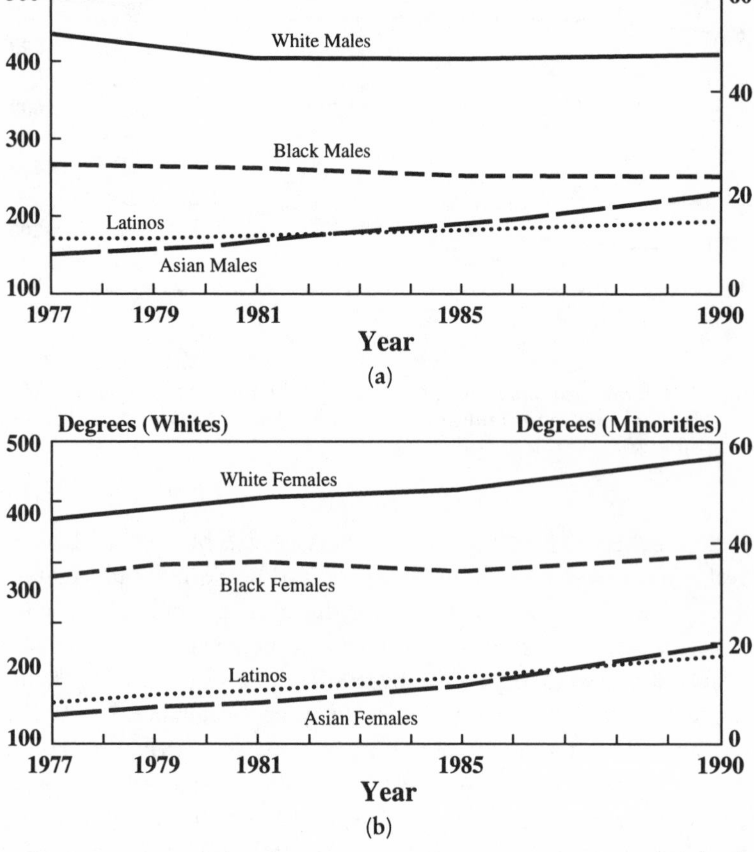

Figure 4.2. Bachelor's degrees awarded, by race and ethnicity, 1977–90 (thousands): (a) men; (b) women. From National Center for Educational Statistics, *Digest of Educational Statistics, 1993,* Table 255.

than whites to attend four-year college, they were somewhat more likely to drop out once enrolled.[11]

This educational stagnation at the college level among blacks in recent years has given credence to the notion that individual responsibility is the root cause of racial inequality. Now that the civil rights victories have been won and blacks have the additional advantage of affirmative action, individual-responsibility proponents claim that blacks should be flooding into colleges and completing at rates comparable to whites. But individual responsibility tends to ignore the data showing that blacks' high school completion rates are increasing more rapidly than Latinos' and that Latinos and poor whites are also having trouble completing college. In the 1980s, blacks were not doing worse, in terms of educational attainment, than other low-income groups, and blacks continued to catch up with whites in average years of education in the labor force.[12] So what is keeping blacks and Latinos away from college? Do they lack motivation or are there more subtle barriers at work?

INDIVIDUAL RESPONSIBILITY AND BLACK ACHIEVEMENT GAINS IN THE 1980S

Educational achievement is another litmus test that the individual-responsibility argument uses to blame blacks for their low economic performance. Although related to educational attainment in that higher-achieving pupils are likely to go farther in school than others, achievement is a better measure of what individuals are willing and able to learn. In many people's minds, it is an even more vivid symbol of competence than level of schooling.

Black pupils have scored much lower than whites on standardized school achievement tests as long as test score results have been recorded by ethnic group.[13] No doubt, lower reading and math ability at every level of schooling are both a reflection of and have contributed to minority economic and social problems. It is not fun to be in school when you are doing poorly – schools stereotype children early and unconsciously try to push out those who do not fit the middle-class ideal of a cooperative learner. At the same time, many – probably far too many – blacks accept the stereotype of the nonlearner even when they could do well in school.[14]

It is all the more surprising, then, that differences in minority and white scores declined dramatically between the late 1960s and the late 1980s even while white student achievement remained unchanged. African-Americans made larger gains than Latinos, but this was due at least partly to the influx of "language-handicapped" Latino immigrants after 1965.[15] The Latino–white gap also closed but to a lesser degree than the black–white gap.

The data in Tables 4.3 and 4.4 show just how great the changes in academic achievement, as measured by reading and mathematics scores, were. The scores are presented by birth cohort and by the age at which the test was taken. Black children born in 1962, for example, scored 170

Table 4.3. *NAEP reading scores for African-American, Latino, and white students, by birth cohort and age test taken*

		Age test taken		
Birth cohort	Ethnic group	9	13	17
1954	White			291[a]
	Black			239
	Latino			—
1958	White		261[a]	293
	Black		222	240
	Latino		—	252
1962	White	214[a]	262	293[c]
	Black	170	226	242
	Latino	—	232	261
1966	White	217	264[b]	296
	Black	181	232	264
	Latino	183	237	268
1971	White	221	263	295
	Black	189	236	271
	Latino	190	240	271
1975	White	218	261	297[c]
	Black	186	243	267[c]
	Latino	187	240	275[c]
1979	White	218	262[c]	
	Black	188	242[c]	
	Latino	194	238[c]	
1981	White	217		
	Black	182		
	Latino	189		

Note: Data from six assessments are reported; they were given in 1971, 1975, 1980, 1984, 1988, and 1990. The scores are the reading proficiency scale scores. The standard deviation for the age 9 scores is about 40 points; for the age 13 scores, about 35 points; and for the age 17 scores, about 40 points.
[a]"White" scores for the 1971 assessment (1962 cohort of 9-year-olds, etc.) included Latinos.
[b]The 17-year-old scores assigned to the 1962 birth cohort are from the 1980 NAEP and so should be for a 1963 birth cohort. The 13-year-old scores assigned to the 1966 birth cohort are also from the 1980 NAEP, so should be for a 1967 birth cohort.
[c]The 17-year-old scores assigned to the 1975 birth cohort are from the 1990

at 9 years old, 226 at 13 years old, and 243 at 17 years old. The gaps between their scores and those of the white cohort born in the same year were 44, 36, and 50 points at the three testing ages (Table 4.4). In the decade between the 1962 and 1971 birth cohorts, the gaps at all three testing ages fell sharply to 32, 27, and 21 points. Thus, in 1988, black 17-year-olds scored 274 on the reading test, having cut the reading achievement gap between them and white pupils by more than half during the 1980s. Blacks also made gains relative to Latino youth, though they were not quite as dramatic.

The data suggest not only that the gap narrowed for blacks, but that in the 1970s and 1980s, the gap narrowed across school years, getting progressively smaller from ages 9 to 17. The narrowing effect seemed to pick up steam in the 1980s. For the 1966 cohort, the decrease in standard deviations from age 9 to age 13 is only 0.10, for the 1971 group, it is approximately 0.28; and for the 1975 group, about 0.35.[16]

The gains are not limited to reading scores. Blacks reduced the difference between their math and science scores and those of whites in this same twenty-year period (see Table 4.4 for differences in mathematics scores). According to Smith and O'Day, a very conservative estimate of the reduction in the mathematics gap for black youth would be "on the order of 25–40% and for science roughly 15–25%."[17] For Latinos, the gains in math were slightly higher, about 33 to 45 percent.

What makes the reduction in the black achievement gap all the more impressive is that it occurred (1) during a period of increases in the percentage of blacks who were completing high school and (2) during a time of "crisis" in U.S. schools – a time when, for example, whites' reading scores stayed almost constant. The 1980s were also a period of in-

Notes to Table 4.3 (cont.) NAEP and so should be for the 1973 birth cohort. The 13-year-old scores assigned to the 1979 birth cohort are also from the 1990 NAEP and should be for the 1977 birth cohort.
Source: Educational Testing Service, *The Reading Report Card,* 1971–88 (Washington, D.C.: U.S. Department of Education, Office of Educational Research and Improvement, January 1990). I. V. V. Mullis, J. A. Dossey, M. A. Foertsch, L. R. Jones, and C. A. Gentile, *Trends in Academic Progress: Achievement of U.S. Students in Science, 1969–70 to 1990; Mathematics, 1973–90; Reading, 1971–90; and Writing, 1984–90,* prepared by the Educational Testing Service for the National Center of Educational Statistics, U.S. Department of Education, Report No. 21-T-01 (Washington, D.C.: U.S. Government Printing Office, 1991). See also Smith and O'Day, *Educational Equality,* Table 3.

Table 4.4. *The NAEP reading and mathematics achievement gap for African-Americans and Latinos, by birth cohort and age test taken (absolute point differences)*

	Age test taken					
	9		13		17	
Birth cohort	White–black	White–Latino	White–black	White–Latino	White–black	White–Latino
Reading						
1954					52	—
1958			39	—	53	41
1962	44	—	36	30	50	32
1966	36	34	32	28	32	28
1971	32	32	27	23	21	24
1975	33	31	18	21	30[a]	22[a]
1979	29	24	20[a]	24[a]		
1981	35	28				
Mathematics[b]						
1956					40	33
1960			46	35	37	30
1964	35	23	42	34	32	27
1969	32	21	34	22	29	24
1973	29	20	24	19	21	26
1977	25	21	27	21		
1981	27	21				

[a]Refers to 1990 NAEP, so 13-year-olds are born in 1977 and 17-year-olds are born in 1973.
[b]The NAEP mathematics assessments were given in 1973, 1978, 1982, and 1986, so the birth cohorts are approximate (within one year).
Source: Educational Testing Service, *Accelerated Academic Achievement* (Washington, D.C.: Department of Education, Office of Educational Research and Improvement, September 1990). See also Smith and O'Day, *Educational Equality,* 1990, Table 2. For 1990 NAEP results, see National Center for Education Statistics, *The Condition of Education, 1993* (Washington, D.C.: U.S. Department of Education, 1993), pp. 40 and 44.

creasing poverty in both the black and Latino communities. Yet it was precisely "disadvantaged" students who were making gains relative to the advantaged (as measured by parents' education), at least until the 1990, National Assessment of Educational Progress (NAEP) test, when 9- and 17-year-olds lost major ground.[18]

These gains can be explained in large part by the increased education of low-income parents. The variation in parents' education has declined sharply in the past twenty-five years. When today's low-income minority parents were going to school in the 1950s and 1960s, at least some years of high school had become a "normal" minimum education. Poverty also declined rapidly in the 1960s and early 1970s, which means that the disadvantaged children whose scores began rising in the 1970s and 1980s were living in better (and more hopeful) surroundings than children even a decade before. This reasoning is supported by another way of dividing the NAEP sample: into extreme rural, disadvantaged urban, advantaged urban, and other. If we compare the middle two categories, differences between them declined from the 1975 testing date (about 45 points in each of the three age groups) to 1988 (26 to 30 points' difference). In 1990, there was a sharp increase to 41 points' difference for 9-year-olds.

Improved schools probably also made a contribution to the closing gap. Minorities had greater access to preschool education, and although there is little evidence that increased spending per pupil made a difference in performance, curriculum and instructional homogenization seems to have had some equalization effect on the lowest-performing groups. There was a focus in this period on achieving equality of educational opportunity by improving resources for minority and low-income students. The biggest impact, however, may have come from regional equalization.[19] When reading test scores for 1971–88 are broken down by region, the Southeast shows by far the largest gains, and it was the Southeast that had the biggest educational changes in these years, especially in black education. The most important was massive school desegregation and the equalization of educational resources for blacks and whites. Another was the South's rapid economic growth and urbanization in the 1970s and 1980s. School resources increased concomitantly and began to catch up with those of higher-quality schools in the North. O'Day and Smith summarize it this way:

> Between 1960 and the early 1980s, the social and economic conditions of many minorities and the poor changed greatly for the better. The percentage of children

in poverty decreased from 26.5% in 1960 to 18.3% in 1980, the health of infants and young children greatly improved, preschool attendance rose dramatically, schools in the South desegregated, and the average education level of the parents of minority children greatly increased. At the individual level, each of these factors has a small but positive relationship to achievement for poor and minority children. Taken together they appear to have contributed in a substantial way to the narrowing of the achievement gap between 1960 and the late 1980s.[20]

The individual-responsibility argument does not do well here. Contrary to its implicit claims that blacks do not take advantage of opportunities, black youth graduating from high school are, on average, reading better than they were ten years ago and also performing better in math and science. This does not mean that minority scores are improving everywhere in the country, or that the prevailing, negative view of inner-city schools is false, or that minority graduates' average performance is all that high. One serious problem is that white scores have not been rising and that minority scores still show a very low proportion of students who are adept readers and problem solvers. Only 4 percent of black 13-year-olds were rated "adept" readers, compared with 12 percent of whites.[21] But even with all these caveats, it cannot be denied that the achievement gap has closed substantially.

The gap has also closed most where the opportunities, in the form of better schools and decreasing poverty, have increased the most. Again contrary to individual-responsibility claims, these gains undoubtedly resulted not mainly from increased self-motivation or self-awareness, but from improved material and educational resources within minority families and from equalization of access to higher-quality education, especially in the South. Both factors are affected by public policy.

Yet given what happened socioeconomically in the 1980s, these very explanations for changes in black achievement do not bode well for future changes. More children now live in poor families than in 1980 or 1973, and poverty has become increasingly concentrated in inner-city schools; the average educational attainment of minority parents is rising at a lower rate than in the 1960s and early 1970s; drug use is up among pregnant mothers; and the inner city has deteriorated socially. If poverty reduction and minority parents' increasing education during the 1960s and 1970s meant better resources at home for low-income families, the increased poverty of the 1980s will translate into a decline in achievement gains. The first indication of this effect appeared in the lower 1990 reading scores for black 9-year-olds born in 1981, when poverty rates had risen sharply.[22] The economic conditions of the 1980s may produce their most dire educational effects on minority youth in the 1990s and beyond.

DID BLACK EDUCATIONAL GAINS MEAN ECONOMIC GAINS?

A fundamental assumption of the individual-responsibility view is that black educational gains translate into economic gains. A free market pays workers according to their abilities, and abilities are closely identified with school attainment and achievement.[23] What effect did gains in minority educational attainment and achievement have on black incomes? Did catching up in school help blacks get better jobs and reduce the differences in earnings between them and whites, as the individual-responsibility argument claims?

On the basis of their extensive study of black–white male income differences, James Smith and Finis Welch argue that educational attainment is the single most important factor in black gains between 1940 and 1980.[24] But their conclusion is founded on the entire forty years as a whole, and although it may still be correct, it misses the important changes in the role of education between the first and second halves of the period. Nor does it cover the 1980s, when blacks' attainment compared with whites' slowed down. To get at these changes, a group of us at Stanford did a somewhat different kind of analysis. We estimated hypothetical black incomes for various census years using the payoffs of schooling for whites to measure the effect of changing education levels on black–white income differences in each decade. We also compared the effect of educational gains on black income gains with their effect on Latino income gains.[25]

This exercise shows a much more complex pattern of educational contribution. It confirms that differences in education have accounted for much of the difference between minority and white male incomes (Table 4.5). But changing minority education levels had most of their positive effect on minority economic standing in the 1940s, a more gradual positive impact between 1949 and 1973, and a more questionable role after 1973. The education gap is generally more important in explaining Latinos' economic standing than blacks'.

Here is how to read Table 4.5. For each year and each ethnic/gender group, the figure represents the percentage point increase in average income that the group would have had if its education had been equal to that of white males in the same year. For example, in 1939, black males would have had a 27 percentage point higher income if their education

Table 4.5. *Percentage points of income gain that would result from equalizing minority education to white male education, by ethnicity and gender, full-time-employed, 1939–89*

Year	Latino males	Latina females	Black males	Black females	White females
1939	29	18	27	22	-9
1949	17	12	18	11	-8
1959	15	10	15	9	-2
1969	12	9	14	7	0
1973	16	9	12	5	0
1979	16	8	11	6	2
1982	15	10	11	6	2
1985	15	10	11	6	2
1987	15	8	10	6	1
1989	20	14	10	7	0

Note: The education variable is measured in 1940, 1950, 1960, 1970, 1974, 1980, 1983, 1986, 1988, and 1990; incomes refer to the previous year – hence the years in the table refer to the income year. The education gap is estimated from a simulation using a regression equation with human capital variables (years of schooling, labor force experience, and, in census years, native or foreign born). The percentages in the table should be read as the number of percentage points that a given group would have gained just from getting the same distribution of education in its labor force as white males. A negative sign means that white females would receive lower incomes, all other variables equal, were education equalized with that of white males (white females in the labor market in those years had higher average education than white males).
Source: Department of Commerce, U.S. Census, Public Use Sample, 1940, 1950, 1960, 1970, 1980, and Current Population Survey, 1974, 1983, 1986, 1988, 1990.

had been equal to white males', taking account of work experience differences. White females, on the contrary, would have had a 9 percentage point lower income if they had had the same education as white males, implying that working white women were much more highly educated than men in the 1930s.

Moving down through the years, the potential percentage point increase in income that could be achieved by equalizing educational attainment between each group and white males tends to decrease. What I call the "education gap" – the income difference attributable to education differences in a given year[26] – was similar for blacks and Latinos until the 1970s, when a new, large immigration of poorly educated Latinos began. That influx of cheap labor drove down the average level of schooling in the Latino labor force relative to that of both whites and blacks, increasing the Latino education gap. In contrast, the education gap for blacks steadily declined over time, leveling off only in the 1980s. Since educational attainment generally became more equal in each decade, the effect of differences in education on income differences also generally became smaller. At the same time, differences in income themselves became smaller, in part because educational differences declined.

However, to estimate the contribution of *changes* in the education gap to changes in relative income by decade, we need to correct for changes in the white male income weights for various levels during each decade. For example, if white incomes associated with low levels of education rose rapidly relative to incomes associated with high levels, as occurred in the 1940s, this alone would reduce the education gap between blacks and whites even if blacks made no gains in education relative to whites. Such changes in income weights represent the equalization or disequalization of income distribution among white men during the ten-year period.[27] Taking out the change in income distribution during the decade leaves us with the "pure" effect of increases or decreases in minority education compared with changes in white education in each decade.

The education gap corrected for this income distribution effect is shown in Table 4.6. A comparison betweeen Tables 4.5 and 4.6 suggests that the income distribution effect was large only in the 1940s, although it had some negative effect on relative incomes in the 1980s. Black males, for example, reduced the income gap 3 percentage points in 1939–49 by increases in relative education and 6 percentage points because of changes in income distribution. In 1949–59, they reduced the income gap 2 points by increases in relative education and 1 point because of income distribution changes.

Blacks appear to have used education up until the 1970s to catch up to white earnings, but even the adjusted numbers in Table 4.6 do not necessarily mean that increased education for blacks (and Latinos) *caused* the income gains. For both men and women, blacks and Latinos, much of the income gain associated with education occurred in the 1940s, when there was also a continuing large migration of black workers from agriculture to manufacturing (and South to North). Changes in relative minority income seem related as much to such sectoral shifts as to the simulta-

Table 4.6. *Change in education gap adjusted for changing income weights, by decade, full-time workers, 1939–89 (percentage points of income)*

Year	Latino males	Latina females	Black males	Black females
1939	29	18	27	22
1949	23	16	24	15
1949	17	12	18	11
1959	16	10	16	9
1959	15	10	15	9
1969	12	9	14	7
1969	12	9	14	7
1979	16	8	11	6
1979	16	8	11	6
1989	19	13	9	7

Note: See Table 4.5 for figures based on the education gap estimated using same-year white male income weights. This table compares the education gap in 1939 from Table 4.5 with the gap in 1949 based on average education differences between ethnic groups in 1949 weighted by white male coefficients estimated using 1939 census data. It also compares the 1949 figures from Table 4.5 with 1959 figures based on average education differences in 1959 weighted by white male coefficients using 1949 census data, and so forth, for various census years. This permits comparison for each decade of the effect on income of the education gain net of changes in the distribution of income among education groups in that particular decade.

neous educational gains.[28] True, workers can make better use of education in nonagricultural jobs, but that still means that for more education to pay off income-wise, jobs requiring higher education have to be available. The results for the 1950s show that blacks made big educational gains on whites with minimal income gains (see Figure 2.1 and Table 2.2 for data on black income gains). In the 1960s and early 1970s, the black income gap narrowed substantially more than the black education gap. Together, the numbers for the 1950s, 1960s, and early 1970s suggest that, at least for African-Americans, the rise in relative incomes came not only from changes in the education gap, but from other important changes – changes in income distribution, equal employment opportunity, and affirmative action, for example. Such changes had as much to do with how much blacks were paid for their work as with their education.

Booker T. Washington had it right: more education works best in improving blacks' economic condition when they have access to better jobs. The big changes in the income gap in the 1940s and 1960s occurred at a time not only when African-Americans and Latinos were getting more education, but when other factors, such as shifts from rural to urban jobs and more equal income distribution in the 1940s and changing wage discrimination in the 1960s, came into play.

Black–white male income differences increased slightly after 1979, even as the education gap continued to fall. What happened? After all, as measured by average *years* of schooling, blacks (and native-born Latinos) continued to reduce the difference in educational attainment in the 1980s.[29] There were still large differences in the percentage of whites and minorities (particularly Latinos, and even native-born Latinos) in the labor force who dropped out of high school, but this difference was still slowly declining during the decade – more and more minorities were, in one way or another, finishing high school.

Important as high school dropout differences are, the answer to the 1980s education gap puzzle lies mainly somewhere else – at the college level. The reasons are fairly simple. First, incomes of college graduates, regardless of ethnicity, race, or gender, rose in the 1980s, while incomes (corrected for inflation) of high school graduates fell. This made college education relatively more valuable – gave it a greater "weight" in assessing the overall average value of an ethnic group's education and the kind of jobs members of that group could get in a changing job market. Second, it was just in the 1980s that blacks' surge into the nation's colleges drastically slowed down. Blacks did not respond to the "new" structure of incomes. Even though they were increasing their educational attainment, they were doing it mainly by increasing their high school completion rate. Whites, in contrast, were increasing their average education by continuing on, raising the percentage that completed college. There was an increase in the proportion of the age cohort that completed college among all minority groups. But apart from black women, it was still only about 12 percent – half the white percentage. As the real incomes of the college-educated held steady and incomes of the high-school-educated fell in the 1980s, the income-weighted gap in years of schooling (the income distribution effect) increased between minorities and whites.

In our increasingly high-tech, information society, the economic implications of the college barrier turn out to be more important for blacks than even their high school dropout or high school achievement gap. By not moving up educationally, blacks get bunched up in jobs where real wages are declining and are left out of those where wages are at least holding constant.

Can we blame blacks' motivation for their failure to go on to college? Or are other factors, such as lack of financing and declining real incomes for the bottom 60 percent of black families, more important? One clue lies in the fact that blacks are not the only ones to get caught in this trap. Mexican-origin Latinos, including those native-born, are also missing the college boat, suggesting that there more than blacks' poor motivation is involved. Blacks and Mexican-origin Latinos, for all the differences in their culture and family formation patterns, apparently share this serious educational problem.

DID BLACK ACHIEVEMENT GAINS MEAN INCOME GAINS?

This still leaves us with the issue of how – beyond the effect of more *years* of education – increasing minority school *achievement* contributed to minority incomes. Even if the education gap in terms of educational attainment did not close in the 1980s, maybe *within* education level – especially among high school completers – young minorities began to earn more income relative to whites because of higher achievement scores.

Recent research on the contribution of relative "quality" of black and white schools in the South to black relative income gains suggests that we should find such a positive relation between achievement and income. Economists David Card and Alan Krueger use three measures of school quality – the ratio of pupils to teachers, length of school term, and teachers' pay – to compare the quality of black and white schooling by state over a fifty-year period, from 1915 to 1965. They find that changes in the composite index of school quality affect earnings. Men who were educated in states with higher-quality systems tended to earn a higher economic return for their years of schooling. The results also suggest that changes in school quality over time explain from 45 to 80 percent of the relative increase in the payoff of schooling for black workers born in 1940–9 over those born in 1910–19, and this in turn explains about one-fourth of the convergence of black and white educational payoffs between 1960 and 1980.[30]

Although there is no definitive evidence linking Card and Krueger's measures of school quality to test scores, many studies suggest a relationship between school improvement interventions and pupils' school performance.[31] Yet when it comes to the impact of school "quality" on labor market performance, the results are less clear. Card and Krueger estimate a positive and statistically significant correlation of higher school quality, as measured by school *inputs*, with income returns to schooling across states,[32] but other studies show little or no relation between higher achievement scores (school *outputs*) and earnings for those with the same level of schooling.[33]

In the individual-responsibility view, black reading and mathematics gains in the late 1970s and early 1980s should have had two effects. First, they should have made young black high school graduates more valuable in the labor market relative to young whites. Second, they should have significantly increased black college entrance and completion. The second effect did not occur, as shown earlier. But did young (16- to 24-year-old) black and Latino high school graduates begin seeing income gains in the middle and late 1980s?

Recent work by Frank Levy and Richard Murnane, using data from the National Longitudinal Survey on 1972 high school seniors and the High School and Beyond survey of 1980 high school seniors, shows that those seniors with higher mathematics scores in both surveys earned significantly higher wages six years later (at age 24) than those with lower scores even when correcting for the amount of schooling they had received. The relation was much stronger in the 1980s than in the 1970s, reaching 16 percent higher wages for one standard deviation increase in test score in the later period and about 5 percent in the 1970s. Furthermore, the impact of higher math scores on income was similar for black and white men and was greater for women of both races. Analogous results with a smaller increase were found for reading test scores.[34] These relationships would seem to support the individual-responsibility view that improving educational achievement by young black people can have some effect on their income. If black male youth could attain the same scores as whites (they are now about one-half deviation apart) they could reduce by about one-half the difference in income between black and white male 24-year-olds in 1986. But there is a problem: Levy and Murnane also show that those graduates who had scored one standard deviation above those with low mastery of math skills in 1980 earned much less in 1986 than the wages in 1978 of those seniors graduating in

Table 4.7. *Ratio of minority to white mean hourly income, high school graduates at 20 years old, all workers with income, by ethnicity, gender, and birth cohort, 1953–71*

	African-American		Latino	
Birth cohort	Males	Females	Males	Females
1953	0.87	0.98	0.89	0.96
1959	0.92	1.05	0.97	0.98
1962	0.75	0.97	0.87	1.04
1965	0.79	0.86	0.93	0.92
1967	0.90	0.86	0.96	0.98
1969	0.92	1.04	0.93	1.01
1971	0.90	0.92	1.01	0.98

Source: Public Use Census Samples, 1980; Current Population Surveys, 1974, 1983, 1986, 1988, 1990, and 1992.

1972 who had low mastery of math skills. This suggests that higher math skills do not in and of themselves yield higher wages – only higher wages compared with the wages of those who graduated in the same year. An improvement in math skills therefore seems to have a relatively small effect on earnings over time.

What do we observe when we measure the relative wages of young people over time? The data in Table 4.7 do not preclude the possibility of a positive relationship between relative wages and improving school performance, but they are hardly convincing. Young black high school graduates (average age about 20 or 21 years old) with income did show gains compared with young whites in the late 1980s and early 1990s.[35] Yet because blacks' relative wages first declined and then rose in the 1980s, they were more likely the result of business cycle demand for young black workers than of blacks' changing academic performance.[36]

Did academic gains have any effect on these young blacks' relative wages? They may have, but if so, that effect is buried in the cyclical fall and rise of relative wages. Such a pattern is more consistent with the relatively greater difficulties young blacks face compared with whites during recessions and the downward pressure that higher black unemployment put on the wages of young blacks in the period 1980–5. The movement of young Latino men's relative wages supports this explanation. Their wages also fell during the 1980–2 recession but tended to recover more rapidly than those of young blacks. This is what we would expect – Latinos traditionally have had much lower unemployment rates than blacks.

Our result confirms Murnane and Levy's in an unexpected way. They found that macroeconomic effects, such as secular declines in male wages, tend to overwhelm the effects of higher test scores. Our data suggest that the business cycle and relative unemployment rates also appear to have a greater impact on relative wages than longer-term increases in test scores.

Table 4.7 also raises questions about Card and Krueger's earlier research showing the positive effect of school quality on the equalization of black–white income differentials and on the return to black education. Their result may have depended heavily on the large economic gains blacks made during the period Card and Krueger analyzed – from 1960 to 1980. Had they looked at the 1950s or 1980s instead of the 1960s and 1970s, the effect of improvements in black education might have been much smaller.

The swing in relative wages of blacks from the early 1970s to the early 1990s is not necessarily inconsistent with an argument for educational improvement leading to higher wages. As Murnane and Levy show, even as real wages decline for male labor as a whole, if individual blacks raise their test scores they will do better economically than their lower-scoring colleagues. That said, Table 4.7 suggests that the economic situation of blacks is greatly influenced by labor market forces out of individual blacks' control.

Even if we argue that higher test scores might have led to higher relative wages for blacks in the late 1980s, the individual-responsibility view would not necessarily be supported by the argument. Black test scores did not necessarily go up because black students and their families were trying harder, but because *government policies* in the 1960s and early 1970s equalized income and school opportunities for black children. This is contrary to what individual responsibility predicts should have happened. Similarly, the increase in poverty and the absence of continuing improvement in blacks' schooling in the 1980s – this time, because of *government deregulation* – produced lower black scores. Incomes for black male youth may therefore decline. Again, this is inconsistent with what individual responsibility predicts should happen.

DO BLACKS EARN LESS BECAUSE THEY DON'T WORK AS HARD?

If black educational attainment and performance make a relatively weak case for the individual-responsibility explanation of black–white economic inequality, what other case can be made? The most popular argument is that black men do not want to work as much as other groups. Individual-responsibility proponents use labor force participation rates to argue that much of the black poverty problem lies in black male withdrawal from the labor force. True, young, low-income blacks do have low labor force participation rates, and that undoubtedly does contribute to black poverty, black crime, black drug use, and the deterioration of black nuclear family life.

But a high percentage of black men do work, they are still poor, and they have become poorer over the past twenty years. This is due only in small part to their having fallen behind whites because they work less. It is mostly the result of sharp declines in what both blacks and whites earn after correcting for inflation. These declines have been greatest for black and white high school dropouts, but they have also hit high school graduates. The general trend to hold wages down in the 1980s expansion left even male college graduates with about the same median earnings in 1989 as in 1979 when adjusted for inflation.

Yet the individual-responsibility argument seizes on the very small fraction of the decline in total black male income that comes from fewer hours worked to establish the case for lower effort. The argument goes that among black men there has been a steady drop of full-time workers. As a result of blacks' working less, black male incomes are falling relative to white incomes, increasing the likelihood that blacks will be poor and that black families will disintegrate.

What are the facts?

1. If a black man gets full-time work, he greatly reduces the chance of being poor, especially if he has graduated from high school or gone on to college. In 1989, a black male high school dropout, about 30 years old, earned a median $9,100 a year, compared with his white counterpart's $13,600. If they were employed full time (thirty-five or more hours per week and fifty weeks per year), their median incomes would have been $12,750 and $17,750, respectively. A black male high school graduate about 30 years old earned a median $13,600. His white counterpart made $19,400. Just as for high school dropouts, getting full-time work made a bigger difference for blacks than for whites: black full-timers

made $17,500 compared with $22,400 for whites. The implication is that a higher fraction of blacks than whites work part time. For college graduates, however, the gain of moving to full-time work is about the same for blacks as for whites.[37]

2. Not only did fewer blacks than whites work full time at the end of the 1980s, the difference between the two groups' probability of getting full-time work used to be much lower in the past. For example, the ratio between the median income for all workers and full-time workers widened in every educational category in 1973 to 1989, with most of the widening for black high school and college graduates taking place in the 1980s. Thus, it looks as though blacks moved out of full-time work at a more rapid pace than did whites.

But let us assume that the ratios for blacks remained the same in 1989 as they were in 1973. How much would that help? The median black high school dropout would earn $11,300 instead of $9,100; the median high school graduate, $15,000; and the median college graduate, $22,600 – still much less than their white counterparts, and less than blacks would have earned had wages not fallen so drastically since 1973.

Assume that the proportion of blacks working full time was the same lower percentage as in 1989, but wages per hour stayed the same as in 1973. This age group of black high school dropouts would be earning $11,400 in 1989, even with the much lower average hours they worked compared with 1973, high school graduates would earn $16,600, and college graduates, $23,600. In each case, the effect of wage decline on median income is greater than the effect of lower labor force participation.

The second comparison is between the incomes of full-time-employed black and white men with the same level of schooling. Here, the issue is not work time; it is wages per hour. In 1979, a black male 30-year-old high school dropout earned 72 percent of a white male's median income. A black high school graduate earned 80 percent of white median income, and a black college graduate, 72 percent. All these ratios stayed constant or decreased in the 1980s – to 71 percent for a dropout, 77 percent for a high school graduate, and 72 percent for a college graduate – contradicting the individual-responsibility argument that free-market-stimulated economic growth can equalize racial differences in earnings. These blacks got full-time jobs yet in terms of wages lost ground to whites. As government got off the backs of employers, the market for black labor weakened rather than strengthened – black men did worse rather than better.

The final question is whether black men have *chosen* to take less full-time work or whether working part time has been forced on them by "the economy." The March sample of the Current Population Survey of the U.S. Census, taken every year, regularly asks those who work part time whether they do so voluntarily. The responses show that males as a whole, including black males, have an extremely high rate of involuntary unemployment.[38]

If this survey is at all accurate, the labor market is increasingly penalizing an ever-larger group of blacks. They not only are getting fewer hours of work but are being paid less than their white male counterparts. The sample of all those 25- to 34-year-old black males who worked lost even more ground to whites in the 1980s than fully employed blacks. All black high school dropouts who worked earned 70 percent of median white income in 1979 and only 67 percent in 1989; high school graduates earned 72 percent in 1979 and 70 percent in 1989; and the earnings of black college graduates dropped precipitously from 85 percent to 72 percent of median white income. The key point is that new divisions in the labor market are springing up that may well be forcing many black men who would like to work full time even at fairly low wages into the part-time labor market. Considering that we have been discussing 25- to 34-year-olds, not black teenagers, the signs are not encouraging.

Most surprising in terms of the individual-responsibility argument is that the largest impact of the 1980s on black male incomes in both full- and part-time work has been among black college graduates. This is all the more impressive because the market for white male college graduates "tightened" in the 1980s but "loosened" for blacks. Since black college graduates are the most successful of young blacks, according to the individual-responsibility argument they should have done best in the deregulated 1980s. Since they did not, it raises questions about the argument itself.

Nor is this sharp decline in median income for college-educated black males relative to whites consistent with the class explanation of racial inequality. If class were the issue, the large increases in black–white income inequality would have occurred in the high school dropout group and especially among high school graduates, who form the vast majority of today's younger working-class labor. That was clearly not the case. Younger black high school graduates did worse in the expansion of the mid-1980s, but came out of the decade about the same as they came in, at

70 percent of white income. This was not so for black college graduates, who declined through the decade.

Individual-responsibility proponents could claim that black college graduates are doing worse because affirmative action allowed lower-quality blacks to get a college education in the 1980s and gave underqualified college-educated blacks good jobs in the 1970s and the early 1980s. With deregulation of labor markets, employers "rationally" gave lower wages to workers of such declining quality. But blacks' SAT scores rose sharply in the 1980s compared with whites' scores,[39] and so did blacks' relative scores on the GRE.[40] Employers may well have been willing to offer worse jobs to black graduates as government became more slack in enforcing affirmative action. Yet this was more likely to be a return to old habits than a "rational" market response to "lower-quality" black graduates seeking these jobs.

WHY DIDN'T BLACKS DO AS WELL AS ASIAN-AMERICANS?

When individual-responsibility proponents lay responsibility on blacks for their inability and unwillingness to "use" the system, they have in mind other minority groups who have succeeded where blacks (and Latinos) have failed. The "model minority" usually referred to is Asian-Americans. For a group that faced severe economic, social, and political discrimination before the end of World War II, Asian-Americans did indeed make great strides in the postwar period. On average, they now earn as much as or more than whites in many states,[41] and their success is largely the result of their having reached much higher average educational levels than whites.

Why have Asian-Americans received so much more schooling than blacks (and whites)? A typical argument put forth by Asian-Americans themselves is that they have a powerful drive to overcome discrimination, and education is the means to do it.[42] Does this imply that blacks do not have this drive, as individual-responsibility proponents claim? Perhaps. But Asian-Americans have also been able to build up a powerful network of connections in the labor market. As a group, they own or manage many businesses. That is more indicative of a significant interaction effect between the commercial talents of Asian immigrants, the historical existence of Asian economic enclaves in the larger U.S. economy, capital accumulation in the enclaves, and the relative economic success of educated Asian-Americans even before World War II because of such en-

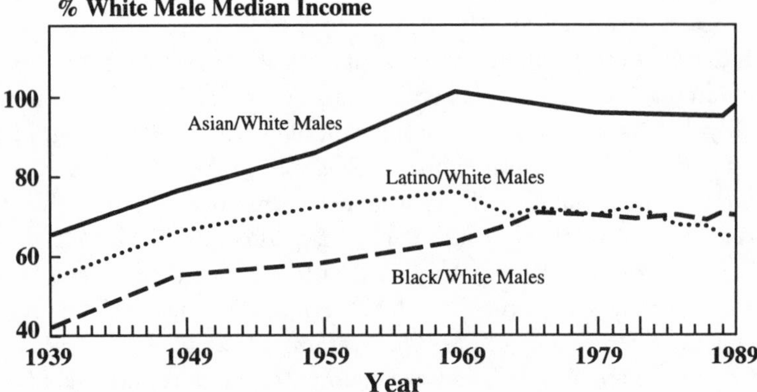

Figure 4.3. Minority–white male median income ratios, by race and ethnicity, full-time workers, 1939–89. From U.S. Census Bureau, Public Use Sample, 1940, 1950, 1960, 1970, and 1980, and Current Population Survey, March Survey, various years, full-time-worker sample.

claves.[43] The existence in an earlier time of an extensive network of Asian-owned businesses employing Asians could explain much of the high payoff of their educational investment even while blacks faced much lower educational payoffs before the late 1960s.

Have Asian-Americans done so much better than blacks in the past fifty years or did they just begin at a higher level? Asian-Americans already had much higher education and incomes than either blacks or Latinos in the 1940s. Asian incomes also rose more in the twenty years between 1949 and 1969. But since that time, increased immigration from Asia and probably certain barriers, such as the so-called glass ceiling, have slowed Asian-American advancement. So despite having received much more education than whites – almost one-half of the Asian-Americans in the labor force have completed college or more, compared with less than one-fourth of whites – the "model minority" still earns about what whites earn. Apparently high motivation and taking advantage of educational opportunities will get you only so far (Figure 4.3).

There is another irony here. The Asians' success story did not become popularized until the 1970s, based on their extraordinary gains in the earlier two decades. With the education-intensive, information-technology-led development of the 1980s, these gains should have been extended, but they were not. Even college-educated Asian-Americans

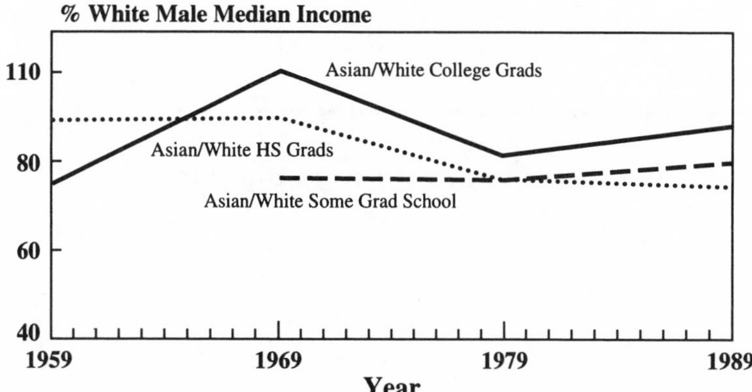

Figure 4.4. Asian-American–white male median income ratios, full-time-employed, 25 to 34 years old, by level of education, 1959–89. From U.S. Census Bureau, Public Use Sample, 1940, 1950, 1960, 1970, and 1980, and Current Population Survey, March Survey, various years, full-time-worker sample.

reached their peak median earnings relative to whites in 1969 (Figure 4.4).

The blame that the model-minority argument casts on blacks for their disadvantaged earnings and employment situations would have much greater validity were not the history of blacks in the United States so different from that of Asian-Americans. Blacks have always been at a greater disadvantage in the labor market because they did not bring commercial skills with them from the "old country." They were always more dependent on white employment and white government policies for their economic well-being. When those policies changed in order to reduce barriers to education and jobs, I will argue, the black community responded quickly. It made gains that might have been as rapid as those of Asian-Americans had the policies been supported over a long enough period of time.

5

Is the economy to blame?

Economies go through changes that hurt some groups and benefit others. In the 1970s and 1980s, the U.S. economy entered an era of international competition that it had not known since the 1920s, when we were the ones exporting to others at low prices, able to exploit the economies of scale of a large domestic market so vital to assembly line production. In these past two decades, however, the tables have turned. Japan, Germany, and newcomers, such as Korea and Taiwan, now complete successfully in the U.S. market. Furthermore, U.S. companies are using other countries' lower-wage labor forces to produce manufactured goods for sale at home. The main fallout of this rapid change has been the "declining middle" – a sustained decline in high-wage manufacturing production jobs – and an expanding bottom and top – low-income and high-income service jobs. The high-income jobs require a college education, so only a small fraction of blacks are even eligible for them. And many of the new low-income (and many of the high-income) jobs have gone to women and immigrants, ready to work hard at lower wages than black men.

Is the changeover from a factory-based, domestic-market-oriented, manufacturing economy using a domestic labor force to a globally oriented information economy the reason that the less-schooled, more manual-labor-intensive African-American labor force has stopped making gains?

Again, taking a close look at historical processes of change helps us understand where we are today. When the U.S. industrial economy totally dominated world markets for more than a generation, from the 1940s to the early 1970s, blacks (and the other large, low-income minority – Latinos) were incorporated into the industrial labor force, mainly into semiskilled and some skilled factory jobs. Just as important, wages for these *and all other jobs* in the economy were rising steadily in this period, fueled by a symbiotic relation between rising productivity and a government policy that endorsed rising wages. U.S. companies were building many factories in other countries, but to supply growing foreign markets, not to reexport to the United States. The U.S. market was growing so fast that there were few worries about jobs going overseas. And until the mid-1960s, immigrants were mainly Europeans, though there were temporary agricultural labor immigration agreements with Mexico. For twenty-five years, blacks were the major new source of low- and semiskilled industrial labor.

So it makes sense that economic restructuring would hurt already low-income black males by shutting down access to skilled manufacturing jobs. William Wilson is right in stating that the economic environment of the 1970s and 1980s was unfavorable to blacks – especially those living in inner cities. Their poor preparation for what Robert Reich calls "symbolic analysis,"[1] or processing information from computers, and their location far from the suburbs, where such work is done, put them at a real disadvantage.

But the changing structure of jobs was not the only "economic" reason that black male and female incomes stopped rising relative to whites' after the mid-1970s. Wages adjusted for inflation fell for all but high-paying professional and managerial jobs. Wage declines also occurred in semiskilled and skilled manufacturing work. Difficult access to higher-paying jobs hurt certain groups of blacks, but lower wages overall, and the fact that with new, massive immigration there was a labor force ready to work for low wages, probably hurt blacks just as badly.

The census data analyzed in this chapter confirm that sectoral and employment restructuring in the economy did hold back the growth of black incomes relative to whites'. But on the basis of the same data I show that such structural change is an incomplete explanation of why the slowdown in incomes took place. Black incomes faced other, more direct pressures – namely, changing government economic policies that explicitly and implicitly emphasized cheap labor as a key to U.S. economic health in the new, competitive environment. Those changing strategies are discussed in a later chapter; here we simply make the case that shifts in employment structures were not the main reason that blacks stopped gaining on whites.

In making this case, it helps to compare the black experience not only

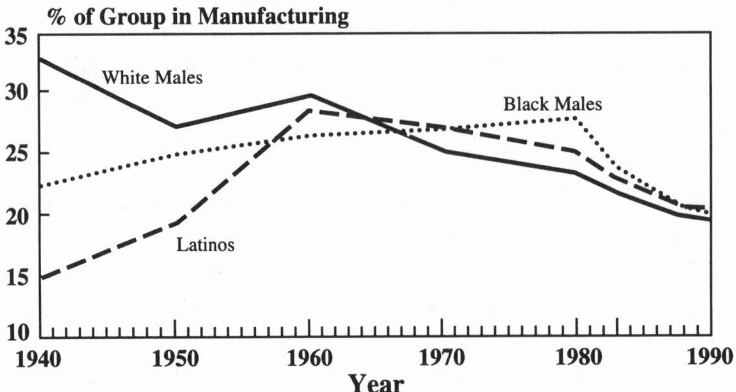

Figure 5.1. Manufacturing-sector employment, all males with income, by race and ethnicity, 1940–90. From U.S. Census Bureau, Public Use Sample, 1940, 1950, 1960, 1970, and 1980, and Current Population Survey, March Survey, various years, all-worker sample.

with the white, but with that of another major minority of color – Latinos – especially after 1970, when Latinos began a new migration into the very urban job markets where blacks had made large income gains for thirty years. How did the changing structure of employment affect the two groups? Does the way it affected them tell us anything about the impact of employment change versus overall wage declines? What do differences in the black and Latino male and female experience with economic restructuring tell us about what slowed black income gains?

THE CHANGING STRUCTURE OF EMPLOYMENT

The industries in which Americans worked changed drastically between 1940 and the late 1980s, and the change was greater for blacks than for whites. In 1940, 22 percent of black males (and 35 percent of Latinos) worked in agriculture, far more than the 14 percent of whites. By 1960, these percentages had become much more equal as minorities moved out of agriculture, and by 1970, agricultural work had ceased to be an important occupation for any group. Simultaneously, blacks were rapidly incorporated into manufacturing, nearly reaching proportional parity with white males in 1960, and then moving higher as the white percentage steadily declined (Figure 5.1). After 1980, however, blacks rapidly lost

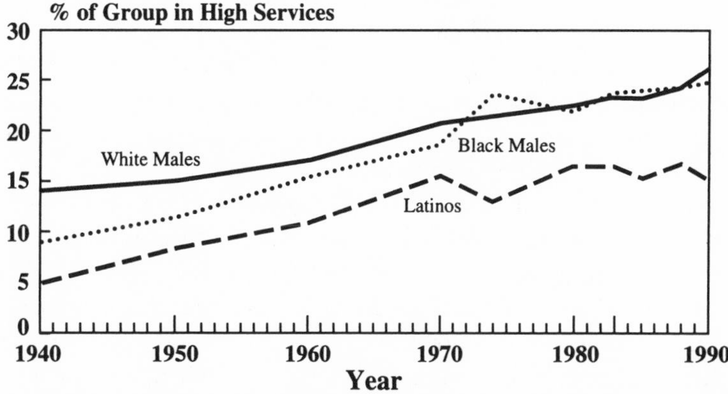

Figure 5.2. High-value service sector employment, all males with income, by race and ethnicity, 1940–90. From U.S. Census Bureau, Public Use Sample, 1940, 1950, 1960, 1970, and 1980, and Current Population Survey, March Survey, various years, all-worker sample.

manufacturing employment. By 1990, about 20 percent of total jobs held by black men were in manufacturing, the same proportion as whites.

The data are not controversial: there *was* a rapid shift of black men from agriculture to manufacturing from 1940 to 1960, and blacks held their jobs in manufacturing into the early 1970s, even as whites were moving out. After that point, the shift out of manufacturing was sharper for blacks than for whites.

But the popularly held notion that blacks as a group were most whiplashed by sectoral shifts after 1970 is not true: the difference between blacks and whites is not nearly as large as that between Latinos and whites. This is borne out by the gradual shift into high-value service jobs[2] throughout this period. Black and white males followed a similar path into service jobs after 1974, while Latinos continued to lag behind both groups, falling even farther back in the 1980s (Figure 5.2).[3] For women, the opposite is true: black women lost ground to both white and Latina women after 1974 in this sector, shifting into lower-paying retail trade and low-end services.

As a first impression, it is not so evident that the "pure" deindustrialization argument is correct for the black labor force as a whole, although it may be valid for certain northern urban groups. About one-half of all black jobs are in the South, and about one-third are in the old industrial north central–northeast corridor. The sharp deindustrialization process in the old, industrial North, therefore, affected only a part of the black labor force – an important part, but a minority nevertheless.[4]

The surprise is that changes in the sectoral composition of the labor force may be as important in explaining the economic problems of Latino men and black women in the 1980s as in explaining those of black men, especially when it comes to wages. Even with the large sectoral shifts that began in the 1960s, black male workers found employment in the high-end service sector along with white males and, incidently, also began to move out of the Rust Belt to the South and West. Latinos were also moved out of manufacturing jobs but, on average, this growing new immigrant population was not able to get into high-end services to nearly the same degree as blacks. Instead, they tended – much more than black men – to find work in low-paying sectors such as agriculture, retail trade, and construction and – like blacks – in personal and restaurant services.

THE IMPACT OF EMPLOYMENT SHIFTS ON BLACK INCOMES

We can estimate the impact of these shifts on minorities' incomes relative to those of whites by simulating what minority incomes would have been in each year if they had had the same sectoral distribution of jobs as white males.[5] The simulation gives us two pieces of informaton: (1) it tells us how many percentage points of relative income an ethnic/gender group could gain (or lose) on average in a given year if its members worked in the same industries as white males, assuming that they were paid the same as white males in each industry; and (2) it tells us how much the effect on minority incomes of changing sectoral composition of employment increased or decreased over time.

The results (see Table 5.1a) tell us that the income gap due to differences between the sectoral distribution of male and female black workers and white male workers was very large in 1939, but by 1949, as more minority male workers moved out of agriculture and low-level service jobs into manufacturing and clerical work, the potential percentage point gain in income from the "sectoral gap" declined. The opposite happened for white and Latina women in the 1950s. They tended to move into lower-paying sectors relative to white men, and that trend continued into the 1960s.

Since the estimate of every group's sector gap used white male income weights in the corresponding year, sector gap comparisons with previous years require adjusting for changes in the "prices" (white male income

Table 5.1a. *Income gap due to differences in industrial-sector employment among white, Latino, and black workers, all workers with income and full-time-employed, 1939–89 (percentage of white male income)*

Year	Latino males	Latina females	Black males	Black females	White females
All workers with income					
1939	29	9	19	14	-9
1949	13	-4	5	8	-8
1959	8	2	5	12	-4
1969	3	0	2	4	0
1973	4	-1	-2	-1	-1
1979	4	4	0	0	1
1982	7	2	0	-1	1
1985	8	3	1	1	0
1987	8	4	2	-1	0
1989	9	4	0	-1	1
Full-time workers					
1939	20	8	15	15	-5
1949	6	-6	3	2	-8
1959	4	-2	2	2	-6
1969	1	-4	2	-2	-5
1973	3	-3	-1	-4	-4
1979	3	0	1	-2	-3
1982	4	-2	1	-3	-3
1985	4	-1	0	-4	-4
1987	5	0	1	-4	-5
1989	7	0	1	-4	-3

Note: A negative sign indicates that when the other group's industrial-sector employment distribution weighted by white male "prices" is compared with white male incomes, the other group's estimated mean is higher by the number of percentage points indicated.
Source: Department of Commerce, U.S. Census, Public Use Sample, and Current Population Survey.

Table 5.1b. *Sector gap changes due to differences in industrial-sector employment among white, Latino, and black workers, adjusted for changes in white male income weight, all workers with income and full-time-employed, 1939–89 (percentage of white male income)*

	Latino males	Latina females	Black males	Black females	White females
All workers with income					
1939	29	9	19	14	–9
1949	22	–9	8	1	–2
1949	13	–4	5	8	–8
1959	7	–1	4	6	–5
1959	8	2	5	12	–4
1969	3	0	2	4	0
1969	3	0	2	4	0
1979	4	4	0	0	1
1979	4	4	0	0	1
1989	9	4	0	–1	1
Full-time workers					
1939	20	8	15	15	–5
1949	10	–9	4	–1	–15
1949	5	–6	3	2	–8
1959	4	–2	2	2	–6
1959	4	–2	2	2	–6
1969	1	–4	2	–2	–5
1969	1	–4	2	–2	–5
1979	3	0	1	–2	–3
1979	3	0	1	–2	–3
1989	5	0	1	–1	–2

weights) of sector distributions from one year to the next. Such adjustments are negligible in most decades, but are important in the 1940s and 1950s for the all-worker sample and in the 1940s and 1980s for the full-time-worker sample. The "true" sector gap changes are shown in Table 5.1b.

The income-distribution-adjusted "sector gap" is much larger than the adjusted "education gap" in the 1940s for both blacks and Latinos. Thus, sectoral shifts in the 1940s had a much more powerful impact on minority males' relative economic position than did relative education gains. After 1949, the decline in sector gap becomes generally less significant in explaining relative income gains for blacks and, although still important for those minority workers not fully employed and for full-time-employed Latinos, is generally smaller in the 1950s and 1960s than the adjusted education gap for full-time workers. The sector gap becomes a factor in explaining the income gap again in the 1970s and 1980s, and then primarily for Latinos.

In the great wartime and postwar expansion, then, the shift into urban jobs was a major reason that minorities' incomes drew closer to whites'. This job shift was accompanied by an increase in minority education. It is not easy to separate out which was "causal": did more education lead to industrial employment, or did industrial employment in urban areas raise educational levels? Probably both. But as the slowdown of black income growth relative to whites' in the 1950s suggests, without job mobility, educational gains cannot have much effect.

What effect did post-1973 economic restructuring have? Did sectoral shifts hurt minorities' incomes more than whites'? Table 5.1b suggests that they did, but mainly the incomes of Latino males. Changing sectoral employment had a negative effect on Latino incomes, very much smaller than the earlier positive impact when corrected for changes in the distribution of wages across sectors, but still a significant fraction of the increas-

Note to Table 5.1b: Since the estimate of every group's sector gap uses white male income weights in the corresponding year, sector gap comparisons with previous years require adjusting for changes in the "prices" (white male income weights) of sector distribution from one year to the next. Such adjustments are negligible in most decades, but are important in the 1940s and 1950s for the all-worker sample and in the 1940s and 1980s for the full-time worker sample. These figures represent the "true" sector gap changes in those decades.
Source: Department of Commerce, U.S. Census, Public Use Sample, and Current Population Survey.

ing total Latino income gap. As Latino employment after 1969 shifted out of manufacturing and was increasingly absorbed in relatively low-paying construction, restaurant and custodial services, and retail trade, the income gap explained by sectoral employment shifts increased from 3 to 9 percentage points for Latino men in the all-worker sample and from 3 to 5 percentage points for those in the full-time-employed sample.

Because the decline in total measured relative income for minority males was not large in the 1970s and 1980s,[6] the increases in the sectoral income gap shown in Table 5.1b tell us that whatever happened to minorities income-wise in the 1970s and 1980s was explained in large part by job shifts. But here is the surprise and in the surprise, perhaps a clue as to why job shifts were important. Sectoral employment shifts explain a much larger fraction of the decline in Latinos' income than in blacks'.[7] For black male workers, changes in sectoral composition had essentially no impact throughout this period. And the relative income position of black women in the 1970s and 1980s also is related less to sectoral employment shifts than is Latinas'.

All of this tells us that the employment shift in the 1970s and 1980s hit those workers – Latinos and Latinas – whose average education was falling farthest behind whites and were most likely to get jobs where wage growth was slowest. Sectoral shifts did not appear to affect black men and women, even though the income gap for black men compared with white men and for black women compared with white women grew in the 1980s. To figure out how this happened, we have to take a closer look at the changing job market of the 1970s and 1980s. More than sectoral shifts, changing job structures within various industries in the 1980s worked unfavorably for blacks.

THE DECLINING MIDDLE

The sectoral composition of jobs was not the only thing about the job market that changed after 1973. "Good," managerial, white-collar, and technical jobs continued to expand as a proportion of total jobs, but "bad," low-paying, service jobs made a comeback after many decades of decline. And mainly because of deindustrialization, the "middle" continued to disappear. Yet it was in the 1980s that this change in the job market became most apparent for blacks and Latinos. Unlike the 1970s, when the middle was also declining, black male and Latino job mobility in the 1980s was adversely affected. Jobwise, minority and white males went in opposite directions.

The figures in Table 5.2 show what has happened to minority men and women compared with whites in the three decades since 1960. The percentages in the table are estimated by dividing all workers with income into the fourteen industrial sectors in which they work, ranked by employees' average annual income, along one axis, and ten occupational categories for the jobs workers hold, also ranked by average income, along the other axis. The cells in this matrix were divided into three groupings called high-paying jobs, middle-paying jobs, and low-paying jobs. The groupings were somewhat different for men and women, but in general professionals and managers were in high-paid jobs; craftspeople, operatives, and clerical and sales workers were in middle-paid jobs; and low-end service workers and laborers were in low-paid jobs.[8]

Between 1970 and 1990, and especially after 1980, the proportion of workers in middle-paying jobs declined, mainly because of the decline in manufacturing. The proportion of higher-paying jobs increased, mainly because employment in information-based services increased. And the proportion of lower-paying jobs stayed about the same.

But the way blacks and Latinos experienced these changes was very different from the way whites did. For whites, the proportion and number of high-paying jobs increased rapidly in the 1980s, even as middle- and low-income jobs declined or grew more slowly. But for minority males and black females who had moved up rapidly into rapidly expanding middle- and high-paying jobs in the 1960s and 1970s, the job market changed in the oppostie direction in the 1980s. High-paying jobs continued to open up in somewhat larger numbers than in the 1970s, middle-paying jobs declined (as for whites), and low-paying jobs exploded. Instead of moving into expanding middle-income jobs in the 1980s, minority males found more work in low-paying jobs (Table 5.3). More jobs were created for minority males in the 1980s than in the 1970s (and fewer for white males), but the jobs created were mainly at the low end. This reversed two decades of a rapid upward job trend, especially for blacks.[9]

Aside from deindustrialization and the growth of service employment, changes *within* industries also caused occupational shifts. On the surface, these seemed favorable to minorities. A high fraction of all workers were employed in traditional manufacturing (16 percent in 1990) and high value-added (or office-based) service (30 percent). Firms in both sectors

Table 5.2. *Employment shares by industry/occupation and ethnic/gender group, all workers, 1960–90*

	1960	1970	1980	1986	1988	1990
Total employed						
I (high wage)	24.6	25.5	28.2	30.9	32.4	32.9
II (middle wage)	40.2	39.6	38.2	34.5	34.2	34.4
III (low wage)	35.1	35.0	33.6	34.5	33.4	32.6
White males						
I	28.4	29.4	32.3	35.6	37.2	39.5
II	41.2	38.9	36.5	32.3	32.1	29.9
III	30.4	31.8	31.3	32.1	30.7	30.5
Black males						
I	7.9	9.1	13.8	15.4	16.3	18.0
II	30.8	40.3	42.6	37.2	37.0	35.5
III	61.4	50.7	43.5	47.3	46.7	46.4
Latino males						
I	10.5	13.9	16.2	15.5	16.9	15.6
II	37.8	40.2	37.8	34.8	33.7	30.6
III	51.6	45.8	46.0	49.6	49.4	53.8
White females						
I	19.2	20.2	24.6	28.6	30.5	32.1
II	47.5	46.0	43.7	40.2	39.4	38.8
III	33.2	33.8	31.7	31.2	30.4	29.1
Black females						
I	9.1	13.5	17.8	18.5	18.8	20.4
II	19.0	33.3	42.2	39.8	41.1	40.7
III	71.8	53.1	40.0	41.8	40.2	38.9
Latina females						
I	5.2	11.5	13.6	15.6	17.3	18.2
II	50.0	52.3	46.1	44.8	42.5	43.0
III	44.9	36.2	40.3	39.7	40.3	38.9

Source: U.S. Department of Commerce, Bureau of the Census, 1/1000 Public Use Sample, 1960, 1970, 1980; Current Population Survey, 1986, 1988, 1990.

Table 5.3. *Employment gains by type of job and ethnic/gender group, all workers (thousands of additional jobs)*

Type of job	1970/60	1980/70	1990/80
White males			
I (high wage)	1,600	2,900	4,600
II (middle wage)	500	1,100	-2,200
III (low wage)	1,700	1,600	600
Black males			
I	100	300	400
II	600	300	50
III	-100	—	650
Latino males			
I	150	250	300
II	350	450	400
III	300	600	1,400
White females			
I	1,400	3,400	5,000
II	2,700	3,500	1,300
III	2,300	2,400	1,300
Black females			
I	200	350	400
II	600	800	550
III	-50	50	550
Latina females			
I	50	200	350
II	250	500	500
III	150	550	500

Source: Table 5.1 percentages multiplied by civilian employment, by race and gender, from *Economic Report of the President,* January 1993, Table B-32. "White" figures corrected for present Latinos in labor force from the proportion of Latinos in the all-worker sample in the Current Population Survey.

restructured after 1970, adopted new technologies, and in many cases reorganized their production processes.

The current mythology is that, through restructuring, U.S. industry became leaner, especially at the management level. Speaking before the National Education Association in March 1989, Lee Iacocca told the five hundred teachers that Chrysler had succeeded because twenty thousand "managers" had been fired. The overall data for manufacturing suggest something quite different. If anything, restructuring has meant a shift to white-collar jobs in manufacturing, especially at the management and professional levels. The real paring down has taken place on the shop floor.

The gradual white-collarization of manufacturing had a significantly different impact on minorities than on whites. Whites moved up into the expanded ranks of managers and professionals, but for both blacks and Latinos little movement occurred, and only from unskilled to semiskilled blue-collar jobs to clerical positions.

Similar movements took place in office-based services. Again, the greatest growth was in management positions, and this occurred for every ethnic/gender group. But almost all of this change came from a decline in professionals, especially among minority men and women. In an industry already dominated by managers and professionals, white males continued to move up into these higher-paid jobs as services expanded. In 1970, 58 percent of all white males employed (part time and full time) in office-based services were in managerial or professional jobs; in 1990, the figure was 62 percent, with all the growth coming in managerial positions. A smaller percentage of minority males held such jobs in 1970 and their percentage barely increased. Thirty-eight percent of Latino males and 30 percent of black males had a managerial or professional job in the office service sector in 1970 and both increased only 1 percent by 1990. For both groups, managerial jobs also grew at the expense of professional jobs. About 42 percent of white women and 30 percent of black and Latina women fell into these categories, and a high proportion of them were in teaching and health care. For Latino males, there was upward job mobility within the service industry, but it was low-skilled labor and custodial services into jobs such as truck driving and those employing skilled crafts workers. Black men and black and Latina women moved up into clerical jobs. Much more than in the manufacturing sector, restructuring in high-value-added services meant eliminating low-skilled jobs, especially for black men and black and Latina women.

If manufacturing and high-value-added services were eliminating low-skilled jobs in the 1980s and, at least in services, creating some middle-level work for minorities to move into, why was there also an increase in the overall percentage of minorities working in low-level jobs? For one thing, the nation-wide shift of employment from manufacturing to office services meant that workers moved from an industry where only 10 to 20 percent of minority males hold low-level jobs to an industry where 25 to 30 percent of minority male jobs were at that level, even in 1990. For another, an increasing proportion of all workers, white and minority, moved into custodial and restaurant services (low-end services), where an even higher percentage of jobs were low-paying and low-skilled.

Deindustrialization and restructuring definitely slowed job mobility for minorities despite continued changes in job structures within industries. Minority men and women were getting more white-collar jobs in manufacturing and office services and moving out of lower-paying, less-skilled jobs. Yet overall, as workers moved out of manufacturing and found employment in services and as both manufacturing and high-value services were restructured to reduce the number of lower-paying jobs, a high proportion of minorities stayed in low-paying work, either in high-value services or in expanding low-value services.

If the heyday of affirmative action and minority gains was the late 1960s and 1970s, the 1980s were the decade of white job mobility. White women did especially well, because as they moved up, their average real incomes increased. For whites, the disappearing middle meant that many more men would be getting professional and managerial jobs instead of work on the factory floor and that women would get professional and managerial jobs instead of clerical work. For minority men, it more likely meant some mobility from factory jobs into professional and managerial jobs and from factory into clerical jobs. But it mainly meant expanding "opportunities" in lower-paying construction, retail trade, or custodial services.

THE GROWTH OF DEMAND FOR SYMBOLIC ANALYSTS

The job shift can be described in a different way: the restructuring of the U.S. economy increased demand for workers who could process and analyze information and reduced the need for assemblers and workers with other kinds of manual skills (noninformation jobs). The main feature of the symbolic analysts is that they have high levels of education and tend to specialize in math and science. Their economic value in the new information economy is on the rise, while the value of workers with manual skills is in decline.

Robert Reich argues that blacks stopped making economic gains in the 1980s mainly because they did not have access to the good jobs in symbolic analysis.[10] African-Americans and other groups in this same situation could not take advantage of such new, high-income opportunities. They had relatively low levels of schooling and, when they did finish college, were greatly underrepresented in scientific and mathematical fields. Worse, their own economic base was deteriorating rapidly.

Is the growth in employment of symbolic analysts important in explaining why blacks have done worse in the past two decades? Let us examine this question in two steps: (1) the shift in employment itself and (2) the relative incomes of symbolic analysts compared with those who do not work with information, taking account of gender and race.

Between 1970 and 1990, whites and Asian-Americans sharply increased their participation in jobs requiring symbolic analysis. Blacks and Latinos not only started out farther behind, they lost ground. Figure 5.3 shows two categories of information jobs: primary producers of information and secondary users of information.[11] These can be considered symbolic analysts in Reich's terms.

The graph makes it clear that Reich's basic premise is correct: there is a great divide ethnically between who analyzes symbols and who does not, and this divide is much greater among men than women. By 1990, white and Asian-American males had about a 50 percent chance to be primary producers or secondary users of information – such workers were paid 50 to 100 percent more on average, depending on the ethnic group, than non–information users.[12] Black and Latino males had only about a 20 percent likelihood of being in those two symbolic analyst categories.

Blacks did much better at catching up to whites as symbolic analysts in the 1970s than in the 1980s, partly because blacks were doing better at catching up in college education in that earlier decade. That was not the only reason. Young, educated blacks had much more occupational mobility in the 1970s than in the 1980s, and this showed up in access to symbolic analyst jobs as much as anywhere else.

Is Reich correct in claiming that the symbolic analysts have made large income gains in the past twenty years compared with those in jobs that don't require information production or use? Probably not. Table 5.4

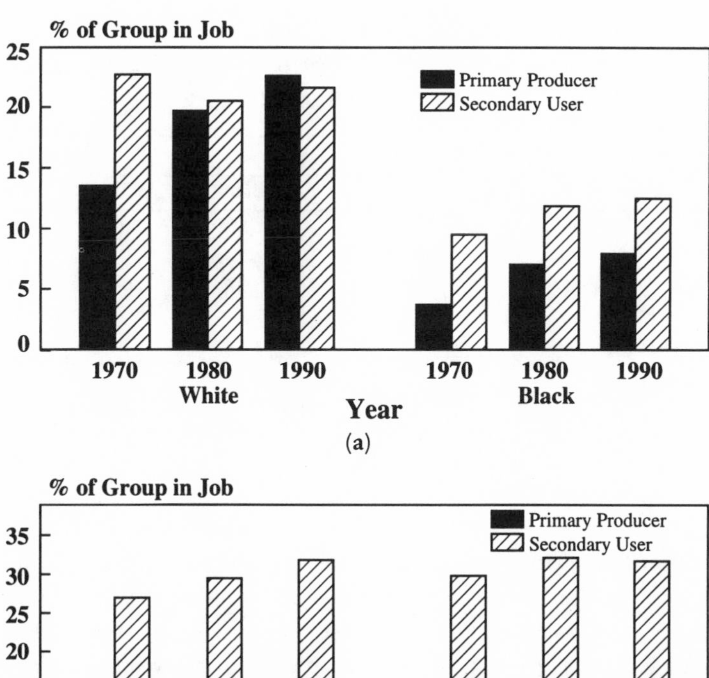

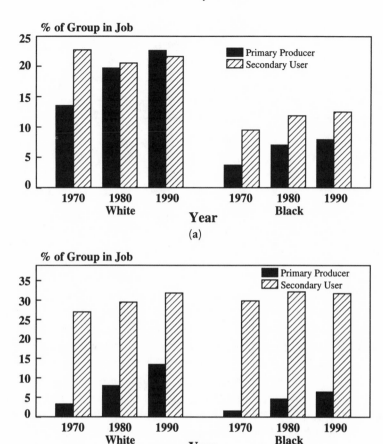

Figure 5.3. Full-time (a) male and (b) female workers in information-analyzing jobs, by race, 1970–90. From U.S. Census Bureau, Public Use Sample, 1970 and 1980, and Current Population Survey, March Survey, 1990, full-time-worker sample.

shows that white *and* black male nonusers earned the same relative to primary producers of information in 1969 as in 1989 (60 and 65 percent). Nonusers made gains relative to symbolic analysts in the 1970s, then lost ground in the 1980s. Which of these income movements is the "secular trend"? I think there is none. How incomes change depends as much on national politics as on changes in the world economy.

As meaningful as the nonuser to primary producer income ratios are the

Table 5.4. *Mean income ratios, by race, ethnicity, and type of occupation, full-time males, 1969–89 (percentage of income of primary producer of information)*

Occupation type	1969		1979		1989	
	White	Black	White	Black	White	Black
Primary producer	100	100	100	100	100	100
Secondary user	94	96	91	88	94	97
Repairer–maintainer	76	82	79	84	75	81
Nonuser	59	65	61	72	59	65

Source: U.S. Census, 1970, 1980; Current Population Survey, March 1990.

large differences in income between black and white male primary information processors and between black and white secondary users of information. The gap has declined over the past twenty years, but is still about 25 percentage points. Among full-time-employed primary information producers, a black male earned 65 percent of white male income in 1969, 67 percent in 1979, and 73 percent in 1989. Among secondary users, blacks rose from a 67 percent salary ratio in 1969 to 75 percent in 1989. Differences were higher in symbolic analyst jobs than in noninformation jobs, where blacks earned 80 percent of white male salaries in 1989, up from 71 percent in 1969. Even among college graduates working in high-end services (financial, insurance, and business services), black male primary and secondary information producers/users earned only 60 percent of white salaries in 1989. Overall, a black male primary information producer earned only 20 percent more than a white male in a noninformation job.

The problem for blacks is not just becoming information producers or obtaining the education needed to get such jobs. That helps – in 1989 it meant earning almost $33,000 instead of the $21,000 that a black male earned in a noninformation job. But it also was $12,000 short of what a white or Asian-American earned as an information producer. The fact that white and black men working in these different kinds of information- and noninformation-using jobs have had about the same income structure over the past twenty years confirms that racial inequality is not a problem just in information jobs or nonuser jobs. It is generic to the occupational structure as a whole. Yes, moving blacks into primary information-producing jobs does much to reduce black–white income differences, but in 1989 the best it could do was to move black males from 68 to 75 percent of white incomes.

EFFECT OF DECLINING WAGES ON MINORITY MOBILITY

The data on information versus noninformation incomes suggest that sectoral shift explains only part of the downward pressure on minorities' incomes relative to whites'. With the shift, minorities got jobs in the service sector that paid less than the jobs they were getting in manufacturing in the 1960s and early 1970s. Aside from implementing policies that would have slowed down deindustrialization,[13] the public sector could probably have done little in the short run to avert the effect of that shift on income.

However, despite important pockets of high minority unemployment, the problem for most minority workers in the shift was less that they could not get a job than that they could not get a good, higher-paying job. And from what we have seen, there was a marked difference between the effect that the declining middle had on minorities in the 1970s and its effect in the 1980s. This difference resulted partly from changes in the kinds of jobs blacks and Latinos could get with high school education and the slowdown in minority college completion.

But also significant was a wage effect in the 1980s that hit minorities even harder than the job shift. A job shift had also taken place in the 1970s. In the 1980s, the incomes associated with both middle- and low-skilled jobs grew more slowly than managerial and professional incomes. The growth was even slower in those lower-income jobs for minorities than for whites. Since blacks and Latinos were much more likley to be in lower-level jobs than whites, increased income disparity among jobs hit minorities hard, so hard that their incomes fell relative to whites'.

Much of the explanation for this increasing income disparity lies in the way incomes grew for different kinds of jobs in the 1980s as compared with earlier decades. In the 1980s, the increase in annual incomes for lower-skilled jobs was less than those for higher-skilled jobs. This was even truer for minorities than for whites and applied similarly to the total of employed workers and to full-time workers. The contrast with the 1970s is illuminating. Although the upward move in favor of lower-end jobs took place in the early part of the decade, it was maintained with proportional growth in the Carter years. In the 1980s, exactly the opposite happened. Although the upward move favoring higher-end jobs took place mainly in the 1980–82 "shakeout," it too was maintained until the last years of the decade.

Here is the rub (and much of the explanation for why minorities lost momentum in the 1980s): the incomes of Latinos and blacks in managerial and professional occupations – the category of jobs least accessible to all minority groups except Latinas in the 1980s – increased more than for whites, but the incomes of workers in lower-end services and unskilled labor – the jobs most accessible to minorities – increased least. Blacks and Latinos did not gain on white workers in the 1980s because the job that minorities were getting tended to have smaller nominal income gains. In two major industries, manufacturing and office-based services, there was minority upward job mobility mainly from lower- to middle-level jobs. However, the job categories into which minorities were moving were the ones with lowest income gains. This was not true of all jobs. Minority clerical workers in office-based services did make larger than average gains in the 1980s, and a significant percentage of minority workers in the labor force worked in such jobs. Yet, on the whole, minority upward mobility, such as it was, was offset by real income declines in those jobs. It was also offset by the growth of low-end, low-paying jobs in other economic sectors – jobs filled by a high percentage of minorities – where income growth was as low as or lower than that in manufacturing and office-based services.[14]

The major puzzle is why in the 1980s incomes in lower-end jobs rose less than incomes in higher-end professional, technical, and managerial jobs when income growth was more equitable among lower- and higher-end jobs in the 1970s. Why was such inequality even greater among minority males than other groups? The answers would help us get at the issue of how little or how great an effect government policies can have on minority incomes. Were market forces, out of policy control, doing in minorities in the 1980s, or was the government?

EFFECT OF INCREASED LABOR SUPPLY ON INCOMES

Market proponents claim that business restructuring and the shift to office-based services in the 1980s increased overall demand for higher-end relative to lower-end jobs, but that this increased demand was met with relatively slow growth in the supply of qualified workers (college graduates) to fill these jobs – a sharp contrast with the 1970s, when demand was also increasing and the supply of college graduates surged. The argument makes the crucial assumptions that incomes for different jobs are highly sensitive to the number of people lining up for those jobs with "suitable" qualifications and that incomes of those with different levels of schooling are highly sensitive to the jobs calling for those levels of schooling and the supply of schooled people offering themselves for work.[15]

Technological advances, the thinking goes, require more "control" and "information-generating" employees than production or even clerical workers.[16] Business services expand relative to manufacturing, and services require information creators and maintainers rather than machine operators per se. The claim is reasonable. Although the proponents of the market argument generally do not do a very good job of measuring increased demand for highly qualified workers, most of the demand comes from the growth of what we call "Category I" jobs in Tables 5.2 and 5.3. Since in our base year (1970) about 80 percent of core labor force (25 years old or older, full-time-employed) male college graduates and 85 percent of female college graduates were employed there, the growth of that category is a good indicator of changes in demand. The usual assumption that the percentage of the labor force employed in Category I higher-end jobs rose in the 1980s is correct. And there was a decline in the percentage of workers employed in middle plus lower-end jobs (Category II plus Category III).

According to the market argument, there was a sudden increase in the supply of college graduates in the 1970s, slowing the growth of incomes associated with higher-end jobs, and a slowdown in the supply of qualified high-end workers in the 1980s relative to demand, which drove their incomes up. This is also credible. White male professionals' incomes grew slower than incomes in other occupations in the 1970s, and more rapidly in the 1980s – although managerial income went just the other way (it grew more rapidly in the 1970s for white males and less in the 1980s), and managerial jobs increased much more rapidly than professional jobs in both periods.

But proponents of this argument have a more difficult time explaining why a whole range of lower-end incomes rose so rapidly in the early 1970s, even though there was also a surge in the number of high school graduates and high school dropouts during the decade. Middle-level and lower-end job growth was slower than the growth of higher-end jobs, so their relative incomes should have also gone down, maybe even more than those of professional jobs. And though the growth of middle- and lower-level jobs continued to slow in the 1980s, the absolute number of high school graduates (especially white high school graduates) not going on to college dropped too, while the absolute number of those with bachelor's degrees continued to rise (slowly) in the 1980s. Why didn't relative wages of middle-level jobs keep up better than they did?

Proponents of the argument also run into some problems explaining income changes for minorities. Again, the number of bachelor's degrees conferred slowed sharply for blacks in the 1980s, and this could explain the sharp increase in income growth for black professionals and managers. However, the growth of demand for blacks in those higher-end jobs also grew much more slowly than for whites. And the incomes of 25- to 34-year-old black male and female college graduates grew less rapidly than those of white graduates, suggesting that it was older black college graduates in prime working life and getting their start in the 1970s who made the big gains in the 1980s through professional and managerial income increases. This is indeed the case: 35- to 44-year-old college-educated black males' incomes increased sharply relative to those of their white counterparts between 1979 and 1989, especially among those employed full time. The relative increase was even greater for those with graduate training. Shortages? Maybe just for the "tried and true" or those already "in house." Why didn't declines in the supply of younger black graduates drive their incomes up relative to those of whites?

RAISING THE EDUCATIONAL ANTE

One reason that fewer high school graduates available for middle-level jobs in the 1980s may not have held back new entrants' falling incomes was the "downward substitution" of college- for high-school-educated labor, mainly in services. High school graduates, in turn, were substituted for those with less than high school education in middle- and lower-level jobs. This would continue to increase "shortages" in the higher-end jobs but reduce shortages in middle-level jobs.

The average education in every job category rose sharply in the 1960s, 1970s, and 1980s. For example, in 1960, 78 percent of full-time female operatives and 30 percent of female clerical workers in traditional manufacturing (84 percent of all the women in manufacturing employed full time in that year were in those two occupations) had not completed high

Table 5.5. *Proportion of high school and college completers in core labor force (25 years old or older, full-time worker), 1960–90 (percentage of total core labor force)*

Year	High school complete	College complete (or more)
1960	29.1	13.1
1970	35.0	15.8
1980	36.4	23.1
1986	37.7	27.4
1990	38.2	30.4

Source: U.S. Census Public Use Samples, 1960, 1970, 1980; Current Population Survey, March 1986 and March 1990.

school. Only 15 percent of clericals had completed some years of college or more. By 1990, about 30 percent of clericals had at least some college and 62 percent of operatives had finished high school or more. In office services, the pattern was the same, with female clericals' education becoming increasingly collegiate – 23 percent had some college or more in 1960 and 43 percent in 1990. Even low-end service workers were transformed from 73 percent high school dropouts in 1960 to more than 73 percent high school completers or more in 1990. In the 1970s and 1980s, black female clericals became collegiate even more rapidly than whites.

This pattern also held for men. By the mid-1980s, few categories of jobs could be had without a high school education. Whereas almost 60 percent of workers in manufacturing and 25 percent of full-time workers in high-value-added (office-based) services had not finished high school in 1960, less than 25 percent of manufacturing workers and 7 percent of office-based service workers had achieved that level in 1990.

Another way to see this shift is in the proportion of the core labor force (25 years old or more in full-time jobs) who were high school and college graduates. The percentage who had completed high school rose sharply in the 1960s, but then the increase slowed, while the percentage of college graduates climbed rapidly and steadily, especially after 1970 (Table 5.5). Employers across industries and occupations shifted in the 1970s toward hiring new entrants with college education. The change slowed down in the 1980s compared with the 1970s (the increase in college-educated labor was greater in the 1970s), but it still continued as a dominant labor market theme in both decades.

Russell Rumberger's finding for an earlier period that worker schooling levels were rising more rapidly, on average, than the skills required by their jobs is probably still true.[17] Employers tend to revise upward continuously what they consider to be an acceptable level of education for each kind of job, and in the 1970s that revision had them looking for young applicants with college degrees rather than secondary schooling.

Why would employers increase the amount of education required even when job skills were not rising? Economist Michael Spence explains this phenomenon with a concept called "signaling."[18] According to Spence, employers find through experience that certain amounts of education "signal" the kinds of attributes they are looking for in workers. Workers acquire those attributes because they are aware of what employers are looking for.

Why don't employers hire people with less schooling and pay even lower wages for certain jobs? Why bother raising the ante? I asked several employers this question. Their answers suggested an aversion to the risk entailed in hiring workers who have less than the level of education they "target" for a job. Employers seem less interested in lowering the nominal wages attached to a particular job – which is difficult to do in an organizational framework – than in reducing the risk of hiring an "appropriate" person for that job (which also means a person more or less like the others in the job category) or in keeping wages of job categories from rising more than a certain amount. Rather than lowering nominal wages, they prefer to reduce the risk associated with hiring people having less education than the going signal indicates and to reduce the search costs involved in finding the "right" people with less education.

The market arguments for changes in incomes among higher-, middle-, and lower-level jobs does explain at least in part what happened in the 1970s and 1980s. To the degree that it does, short-term public policy could have little effect on what did and what will happen to minority–white incomes. But even when we include the idea that "signals" changed, the large increase in lower-level incomes in the 1970s and the smaller increase in middle- and lower-level incomes in the 1980s are hard to explain without discussing the great changes in government's spending patterns and its behavior toward labor – particularly toward lower-income earners.

Those government policies, it turns out, are crucial for understanding why blacks' incomes have risen and fallen relative to whites'. I will examine them in Chapters 8 and 9.

6

Have racism and discrimination increased?

For most in the black community and some in the white, there is a simple explanation for the slowdown in black economic gains in the 1980s: deeply ingrained white racist attitudes that have hardened in the past decade. According to this explanation, most whites are not able or willing to deal with their feelings toward blacks and practice racism on a day-to-day basis. Further, such attitudes are ingrained in the nation's most important institutions – schools, offices, factories, hospitals, and sports organizations. Institutionalized racist practices, the argument goes, translate into continued and even increasing discrimination in education and jobs.

The argument can be broken down into two parts: (1) racism and racist practices are as bad as or worse than they were two decades ago despite the Civil Rights Act, affirmative action, and the growth of the black middle class; and (2) such practices are translated into greater educational, job, and other institutional discrimination.

Has racism hardened in the past decade and does that explain blacks' stagnating incomes? Racist attitudes and practices certainly abound, from race baiting at the Federal Bureau of Investigation, to high school guidance counselors' making black students feel unworthy to go to college, to police brutality toward blacks under arrest.

But it is one thing to say that attitudes continue to exist, another that they have hardened, and yet another, that, even if hardened, they have led to increased racial discrimination. In some areas, such as local electoral politics, race relations seem to be better than twenty years ago. In his two runs at the presidency Jesse Jackson garnered many white as well as black votes – the very size of his support nation-wide and his influence in the Democratic Party would have been unheard of even in the 1970s. There also seems to be less racism in the arts, media, and sports. There is much more intermarriage than a decade ago, and more blacks live in the suburbs (even among whites) than ever before. The median African-American income compared with that of whites was nearly the same in 1989 as in 1979. Black male unemployment rates remained high – about 2.5 times those of whites – but the ratio did not increase. All these indicators point to similar or somewhat less racism in the 1980s than in the 1970s.

But some data do support the argument that racism has increased – or at least that pervasive racist behavior is being expressed more overtly: younger, higher-educated black men lost enormous ground relative to their white counterparts during the Reagan expansion. College-graduate blacks were precisely the group that made the greatest gains in the 1970s. Black women also lost some ground to white women. In both cases, white comparison groups did especially well in the 1980s and blacks did not keep up. During the Reagan expansion, beginning in 1983 and continuing until 1989, employers were increasingly willing to pay higher wages to younger whites but not to blacks. Even if race is an important element in employers' profit-maximizing behavior, as some have argued,[1] it is mystifying why employers would have turned most against those younger, highly educated blacks who should have been favored by the increasing demand for higher-educated workers.

All this is complicated by different conceptions of racism in the white and black communities. According to sociologist Bob Blauner, who has studied racial attitudes for more than twenty years, no matter what the economic reality was for blacks in the 1980s, whites have tended to interpret recent trends as evidence that racism is sharply on the decline – they see a growing black middle class, more elected black public officials, and more black students at the better universities as evidence of the great gains that blacks have made in the post–World War II era. They see racism largely as a thing of the past.

Blacks, on the contrary, see race and racism as central to the very existence of the United States, past and present. They do not think that "racism has been put to rest by civil rights laws, even by the dramatic changes in the South. They [feel] that it still [pervades] American life, indeed, [has] become more insidious because the subtle forms [are] harder to combat than the old-fashioned exclusion and persecution."[2]

Thus, for blacks, the absence of overall economic gains relative to whites in the 1980s, the slowdown of the equalization train of the 1960s and early 1970s, and the exacerbated black poverty and disintegration of black communities are convincing evidence of hardening racism, contradicting any signs noted by whites of declining discrimination.

Differences in white and black interpretations are not based just on different views of society. The 1970s and 1980s provided both sides with data supporting their views. When all is said and done, those two decades witnessed the end of a period of large black gains followed by a sharp slowdown – a slowdown that occurred despite increasing expressions of black electoral power and despite little evidence of increasing wage discrimination for most blacks in the labor force.

I claim in this chapter that individual attitudes toward race, as exhibited by individual political behavior, suggest a trend toward less racism. But when it came to blacks' economic situation, "larger" politics may have done much to reduce black incomes relative to whites'. Blacks are right, then, in claiming that pervasive racism was again "allowed" by reduced government regulation to express itself in the labor market by employers' favoring of certain kinds of white workers over blacks. Deregulation served political ends, but the result was deteriorating relative incomes for some blacks. At the same time, whites are right in claiming that in many areas, there is much less institutional racism than in the past.

The corollary of this argument is that individual attitudes may tell us much about race relations, but not about social and economic outcomes. It may seem strange that in a capitalist democracy, where individuals' views on issues should be a key factor in economic results, individual attitudes on race do not explain consistently why the outcomes for blacks change.[3] Race, it turns out, is factored into society and the economy in a complex fashion. Part of the explanation for the slowdown in black gains does lie in *existing* institutionalized racist attitudes. But it is less in their existence than in how politics – especially national politics – uses those attitudes to construct larger economic policies and, through them, allows racial biases to be expressed. Such policies reflect both the vision the government has for society and its economic development strategy. Race cannot help but play a role in the national political vision and strategy. In turn, African-Americans have always depended on politics for their self-definition in society. For national politics to turn away from blacks does not require racist attitudes to harden, only the dominant political project to change. According to this "political" explanation, black economic progress stops when it is not consistent with that project.

RACISM AND ELECTORAL POLITICS

Despite their sense that race is as much as or more of a problem than it was fifteen or twenty years ago, African-Americans continued to make gains in the 1980s that suggest declining rather than increasing racism. The biggest gains were electoral. Most of the nation's major cities have or have had black mayors, and one state, Virginia, now has a black governor. Black victories occurred with large turnouts by multiracial supporters of black candidates.[4] Jesse Jackson, running from the left wing of the Democratic Party, had impressive backing from white voters for his presidential candidacy in 1988. He came into the Democratic convention in Atlanta with a clear minority of delegates but also as more than a mere spokesman for blacks.

One reason for these political successes is that government does not harass blacks in the same way it did fifty or even twenty-five years ago. They also have greater protection before the law. And all signs point to their increased civic status as a result of electoral participation and the increase in minority public officials.

Electoral success of this magnitude can only be interpreted as a clear signal that racism has declined at some level. Blacks are elected from predominantly black constituencies; however, big-city mayors need a sizable white vote to win, and in Douglas Wilder's election as governor of Virginia, he managed to put together a solid coalition of blacks and whites, where white votes were a majority of his total. In many cases, blacks have to play down their blackness in order to win; yet that does not contradict the claim that only in a less racist environment would it be possible for them to win under any circumstances.

There are even more solid examples of African-American political victories on their own terms and white support. When Harold Washington was elected Chicago's first black mayor, he faced years of entrenched opposition within his own party, mainly because he wanted to develop an alternative power base and policies that shifted resources to lower-income neighborhoods. Washington was eventually successful, both because he turned out to be a clever politician and because his policies were clearly destined to help an expanded constituency. He kept his original supporters together by not selling out and added to his white liberal base by making the opposition look corrupt and obstructionist in a city known for its corrupt public officials. But his death showed just how fragile and dependent on his person that success was: no other black politician could step into his shoes.

It is true that most blacks are still elected at the local level and therefore have little to say about national political ideology. Even with the large gains of 1992, only thirty-six members of the House of Representatives are black, and only one senator is black. Several have reached powerful committee positions, and the Congressional Black Caucus is an ideological bloc that speaks out on racial and other issues. Between 1979 and 1992 there were no black senators. So blacks are severely underrepresented at the national level relative to their population.

This goes far in explaining why electing officials has not necessarily translated into an improvement in minorities' economic position. At the local level, the highest political authority – the mayor – usually has considerable discretion in making policy decisions, yet also faces many limitations in collecting and allocating resources. Downtown business interests and other nonminority constituencies still exercise a great deal of power over what happens in cities and towns. Just because a minority mayor is elected does not mean that the city council is minority-controlled. Civil servants may also continue to exercise control over day-to-day decisions, and changing that bureaucracy may not be directly in the mayor's hands. As these limitations become clear, elected minority officials have to choose to fight them, which may mean losing important allies not totally committed to the cause, or cater to them, which may lead to charges of selling out their minority constituency.

Because minorities tend to be poor, the towns and cities where they live in large numbers also tend to be in bad shape financially. They have inadequate schools, housing, and health care, and a relatively high percentage of the population is on welfare. Cities generally have seen their tax base erode as the wealthy escape to the suburbs but continue to make demands for services by commuting into town to work. In order to attract a tax base in the form of new businesses, tourism, and higher-income residents, city governments must keep tax rates low and simultaneously try to improve infrastructure. Some successful city administrations have managed to produce economic progress, but it is a difficult game to play successfully and still improve the immediate lot of low-income residents.

Minority public officials also have to bargain for resources with state and federal officials who may not be in a position to help or may be downright unsympathetic to making local officials look good. State governments play a key role in welfare and education spending, the federal government is the primary source of funds for public housing, and most redevelopment projects get matching funds from the feds. "This complex of pressures gave rise to the seeming paradox by the early 1980s of increasingly conservative fiscal policies at the municipal level at a time when black electoral representation was surging in major cities across the country."[5]

Where electing minority officials does seem to make a difference is in increasing the delivery of certain kinds of municipal services, such as health care, in integrating police forces and fire departments, which probably improves the delivery of those services into minority neighborhoods, in hiring minority municipal employees across the board, and in increasing municipal contracting with minority firms. These last two effects, which are often the clearest expression of minority mayoralties in fiscally constrained cities, are a boon to the upper-income end of the minority constituency but have little impact on the lower-income groups that make up most of the minority electorate.

Where minority mayoralties do have an impact on lower-income groups – for example, in better housing and police protection – it has been necessary to develop strong coalitions among blacks, Latinos, and white liberals committed to change. The local administration has also had to prove that low- and middle-income whites would not pay the price of improving conditions in minority neighborhoods and might even be better off themselves because of such policies. Good minority administrations have had to break through the stereotypes and fears that whites have held concerning potential reverse discrimination.

Electing minorities at the local level is an important expression of newly gained minority political participation and power and, in some sense, must reflect a decline in racism. But the power gained is highly constrained. These elected officials are limited by poor revenue bases and the need to cater to traditional centers of economic and political power outside the minority community, including the private sector and other levels of government. And just because an elected official is black or Latino does not mean that he or she will favor lower-income minorities in distributing the limited economic resources available. Claims by minority entrepreneurs and middle-class professionals may come first and may be easier to satisfy (and yield more financial contributions to future campaigns).

At worst, it has not hurt minorities to have elected their candidates to local political office. Where they occur, such manifestations of softening racism can produce gains for blacks and other low-income minorities. Social services are often better and more frequently directed to minority groups than they would otherwise be. In some cases, poor cities, such as Newark, have been turned around under minority leadership. Even if higher-income minorities are the ones who receive the lion's share of the limited economic resources to be distributed, this is precisely the pattern that many white groups, such as the Irish and Italians, used to establish themselves economically in eastern cities earlier in this century.

However, there are severe limitations to using local electoral victories as a vehicle for economic improvement among the general minority population. Los Angeles is a good case in point. It had a black mayor for twenty years. Not only was it difficult for Mayor Bradley to extend political rights to the growing Los Angeles minority population, but the police remained racist, and he was also powerless to improve economic conditions in the city's black and Latino ghettos.

It is at the state level, now least accessible to minority officials, where economic action is most possible. This is clearest in educational, health, and vocational training policies. Despite large budget deficits in a number of states, many other states are the most financially sound of all levels of government and have the most power in setting the human resource agenda.

The local experience also shows that minority poor are most likely to benefit from minority electoral victories when they are the result of, and are able to strengthen, a political coalition with other minority groups and with white liberals. This requires more than a decline in racism that simply allows for the election of a black or Latino. Coalition politics of the Harold Washington type allows for constructive confrontations with more traditional power bases and for developing alternative institutional approaches to solving social problems. The objective of these alternatives is not patronage for a particular minority group or subgroup, but the use of political power to alter more permanently the way resources are distributed at the local level. This can be achieved only by bringing together a broad base of political support with common social goals. Much of black frustration with local political victories, then, should be blamed less on racism than on interest politics, where black politicians are as unable (and often unwilling) as anyone else to build the kind of coalitions needed to produce change locally.

LABOR MARKET DISCRIMINATION

Did racial discrimination increase in labor markets in the 1980s? This is a difficult question to discuss because of Americans' belief in the ultimate fairness of markets. The American dream is rooted in the ideology of equal opportunity: those who acquire skills will be given the same chance as the next person to use them productively. Logically, this basic tenet of eighteenth-century Liberal philosophy found its most fervent expression in the New World. Free of Europe's feudal institutions, without a landed aristocracy and the psychological fetters of rigid class relations, Americans were easily convinced that anyone who wanted to learn, work hard, and save could make it to the top.

In the democratic electoral system or even the family, the political issue has always been *equality* (among adult individuals), a legitimate, clearly defined Liberal goal, although far from simple to achieve for excluded groups. Because the educational system is part of the public sector, minorities have fought to achieve such equal treatment in the schools, and with considerable success. The market economy, however, begins from the premise that equality is *not* a desirable goal. Instead, the market's legitimacy rests on productive efficiency – efficiency that necessarily requires unequal rewards for unequal abilities. Equality is replaced by a more nebulous notion of "equity," or equal treatment of equal capability to produce (productivity).

It is precisely defining "capability to produce" that has made inequity in labor markets so controversial and difficult to pin down, especially for those who feel discriminated against. In the most extreme interpretations, equity itself is inherent in the perfection of the market's internal value system. The market cannot be wrong – it cannot value labor unfairly because there will always be someone willing to pay more for a worker who is able to produce more than he or she is paid.

If individual worker productivity could be measured accurately, there would not be much of an argument. Workers could exhibit their productivity figures, compare them with one another and with their wages, and prove that owners and managers were not being "fair." Words like "exploitation" and "discrimination" would take on the mantle of empirically measured facts. Unfortunately, individual productivity is extremely difficult to measure in group work processes, and even more difficult to compare *across* production processes. Generally, workers are paid by the kind of work they do, where they work, and the industry they work in.

Individual productivity within jobs enters little into individual wage determination. Rather, particular jobs with particular work requirements have particular wages attached to them. Either an employee can perform them reasonably well or not. The wage negotiation process usually takes place at the industry, plant, and job level for all workers as a group and is often affected more by the political climate surrounding it and company profits than by productivity figures. Yet employers can always argue that certain groups are less productive because of lower "ability" or "trainability" or, in the case of women, because they are more likely to move in and out of the labor force during their work lives.

Since individual productivity and wages are only indirectly connected, it is not easy to show inequity. Workers often feel discrimination, but have a hard time proving it at the individual level. There are ways to approximate statistically what might loosely be called "wage discrimination" and "income discrimination," by estimating the earnings of workers with similar education, experience, civil status, places of work, and time worked but of different race, ethnic group, or gender. True, the differences in earnings estimated this way do not account for all sources of differences in the "capacity to produce." For example, workers with the same education and experience do not necessarily have the same ability. The affirmative action debate has focused mainly on the allegedly high cost to the economy of hiring lower-ability black and Latino workers in the place of whites with the same amount of schooling.[6] But the estimates do suggest much about the changing degree of racial (and gender) discrimination in the labor market over the past fifty years.

Measuring wage discrimination

Suppose that black workers had the same education and work experience as white workers, were distributed across economic sectors and regions of the country in the same way, had the same marital status, and worked the same number of hours and weeks per year, but were paid a black "price" for each of those attributes. Simulating that situation, we estimated what blacks would earn if they were "like" white workers but were paid like black workers. The result is an approximation of the lower "price" that blacks and Latinos would get for their work even if they were like white workers in a number of important ways. We can call this price difference income or wage "discrimination." Agreed, there are

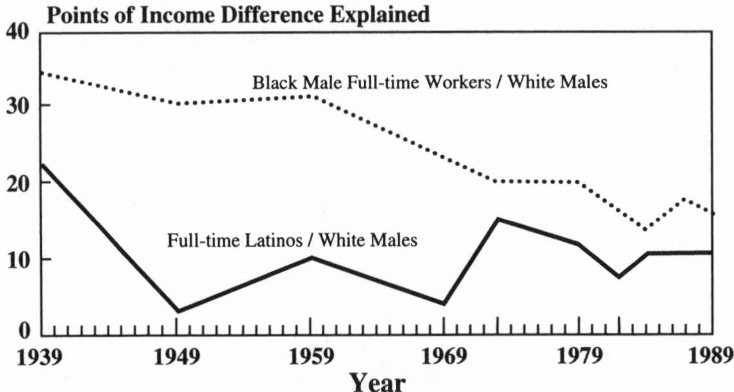

Figure 6.1. Minority–white full-time-employed male income gap explained by wage discrimination, 1939–89. From U.S. Census Bureau, Public Use Sample, 1940, 1950, 1960, 1970, and 1980, and Current Population Survey, March Survey, various years, full-time-worker sample.

problems with equating a residual of this kind with discrimination. Some unknown variables, such as quality of schooling and others, that are important in explaining employability or the capacity to produce, have probably been left out. But I feel that this is a reasonable approximation for understanding whether or not the race issue is fading.

Figures 6.1 and 6.2 show how wage discrimination, measured in percentage points of income difference between fully employed black and white men and between fully employed black women and white men, has behaved in the past fifty years.[7] The figures also compare black wage discrimination with Latino discrimination and, for women, also with white female wage discrimination. Although there are some differences between the full-time and all-worker samples for men, the general trends are the same.[8]

Wage discrimination fell somewhat for African-American men in the 1940s, stopped falling in the 1950s, dropped sharply between 1959 and 1973, and then continued to decline more gradually to the mid-1980s minimum of 14 percentage points. But by the end of the 1980s, wage discrimination was rising again.[9]

Wage discrimination against black women rose somewhat in the 1940s, then fell sharply and steadily from 1949 to the early 1980s, when the decline leveled off. By the early 1970s, black women were discriminated against to the same degree as white women and, for a few years in

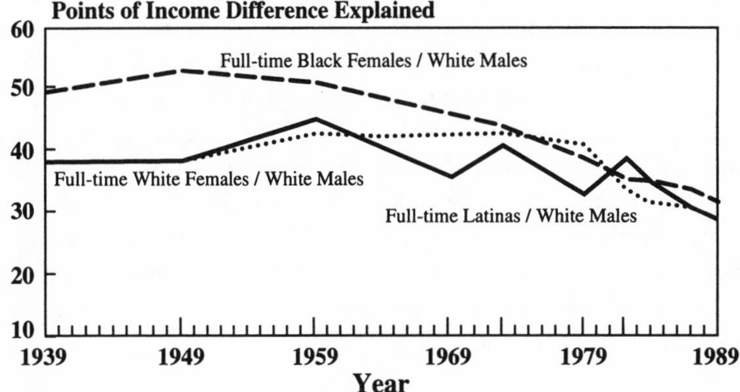

Figure 6.2. Minority female–white male income gap explained by wage discrimination, 1939–89. From U.S. Census Bureau, Public Use Sample, 1940, 1950, 1960, 1970, and 1980, and Current Population Survey, March Survey, various years, full-time-worker sample.

the late 1970s, did better than white women. Black women had closed the race gap but not the gender gap. Yet in the 1980s, the race gap opened again as wage discrimination against black women fell compared with that against white men but increased relative to that against white women. Thus, in the 1980s, the gender gap narrowed further for black women, but the race gap opened.

Those who claim declining race discrimination have a good point. Black men and women closed the wage gap substantially after 1959. Black males at the end of the 1980s faced less than half the 25 to 30 percentage point "pure" wage penalty they faced in 1959, which means, simply put, that when the average African-American male got a job in the 1980s, he made much closer to white male pay. As some contend, part of this decline might have been due to the improved quality of schooling available to African-Americans, not to equal-pay legislation or affirmative action.[10] The average worker in the labor force in 1959 went to school in the late 1930s; workers in the 1980s received their schooling, on average, in the early 1960s. There were large changes in black education during those twenty-five years.

Labor market race discrimination itself declined in the 1960s and early 1970s. This, too, is reflected in these falling curves. One hint that school quality differences are not the main reason for the wage gaps in Figures 6.1 and 6.2 is that Latinos also attended, on average, schools of much lower quality than whites in the 1930s and 1940s but suffered much less wage discrimination than blacks in the 1960s.

But the gains of the 1960s and 1970s hardly meant the end of wage discrimination. The perception by blacks of a slowdown in reducing wage bias in the 1980s was also correct. The "discrimination" curves stopped falling at the end of the 1980s and even rose. Combined with the Reagan tax reform, cutbacks in social services, stagnant college financing, and other policies biased against low-income Americans, young minorities could well have had the sense that society was turning away from them. It would not be difficult to interpret all that as increasing discrimination and rising economic racism.

Where did discrimination increase?

In 1989, according to census samples of all those in the labor force with income, black male high school dropouts 25 to 34 years old earned about 68 percent of their white male counterparts and high school completers earned about 70 percent. The figures for blacks employed full time were higher – 71 percent and 77 percent, respectively – showing that low-paying part-time work is a larger issue for black than for white males (Figure 2.8 and Table 6.1). Young black college completers earned 72 percent of white male college incomes in 1989.

The wage difference between similarly educated blacks and whites working full time, which in 1991 was 20 to 30 percent, was 10 to 25 percentage points higher in 1939, fell sharply in the 1940s when blacks moved from rural to urban industrial jobs, and did not fall much again until the mid-1960s and early 1970s. It was not until the 1970s that college-educated blacks began their major income surge to catch up with whites.

The two periods of gain – the 1940s and 1960s/1970s – reflect changes in three different "discriminatory" phenomena. The first two resulted mainly in the 1940s when blacks moved from a low-paying industrial sector (agriculture) in a low-paying, segregated region (the South) to higher-paying, somewhat less discriminatory industries in the North under conditions of equalizing income distribution. The third resulted mainly from blacks' greater access to better jobs *within* industries nation-wide in the 1960s and particularly from the elimination of segregation in the South. The effect of this later wave of gains was especially great for higher-educated blacks. Just as the 1940s saw the incorporation of blacks into the

Table 6.1. *Black–white median income ratios, by education, 25- to 34-year-old males, 1939–91 (percent)*

Level of education	1939	1949	1959	1969	1979	1982	1985	1989	1991
All workers with income									
High school dropout	62	70	57	69	70	82	64	68	70
High school graduate	56	67	60	71	72	70	67	70	69
Some college	51	61	62	81	74	72	68	79	72
College graduate	59	71	62	58	85	85	83	72	74
Graduate school	62	—[a]	80	81	92	87	81	82	67
Full-time workers									
High school dropout	58	76	63	72	72	82	74	71	75
High school graduate	58	73	69	73	80	83	78	77	77
Some college	55	66	71	79	78	75	75	81	78
College graduate	59	72	67	68	82	81	89[b]	72	76
Graduate school	58	—[a]	72	75	94	92	78	76	105[c]

[a]Those with graduate school and those who completed college are not separated in the 1950 census.
[b]The ratio was 78 in 1987.
[c]The number of observations in this category for blacks was only 20.
Source: U.S. Census Samples and Current Population Surveys.

working class, the 1960s and 1970s represented the beginning of blacks' move into the professional class.

In the 1980s, both these movements gradually eroded – the earlier move into the working class slowed sharply because of the lack of industrial jobs and government polices unfavorable to low wage-earners, and the later move into the professional class because government abandoned civil rights legislation, which had served mainly to bring blacks into colleges and the professions. Even with gains in the 1980s for some education groups, notably younger black males with some college education, income differences between black and white males with similar schooling did not go below 20 percentage points and increased in absolute dollars. A 25- to 34-year-old white male high school graduate working full time earned a median income of $14,800 (current dollars) in 1979, and a black $11,800. In 1989, the corresponding incomes were $22,600 and $17,500. For 25- to 34-year-old male high school dropouts, whites earned a median $12,600 and blacks, $9,100. In 1989, they earned $18,000 and $12,800, respectively.

Does this represent pervasive racism and the success of white backlash in the 1980s? For younger black college graduates and those who went on to graduate school, relative opportunities were clearly worse at the end of the decade than at the beginning. The labor market valued them much less compared with whites than it did ten years earlier. For black males with less education working full time, relative incomes at best stagnated. The total (part-time workers included) of younger black male workers with all levels of education also lost some ground in the 1980s (Table 6.1).[11]

Thus, race remains an important economic issue for blacks, and what happened in the 1980s is not just a matter of class (antilabor policies). It was not only that blacks had less education (lower social class), or that they lost ground only at lower levels of education; on the contrary, it was those young blacks with a college degree who did worse. At the end of the 1980s, they still earned almost 30 percent less than whites.[12] This means that increased wage discrimination was situated mainly in the relatively small group of black males who had graduated from college or had gone to graduate school. Younger blacks with less education may have suffered increased unemployment in the 1980s, but their relative wages fell only slightly, and then mainly for part-time workers – again, largely an employment effect.

What does this suggest about the causes of increased wage discrimination? Contrary to the caste/class thinking which predicts that less-educated black males should have been hit hardest relative to whites and to higher-educated blacks, by the end of the 1980s[13] it was black male college graduates who suffered the greatest relative income decline. This means that the main cause of the decline lay with government policies rather than the structure of institutionalized racism. Since civil rights

Table 6.2. *Black–white median income ratios, full-time workers, by education, 25- to 34-year-old females, 1939–91 (percent)*

Level of education	1939	1949	1959	1969	1979	1982	1985	1989	1991
High school dropout	58	65	62	77	97	113	88	107	91
High school graduate	51	75	73	84	95	93	85	90	86
Some college	55	74	78	102	99	96	80	92	84
College graduate	67	89	71	101	95	92	89	90	87
Graduate school	—[a]	—[b]	—[a]	77	93	94	76	86	77

[a]Fewer than 15 observations.
[b]Included in college graduate category.
Source: U.S. Census; Current Population Survey.

legislation had its greatest impact in the 1970s on young, higher-educated blacks, the retreat from civil rights in the Reagan and Bush administrations should logically also have had its greatest negative effect on this group. Inequality increased not because employers felt most racist about black college graduates, but because, by the 1980s, graduates were most dependent on civil rights legislation for good jobs.

A similar comparison of black women's incomes with those of white women also shows large gains for blacks across levels of education until the end of the 1970s, and then a reversal (Table 6.2). By 1979, black women employed full time earned essentially the same incomes as white women. These were still far less than white male incomes, but the race factor had been eliminated among women. But by 1989 – although still gaining ground *as women* on white and especially black men – full-time employed black women fell behind white women at all but the lowest education level. The data in Table 6.2 show that the decline was general across all but the lowest education levels. The increased participation in the labor force (because they chose not to stay home with their children) of more "talented" (higher-ability) white women in the 1980s relative to the 1970s could explain the decline, but it is just as likely that racial income inequality among women grew in the 1980s.

THE GAP BETWEEN SUBJECTIVE AND OBJECTIVE RACISM

The feeling among blacks (and Latinos) that they are judged by a different, harsher standard, are treated differently on the job, and are usually passed over for promotions is probably as pervasive today as it was in the 1960s.[14] The difference is that race and ethnicity as *white* issues have been swept under the carpet – they have disappeared from most whites' political consciousness. This makes it all that much more difficult for whites, blacks, and Latinos to discuss them openly, even while perceptions of discrimination among minorities intensify.[15] Blauner concludes that "even successful, middle-class black professionals experience slights and humiliations – incidents when they are stopped by police, regarded suspiciously by clerks while shopping, or mistaken for messengers, drivers, or aides at work – that remind them that they have not escaped racism's reach."[16] And in the words of one young Latino professional, "I know that I am often not taken seriously in my work simply because of my Hispanic appearance. Before I say a word, I'm prejudged because I don't have a white complexion. It's not something that's talked about all the time, but it's always there. Every Hispanic thinks about it."[17]

These individual experiences are reinforced by nationally publicized incidents, such as the beating of Rodney King in Los Angeles and the racial strife in Brooklyn. Together, they build a case for unchanging racism and deepen pessimism in the black community about things ever changing. So it is not illogical that blacks feel a greater sense of racial isolation today than they did a generation ago, despite several historical indicators – for example, political gains and wage discrimination data – that suggest a much more ambiguous situation, with most blacks about as well off economically relative to whites as they were in the 1970s and with many more blacks elected to public office.

One plausible explanation for this growing gap between black subjective reality and some key measures of objective reality is the way political ideology defined racial issues in the 1980s and 1990s. National politics increasingly marginalized blacks, identifying them with a broad range of negative symbols, from drugs and gang wars to low test scores and teenage pregnancy. The dominant "gimme, gimme, want, want" ideology of the 1980s cast blacks as the "failures" and "villains" of the American equal-opportunity society. The poor were characterized as just not able to keep pace with the greater demands for success in an accelerated information society. Inevitably the poor were black. The politics of race also became more overt – appeals to racial fears and stereotypes were standard fare in local, state, and national contests.

Whether in reality racism was increasing or decreasing, it is not surprising that blacks felt national opinion was increasingly stacked against them. In this political climate, subjective notions of race as defined by white politics overwhelmed the objective reality of class for middle-class blacks and destroyed any mythical notions of the American classless society for low-income blacks. The black middle class was made to see itself as low caste regardless of its class accomplishments, and the black underclass was made to give up any hope of social mobility. For younger black college graduates – a highly vocal group in their black community – the situation was objectively reinforced by sharply declining relative incomes. They not only viewed the situation as deteriorating in political terms, but saw the expanded opportunities of the 1970s closing down.

In a society that emphasizes the individual consumer and voter as the source of all economic and political power, the role of political leadership and ideology is highly underplayed. Politicians and their policies are viewed as emerging entirely from public opinion. Even in this era of the mass media and persuasive advertising, the concept of political leaders and policies shaping and guiding individual political and social views grates against the deeply held assumption of consumer-citizen sovereignty.

As race has become a more subtle issue in politics, so has its use by presidential candidates and by the winners of elections once they sit in the Oval Office. The transformation of race policy from Roosevelt to Reagan and Bush is mainly the story of changing presidential politics shaping Americans' views about race and economic inequality rather than the other way around. But once those values and policies were changed, so were politics themselves. This symbiotic process has had a profound effect on what happens to blacks economically, on how whites view them, and on how they view themselves. Both the subjective and objective realities of racism have increasingly been formed by presidential politics and policies.

But politics has not just produced subjective images. It may have had a real impact on the relative wages of those very blacks who had made the largest gains in the preceding decade: male college graduates. The increasing national political assault on the black image and the reduced enforcement at the Equal Employment Opportunity Commission did halt black gains and even rolled them back for some. They had economic implications beyond their political usefulness to the Reagan and Bush administrations.

The argument that racial inequality and discrimination still exist as such (and not simply as a class issue) is certainly correct. But the case for increased white racism as an explanation for black economic stagnation in the 1980s is less persuasive. Government changed its policies toward blacks drastically as part of an overall political strategy that exploited racism even while criticizing it. Did the strategy intend greater wage discrimination by the end of the decade? Probably not, but this seems to have been its result. By emphasizing market solutions to social problems, the politics of the 1980s gradually allowed the market to become more discriminatory than it had been in the 1970s or even the early 1980s. This racial politics served larger political goals even as it claimed not to be racial. Inadvertently, it showed that, without active government intervention, black incomes would not become equal to whites'.

It is here that the pervasive-racism argument misses the mark. Racism did not have to harden for wage discrimination to increase. All that had to happen was for government to change its ideological position on racial inequality – from one that viewed government as a force for reducing discrimination to one that declared that discrimination was a thing of the past. Even if racism had declined substantially in the generation since the 1950s, it was still widespread. A government that chose to exploit it subtly for political purposes could still appeal to key parts of the electorate. In the 1980s, this is precisely what happened, with public anti-discrimination policies sacrificed in the name of free-market economics but essentially for political expediency and with predictable results. With the change toward greater governmental deregulation, the gap between black and white incomes increased, even as more and more blacks were elected to public office by white voters. At the same time, national political ideology undoubtedly created an atmosphere in which differences between black and white incomes were blamed on blacks themselves, reducing any sense of racial inequality and racism in the white community, but increasing frustration and anger in the black community.

If government policy is a key to understanding race relations and its effect on blacks' economic possibilities, we need to look much more carefully at government policies in the past fifty years and how they changed. This is just what we will do in the second half of this book.

7

Politics and black educational opportunity

For the black minority in the United States, process is inexorably tied to national politics. For better or worse, government has been a major player in defining how blacks participate in the economy and society. Proponents of both the individual-responsibility and pervasive-racism explanations claim that government intervention holds blacks back, but for very different reasons. According to individual responsibility, this is because government intervention in the free market, even if intended to be helpful, makes conditions worse. According to pervasive racism, it is because U.S. politics *and* markets are biased against blacks – so government can't help but maintain discriminatory practices, by, among other things, tacitly supporting them in private business.

Neither of these explanations correctly characterizes the way politics has affected blacks' position in the economy. Usually in response to changing economic and social conditions (including social movements that raise consciousness on certain issues), voters periodically change our national political leadership. With new presidential mandates and new Congresses come new government approaches to economic and social problems. The Roosevelt administration did not deal with the economic crisis in the 1930s in the same way as the Hoover-led 1920s Republicans. Eisenhower's approach to domestic issues in postwar America was not the same as Truman's before him or Kennedy's and Johnson's after. And Ronald Reagan's position on most issues was philosophically far from John Kennedy's or Lyndon Johnson's.

Changes in national leadership have usually meant distinctly different national policies toward race. Race has always been a primary issue in politics, and no government can avoid taking some stance on it. Although much of the political change on race in the past century has come about because of political action by blacks themselves and the alliances they have been able to build with whites, it has taken government policies to implement change. Depending on what the policies were, they influenced blacks' economic position positively or negatively. There is no reason to believe that this will be any different in the future.

Even accepting that politics has an important effect on blacks' economic position, is government policy toward race really not about race but about class? Is blacks' economic position the outcome much more of class politics than of race politics? The economic-restructuring argument claims that it is, or at least has been since the 1960s. There is no question that as the race issue becomes more diffused and subtle, the distinction between class and race politics also blurs. But even today there are elements of class politics that have a distinct influence on blacks as a particular ethnic group, and the tension of race pervades class politics. William Wilson is right to claim that federal emphasis on fuller employment and urban redevelopment – essentially pro-labor policies – has a disproportionately positive effect on blacks. And when conservatives accuse liberals of "tax and spend" economic policies, this is essentially their political code for the argument that liberals tax the white suburban middle class in order to spend money on welfare for inner-city blacks.

Politics, whether that of class or race or both, affects black incomes in four ways. First, because of residential segregation and regional minority population concentrations, changes in government educational policies that affect certain regions and residential areas (e.g., inner city vs. suburban) can play a key role in blacks' access to good-quality public schooling, and therefore in black economic mobility. Educational policies can have a clearly identifiable positive or negative racial bias.

Second, government macroeconomic policy, especially in job creation, government spending and direct employment, income distribution, and, more recently, health care and urban issues, has much to do with how well lower-income blacks do. Although employment policies are mainly the result of class-based political decisions, the relatively high concentration of low-income blacks in inner cities makes it possible (even necessary) to target employment policies to reach and benefit certain groups of blacks. Similarly, the reorganization of the health care system to provide universal coverage leads to greater benefits for low-income workers with jobs in the least organized sectors.

Third, government legislation on and court interpretation of minority rights to equal treatment, especially in job markets, affects blacks at all levels of income. These policies are specifically aimed at correcting race bias within social class groups.

Fourth, government ideological leadership on policies and attitudes toward race and multiculturalism sets the tone for black economic and social possibilities throughout society. Again, the race element in such ideological leadership is usually not very subtle.

The four are linked by political philosophy. In the past fifty years, two contesting philosophies have fought for political dominance. One puts great faith in the market and in the resolution of social problems, such as race differences, by the "invisible" and just hand of the marketplace. The second believes that the market is powerful but highly imperfect. The free-enterprise system as such is limited in its capability to resolve social problems and economic inequality. Politics therefore has an important role in "leveling the playing field." The conflict between the two approaches has changed somewhat over time, conditioned by the impact of each on social institutions. In the 1980s, free-market forces radicalized their economic program in response to the crisis of the 1970s. They also incorporated the religious right's social program in response to the 1960s social movements on the left. In the 1990s, the regulatory/equalization forces reduced their social expectations because of budgetary constraints imposed by the failure of conservative economics in the 1980s. But the essence of the differences in economic philosophy that emerged from the 1920s and 1930s endures. It is the shifting dominance of one or the other at the national level that has shaped black progress.

THE DOMINANCE OF POLITICS IN BLACK EDUCATION

Nowhere is the role of government more widely accepted and more widely criticized than in education. This isn't surprising. Public education is seen as basic to our democratic political system, because it is both the main vehicle for equalizing opportunity in a diverse society and the major means by which the immigrant population is socialized into American values. As part of the democratic political system, and a part that touches most families directly, it is also contested. Reagan conservatives raised doubts about the "public" in education. They thought it should be privatized, or at least made to compete more directly with private schools. Liberals fell back on the still broad consensus that government should provide schooling to all groups and that the schooling it provides be "equal." Right and Left argued over the meaning of "equal."

African-Americans always took this democratic ideal and the role schooling had in it as seriously as anyone else – because of slavery and discrimination, perhaps more seriously. The amount and quality of public education they could get for their children became the main political issue in their struggle for equality. It was natural that they should see politics and schooling as synonymous. After Emancipation, they had to fight race-biased state legislatures for equal school funding. When that failed, they had to go, hat in hand, to "progressive" white foundations interested in the South's development, such as Carnegie and the Rockefeller Education Board, to fund private education of reasonable quality for a small black cadre. Eventually, almost a century after the Civil War and freedom from slavery, that educated cadre brought the struggle for black education to the level of national politics. Through effective social organizing, they forced school desegregation and greater equality at the local level.

Eventually, government responded to black pressures for more and better schooling. But it took changing government leadership to begin changing educational spending at the state level in the 1940s and then to enforce federally mandated equal access to public resources in the 1960s and 1970s. When that enforcement came, blacks received more schooling and did better in school.

Parent motivation has been less a problem in black education than has state and federal government indecision and the abject poverty of black school districts. The prevailing image is that most blacks go to chaotic inner-city schools and achieve at a low level. True as that is for many blacks, the percentage who graduate from high school is only slightly less than that of whites who graduate. Blacks' test scores are still much lower than whites', but they rose rapidly relative to white scores in the 1980s, partly because poverty among blacks decreased sharply in the 1960s and early 1970s and partly because in the 1960s and 1970s lawsuits forced state legislatures to more nearly equalize educational funding through a shift away from local property taxes toward greater reliance on state aid. A new standard was also imposed by the federal government and many states on local spending for economically disadvantaged children in order to receive federal aid under Title I of the Elementary and Secondary Education Act of 1965.

Even so, the education of blacks is not yet equal to whites', either in terms of the money spent per pupil or the quality of educational resources available to black schools. This is only partly an issue of compensating for more difficult educational conditions in black neighborhoods and schools. Schools attended by black children get fewer resources in absolute terms, and this does not even account for another reality: good teachers are unlikely to work in black urban schools for the same pay as they would get for teaching in white suburban schools.

The effort to equalize resources in the 1970s had less impact than might have been expected, but it was greater in those states that enforced it than in those that did not.[1] Access to funding changed when *Brown v. Board of Education* (1954) mandated equal access in legal terms. But such federal legal interventions never actually equalized the resources black pupils received, either in direct funding per pupil, in the resources that the funding could buy, or in the treatment of pupils by teachers and administrators.[2]

During the Reagan–Bush era, the implementation of equal access to resources slowed down substantially as part of a philosophical move away from equalizing education for the poor and toward improving educational methods in middle-class schools. The decision was largely political, part of the backlash against social spending. Since the 1960s, ambivalence about equalizing black and white education has been directly related to sharp political conflict over government's role in the equalization process. No one denies that government has a key role in schooling, or that improving black social mobility depends on improving the educational system for black children. But how much responsibility should schools take for equalizing opportunity? Education in democratic societies is subject to competing demands. One of its functions is to help students develop the skills needed by the economy, preparing the best students for higher levels of schooling and the highest-skilled jobs. Another function is to enable citizens to participate effectively in a democracy.[3] Producing highly skilled people requires a selective system in which the best survive and everyone else falls by the wayside. Producing citizenship requires that everyone be brought up to some socially desirable minimum of educational performance – schools need to be organized around greater equality. Schools may not meet either of these requirements well because they are organized to meet both of them simultaneously. Both sets of requirements are being placed on them at all times. Teachers and principals are given a double message: produce excellence but make sure that students who have difficulties are brought to higher levels of performance.

American public schools were always more democratically oriented than their European counterparts. Until the 1960s, the democratic goals of education were pursued in a largely race-segregated environment. Yet in that decade, the equality message was delivered louder and clearer than at any time in the history of education in the United States. This time it included blacks. Schools were asked to provide equal education for educationally disadvantaged minorities living in conditions of poverty, separation, and alienation.

This tilt toward such a broad and more "extreme" democratic agenda for schools created a reaction among middle-class white parents, business interests, and conservative politicians. They revolted in the 1970s with the back-to-basics movement, which focused on restoring the first goal of education – "academic excellence" and selectivity – and downplaying the citizenship/democratic goal of greater educational equality for the disadvantaged. But because the 1960s created all kinds of legal and financial incentives to provide greater equity and a reinforcement of the democratic ideal among educators, the back-to-basics movement failed to overturn blacks' greater claims for educational equity. As a result, rather than raising white children's average performance, back to basics may have helped – along with much higher black incomes in the early 1970s – to raise minority test scores significantly at all age levels by the 1980s.

Despite such gains by black children, conservative critics have cast doubt on public schools' capacity to help blacks do better.[4] For more than a generation they have been claiming, with little response from liberals, that school bureaucracies do little more than certify most black children as failures[5] or, at best, that they are ineffective in educating the disadvantaged. Supporters of a strengthened public system have provided few counters to such claims even though black children have done better when increased resources have been available.

The argument I make here is that government efforts to equalize black and white education in the 1970s, in addition to "systemic" educational reforms, did combine with a reduction in poverty – again, in large part through government intervention in labor markets – to improve black education and black performance in school well into the 1980s. But when all those efforts ended with the Reagan administration, black improvement gradually, inexorably ground to a halt. Conservative doubts about public education produced a self-fulfilling prophecy. As the equalization process slowed down in public education and the economic conditions in many black communities got worse, it became increasingly more difficult for education to help black youth move out of poverty.

Education in African-American communities did better in the 1970s and stagnated in the 1980s for three reasons: (1) the resources available per student in schools – which started out much lower for blacks – began to catch up in the 1960s and 1970s but not in the 1980s; (2) programs that improved student performance in school, such as Head Start and back-to-basics instruction, expanded in the 1970s but not in the 1980s; and (3) grants and government-guaranteed loans for low-income college students expanded rapidly in the 1970s but not in the 1980s – the slowdown in college money combined with increased poverty in the black community dampened college enrollment and even the motivation to continue on to college.

THE CHANGING DISTRIBUTION OF PUBLIC RESOURCES FOR EDUCATION

One of conservatives' most persistent criticisms of public education is that it wastes resources. More money for schooling has not produced better results, they argue, and by implication it would not improve poorly performing schools, even those with few resources for their students. For the William Bennetts and Lamar Alexanders, spending more on schools in black neighborhoods would do little to help the children attending them.

But recent studies suggest that more resources do help. Economists David Card and Alan Krueger estimate the impact of pupil–teacher ratio, average term length, and relative pay of teachers on the income payoff of education. They find that men educated in states with fewer pupils per teacher, longer school terms, and better-paid teachers earn more per year of schooling received and that the effect is as large for black men as for white. Since all the factors that contribute to higher school quality require more resources per student in school, their results suggest that when states spend more on their students, there is a greater economic payoff and that spending more on lower-cost black schools would make a major economic difference for their pupils.[6]

Thus, spending matters, and politics' impact on black education is partly measured by the relative amount spent in public education on black pupils relative to white. Equal spending is no guarantee of equal education or of equal outcomes for pupils of different social backgrounds, but it does mean that pupils get access to a similar set of school resources, such as teacher skills, classroom space, and educational materials.

What has happened to educational spending over the past three decades in states with relatively large black populations compared with those with smaller black proportions?[7] Between 1960 and 1970, spending per pupil in public schools increased 70 percent (5.4 percent annually), corrected for inflation. Between 1970 and 1980, growth fell by half, to 35 percent (3 percent annually), and between 1980 and 1989, it also increased about 3 percent annually.

States with a high percentage of black pupils (more than 20 percent) – primarily southern and border states – increased their spending much more rapidly than those with smaller black pupil populations in both the 1960s and 1970s, and although they were still catching up in the 1980s, they were doing so at a much lower rate. During all three decades, states with a high percentage of black pupils raised their spending per pupil more rapidly than the twenty states with less than 5 percent of blacks or the twenty-six states with less than 10 percent of blacks. Even so, the states with a high proportion of black pupils continued to spend less than those with a lower proportion. In 1989, the twelve states with more than 20 percent of black pupils spent $3,950 per pupil and those with less than 10 percent of black pupils spent about $4,600. The slowdown in the 1980s was especially harmful to the majority of blacks who lived in those poorer states.

What about *within*-state spending on black and white schools? According to economists Card and Krueger, the quality of black public schooling relative to white schooling in eighteen segregated states, as measured by relative pupil–teacher ratio, relative school term length, and relative teacher pay, improved dramatically between 1920 and the mid-1950s, with a hiatus in the early 1930s. By 1956, teacher pay and term length were equal and the pupil–teacher ratio was only about 13 percent higher in black schools.[8] Although data after the mid-1960s are harder to come by, there is no reason to believe that these measures of relative quality in public schools would have changed significantly after desegregation.

Some states, such as California, equalized spending across districts under legal mandate. *Serrano v. Priest* (1968) required the state to redistribute local property taxes so that all school districts had equal per student resources. An analysis we did of spending by more than a thousand school districts in California in 1988–91 shows that even in a state that has consciously equalized spending on public schools, wealthier districts spend somewhat more on their students than do poorer districts, but the difference is small. Districts with the largest percentage (more than 17 percent) of Aid for Dependent Children families – a good measure of low-income populations – got about $100 less per pupil from the state in 1989–91 than the districts with the lowest percentage (less than 4 percent). Although the poorer districts got more in federal and other categorical funds, wealthier districts were able to raise "extra" monies from parents through private donations. Schools with a high percentage of economically disadvantaged pupils already need more funds to make up for fewer educational resources at home. Instead, even in an "equalized" state such as California, they get the same or less.[9]

Most states do not equalize spending across districts, and in the 1980s there was no pressure on states to do so from the national government. The National Board of Inquiry, organized by the National Coalition of Advocates for Students in 1984 to hold hearings on educational inequality around the country, found that large differences existed in spending per pupil among school districts in Massachusetts, Kentucky, New York, Texas, and Ohio – states that had not moved toward equalization at that time. "On few issues did we hear such agreement from teacher union representatives, school administrators, school board members, parents and others. Clearly, throughout the United States, great inequities exist in funding levels for different school districts within the same state."[10] Ultimately, in 1990, Texas was forced by the courts to equalize spending across districts.

According to Jonathan Kozol, school funding in the New York City area increased approximately 30 to 40 percent per pupil across a wide range of school districts between the 1986–7 and 1989–90 school years. Funding per pupil started out at a very high $11,300 in the upper-middle-class Long Island suburbs of Manhasset, Jericho, and Great Neck, at $6,400 in the largely working-class suburb of Mount Vernon, and at $5,600 in the high-minority New York City public schools. Three years later, the figures were $15,000, $9,000, and $7,300. Kozol's point is that the relative increases are similar, but the absolute differences greatly favor the already rich districts. It is the absolute differences that make life easy or difficult in the schools.[11] Kozol finds similar differences in school funding between Chicago and the Chicago suburbs.

If New York City schools were assumed to use educational resources as effectively as those in Great Neck, this enormous gap in educational resources would still produce a much lower outcome for those in the city than those in the wealthy suburbs. According to these data and this criterion, the gap should have increased at the end of the 1980s.

The situation is much more serious than the growing gap suggests. Even with the same funding, "land prices, construction costs, and the difficulty of attracting teachers to teach in inner-city conditions often means that the same levels of funding do not go as far in cities as in suburbs. . . . [And] schools educating those students with fewer resources in the home, family, and community that bear on educational success, will need more school resources to reach any given educational outcome."[12] As Kozol shows, the growth pattern of educational spending in the 1980s did little or nothing to correct these three sources of unequal outcomes. Absolute funding differences between low-income minority and high-income white districts grew even as the higher cost of attracting equally effective resources to low-income districts and their unequal needs for educational funding to equalize student achievement persisted.

The much larger needs of inner-city schools versus their relative lack of resources is typified by the educational battle with poverty in Hartford, Connecticut. Ninety percent of Hartford's 26,000 students are black or Puerto Rican, and nearly half are from families on welfare. Few children learn to read at grade level in these schools, many have learning disabilities, and many complain of stomachaches, headaches, and other symptoms of hunger by midmorning. In the words of one teacher, "They need more than other children. . . . It is as if they have a terrible illness and they need all the medicine in the world."[13] In trying to fight poverty, Hartford's teachers and school administrators end up spending precious resources that are drained from basic education. This is in contrast to higher-income, suburban districts, where children come to school ready to learn and all available resources are used to teach them academic skills. Ultimately, unless poverty outside school is sharply reduced, low-income children in inner-city schools like Hartford's will need many more and entirely new kinds of resources in school to achieve significantly higher learning.

The Reagan and Bush administrations ignored this fundamental problem of poor, inner-city districts. They argued that the amount school districts get to spend may not mean much if they use their funds ineffectively. They claimed that low-income school districts are not as well managed as others, using existing funds for financing top-heavy central administrations rather than for direct instruction in schools.

This public school "bureaucracy" argument became fashionable in the

1980s as a justification for public financing of private schools – better known as the Bush "school choice" plan.[14] Our study of California districts shows no such pattern. School administrations in low-income districts may be less effective, but they have no more to spend than wealthier districts. The ratio of spending on administration to spending on instruction is equal for low-, medium-, and high-income districts. We did find that the more money a district gets to spend, the more it spends in administration per pupil. But it also spends more on instruction per pupil and on noninstructional staff, such as custodians, secretaries, and librarians.

California's experience tells us that equalizing school spending downward may not hurt higher-performing students much, but it does not help low-income pupils either. Reducing Great Neck's $11,000 per pupil spending to $6,000 and raising New York City's $5,500 to $6,000 would probably have little effect on school performance at either end. Instead, low-income school populations need significantly more school resources to do better.

The real issue here is not so much how schools can become more effective with the same resources as how they should use additional resources effectively. Most new resources in the past have gone into higher hourly wages for teachers. Is this the most effective use of additional dollars? Or should funds be used to increase the number of hours children stay in school every day, on school snacks, on additional personnel, or on library books and other supplies?

THE CHANGING DISTRIBUTION OF OTHER RESOURCES

Low-income districts need more than equal or better in-school financial resources to catch up to higher-income districts. They also need preschool resources such as Head Start and better in-school management to deal with increasingly difficult conditions in schools, at home, and in the community. This means facing up to the problems those districts have in recruiting teachers and holding them, the difficulty in producing high-quality schooling for illiterate *and* non-English-speaking children, and the lack of school resources for dealing with the social problems of children outside school.

In the 1970s, Head Start grew rapidly from $326 billion in 1970 to $735 billion in 1980, a 35 percent increase in per pupil spending when corrected for inflation. The number of children in Head Start fell by 100,000, partly because poverty levels fell. In the 1980s, funding for Head

Start slowed down sharply to 14 percent corrected for inflation, even with somewhat increasing enrollment. Real expansion occurred only when an inert Congress and the Bush administration finally acted to increase funding for Head Start significantly in 1991. Since poverty rose sharply in the recession of 1980–2 and remained high even during the economic expansion of 1983–9, the result was predictable: a smaller percentage of eligible children were covered by Head Start in 1989 than in 1980.

The new conservatism did not stop at Head Start. Reagan and Bush educational reforms, such as they were, systematically cut out the additional resources needed by school districts hard hit by expanding poverty. Beginning in 1982–3, and in keeping with the anti–government intervention ideology of the Reagan–Bush era, national educational policy tilted toward market approaches to education and a declining federal role. Not much actually changed educationally in the twelve years between 1980 and 1992, but the dominant ideology in the 1980s moved public opinion on education away from policies that would try to improve public education for the disadvantaged – especially policies that would require more resources for education – toward ones that would make education more efficient and competitive in some abstract sense. In theory, such efforts would help low-income schools. But conservative thinking never dealt with the special kinds of reforms needed for greater efficiency in low-income schools or with the possibility that greater efficiency could be achieved only if it was rewarded with more resources.[15]

The educational reforms that did occur in K through 12 public education in the 1980s took place almost entirely at the initiative of the states but within the context of an overall federal ideology. In every case, they tried to get more out of existing spending. The reforms focused first on raising standards in secondary schools (in the early 1980s), then on "restructuring" public schools for greater efficiency in delivering educational services (mid-1980s), then, in the late 1980s, on "choice" – increasingly a euphemism for public financing of private schooling. All of these reforms were a response to the "crisis" of education as identified early in the Reagan administration.[16] They also deemphasized the allocation of more resources for schools and communities in favor of greater efficiency in using existing resources.[17] In and of themselves, higher standards and greater efficiency were legitimate reforms. They spoke to real problems in education. But although by their emphasis on "basics" they may have contributed to higher performance by low-income students,[18] they only went a small part of the way in meeting their home and school resource problems.[19] By the Bush administration, even these reforms were de-emphasized in favor of school choice. The main solution to the minority educational problems being touted by conservative reformers was inner-city private education.[20] It corresponded to solutions proposed across a range of issues, including economic policy, health policy, and urban policy – all of them focused on less government support for public infrastructure and increased private financing.

The conservative movement in the 1970s and early 1980s had two major effects. First, it slowed efforts to solve the serious problems that black and Latino students were still having in schools. Since the conservative agenda had little interest in such issues, disadvantaged blacks and others struggled along at an improving but still dismally low level. Second, it created doubts in the minds of the middle-class white population that public schools could produce the same excellence that they had in the past, mainly because excellence and selectivity no longer seemed to be a primary educational goal. When reforms in the early 1980s failed to change educational outcomes for the white majority, conservatives moved to destroy the legitimacy of public education. With all the inefficiencies of the large educational bureaucracy in addition to its contradictory aims, this was not a difficult task. The public had much less confidence by 1992 that publicly run schooling could solve black educational and economic problems.

The decline in confidence in public schooling in the 1980s did not match the real improvements that were taking place for minorities – both black and Latino students did systematically better on national tests in all age groups until the end of the decade. And the fact is that schools held their own with white students even though changes outside schools – parents working longer hours and spending less time caring for children – made teaching more difficult. But when everybody from the Business Council to the secretary of education to conservative intellectuals bad-mouthed public schools, it diminished the attractiveness of teaching as a profession, lowered expectations in schools, and certainly made it more difficult for states to raise money for education, through either taxes or bond issues.

So the lack of support for minority education in the 1980s affected not only black students adversely. Public elementary and secondary schools had a hard time keeping up with the increasing economic and social stress on all lower- and middle-income families, whether white or black. But because blacks started out behind and seemed to be making progress in the 1970s, the policies of the 1980s were an especially cold shower. Blacks are more likely than whites to be poor, so the slowdown in federal support for education made it particularly difficult for them to overcome their early disadvantage and, even when they completed high school, to buck the financial barriers of higher education. And the same political ideology that deemphasized assistance to minority education also made life in general increasingly difficult for the poor – that, in turn, made it much less likely that poor children would come to school ready to learn.

THE POLITICS OF HIGHER EDUCATION IN THE 1980S

It took until the very end of the Reagan–Bush period for black college enrollment to begin rising after years of stagnation (see Chapter 5). As brought out in the National Academy of Sciences' massive study of blacks in the United States, *A Common Destiny,* for most of the 1980s the military was as attractive financially to black and Latino high school graduates as a college education. For good reason. Despite greater potential demand during the Reagan–Bush years, grants for college students remained constant in inflation-corrected dollars and college loans increased far slower than college tuition and other college costs. In the 1980s, the incomes of college-educated workers rose relative to those of high school graduates. This was true for all groups – whites, blacks, Latinos, men, and women. The rising value of college education also became obvious at the national level: the nation's economy – whether in manufacturing, services, or commerce – was becoming increasingly information- and communications-based in the 1980s. It required many more college-trained workers, and those workers would have to come from low- and middle-income families – including many black and Latino families – who could not afford to send their children to college.

The amount of money in the form of Pell grants – issued by the federal assistance program for postsecondary students from low-income families – given to college students remained constant at $2 billion, adjusted for inflation. Yet the costs of going to college rose much faster than inflation: nation-wide, average inflation-adjusted tuition at four-year colleges (including public colleges) rose 90 percent in ten short years. With median black family incomes only inching up during the decade and higher-education costs skyrocketing even at public colleges, black high school graduates faced a triple disadvantage. They came from homes of lower than average income and had to pay ever-higher costs with less financial aid available.

Although it was possible for all low-income blacks or Latinos to obtain college tuition funding either through grants, loans, or tuition-free public education, low-income high school graduates needed to support themselves and even contribute to their families' livelihood. Self-support while attending college was a much more limited possibility. So with the economic stagnation for low-income families hanging in until 1986–7, the training and income opportunities offered by the military looked very good compared with the uncertainty and forgone income of college.

But from a different angle, the choice not to go to college was illogical. The payoff of a college education rose almost as rapidly for blacks and Latinos in the 1980s as for whites. The decline in payoff for young black male college graduates did not begin until the mid-1980s. Yet the high payoff did not draw blacks and Latinos into college in the numbers it should have – that is, until family incomes in the black and Latino community rose enough in the last years of the decade to make it easier financially to go to college. Ironically, just as it became easier to finance college, it became much less obvious for young blacks that graduation from college would lead to a good job.

What does all this mean? Economists have always understood that borrowing for education is difficult and risky, and that an important role for government is to make it easier for those who have little access to savings or bank loans to go to school. This is especially true when the economic payoff of such an investment may be high for society. That has been the rationale behind public education in general and behind public university education. It was one of the rationales behind the GI bill after World War II. And it was the reason that the Higher Education Act made grants and student loans available especially to low-income students. The failure of all these measures to increase college enrollment among low-income students in the 1980s tells us that when the economy is particularly hard on the poor, the incentives offered to them to acquire additional education – even when the economic payoff is very high – have to increase. Instead, the Reagan administration cut financial assistance. It was not until the economy recovered sufficiently (in 1986–7) that blacks and Latinos began enrolling in much larger numbers. In terms of the labor market, however, the move may have come too late.

Where the educational payoff is

There are many ways to look at changes in the economic payoff of education. One is to look at the average incomes earned by young people with different amounts of schooling. The additional income that comes with more schooling should have a big impact on the way teenagers view education. If workers in their twenties who finish college earn increasingly more income than high school graduates, it should serve as a major incentive to complete a four-year college education.

The greater inequality in income growth among higher- and lower-end jobs in the 1980s had a profound effect on the worth of different levels of education.[21] The fall in real income in low-end jobs during the 1980s in both absolute and relative terms translated into a sharp drop in relative income for the less educated – especially, as it turns out, for younger, less-educated workers.

Even so, younger (25- to 34-year-old) minority college graduates who were employed full time did not fare so well either. White male median income corrected for inflation *rose* slightly from $18,400 to $18,600 (in 1979 dollars) between 1979 and 1989, young Latino male graduate income fell from $16,200 to $14,800, and young black male graduate median income fell from $15,100 in 1979 to $13,300 in 1989.

Yet mean income premiums – the average income gain over high school graduates – for 25- to 34-year-old men and women who completed college rose in the 1980s for all groups (Figures 7.1a and b, respectively).[22] There are differences among ethnic groups as to when the increase in payoff of college began, how much it rose, and (for minority males) whether it had begun to fall away after the middle of the decade, but it seems to have been a general phenomenon in the 1980s. It also seems to have been much more sensitive to the unemployment rate for blacks and Latinos, rising less when the unemployment rate fell. Black high school graduate incomes are even less likely to go up than whites' when unemployment is high.

A more common way of looking at the income gain from additional education is to take account of the income given up by going to school.[23] The "private rate of return" (as economists call this premium) of completing even some years of college fell for whites in the 1970s and rose in the 1980s, but the rate of return to blacks and Latinos of some college and college completion rose and fell with more irregularity in the 1970s, all of which tends to confirm the enrollment figures in Chapter 4. How the rates behaved for blacks and Latinos in the 1970s depends on who was included in the sample – all workers or only full-time workers. The one sure thing is that the rate of return of college graduation rose for everyone

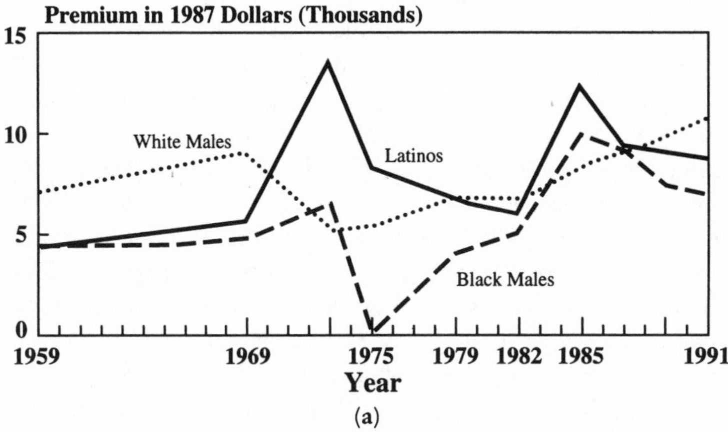

(a)

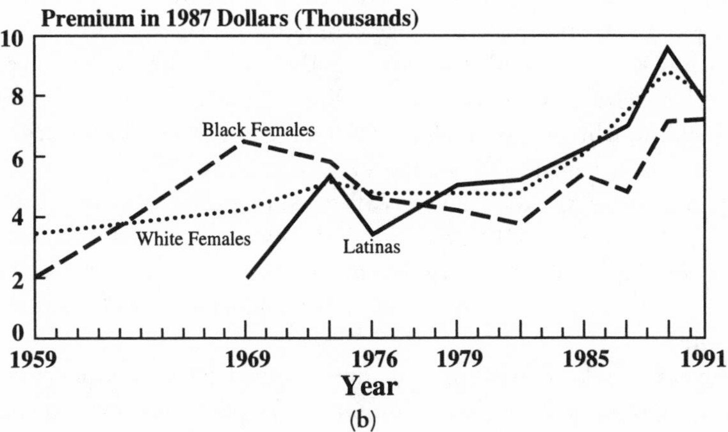

(b)

Figure 7.1. College premium for (a) male and (b) female full-time workers, by race and ethnicity, 1959–91. From U.S. Census Bureau, Public Use Sample, 1960, 1970, and 1980, and Current Population Survey, March Survey, various years, full-time-worker sample.

in the 1980s – men and women, Latinos, whites, and blacks. The premium for completing high school as measured this way rose in the 1970s and into the early 1980s for all men, but then began to fall in the mid-1980s. For blacks and whites, this is true when all income earners are included in the analysis and when only full-time workers are included.

This rapidly growing premium for college graduates results not just from movements in the supply of and demand for educated labor. In part it is due to an income and employment policy in the 1980s that put downward pressure on wages and thus lowered the relative payoff of a high school education. Yet there is no doubt that the demand for college-educated workers also went through a sea change in the 1970s that continued into the 1980s. Employers set new norms for minimum levels of acceptable education for different kinds of jobs, even though the skill requirements of those jobs may hardly have changed. As the majority of young whites entering the labor force came with college education, employers began to consider that having at least some college was a sign of "normality" among young people. Whether the job required a college education was almost immaterial. Some jobs may have become more complex in the past two decades. But what really happened in the 1970s and 1980s is that young whites, still the dominant group in the age cohort, set new standards for the level of education attained. By doing so, they put other groups, particularly minority men, but also minority women, who were less likely to go to college and much less likely to get a bachelor's degree, in an increasingly disadvantaged position. Minorities (and whites) who finished high school but did not attend college began to find themselves outside the job market mainstream.

In that sense, the demand for college-educated labor increased more rapidly than in the 1960s or early 1970s. When combined with a slowdown in the supply of college graduates in the 1980s, increasing demand had to put upward pressure on the relative wages of the college-educated.

However, *why* the payoffs of investing in high school and college education went up or down is unimportant for predicting the demand for more schooling. The high premiums of attending and finishing college for all groups in the 1980s should have brought whites, blacks, and Latinos, men and women, into four-year colleges in droves.[24] College completion rates should also have risen. Since even the returns of high school completion went up in the early 1980s (the real incomes of those who dropped out declined even more than those of high school completers), this should have also decreased the number of high school dropouts in all groups. For whites, these supply responses did occur in the form of increased rates of college enrollment (although after the baby-boom bulge there were fewer whites to go around), but the great "mystery" has been the failure of Latinos and especially blacks to increase their rate of college enrollment and college graduation in the past decade. Why haven't greatly increased payoffs led to a rush of college education among minorities?

Explaining rising and declining minority college enrollment

Harvard economist Richard Freeman argued in the 1970s that the large increase in minority high school graduation and college enrollment in the 1960s and early 1970s was at least in part a response to public policies that raised aspirations among minorities and provided the wherewithal for them to continue their schooling at the university level.[25] These policies did not equalize attendance between whites and minorities at four-year colleges, and the percentage of whites who graduated from four-year colleges remained much higher. But the late 1960s and early 1970s showed that it was possible to create an atmosphere and the financial conditions in which discriminated-against minority groups would catch up educationally even at the college level. The reversal of those policies in the 1980s apparently had a large and negative effect on black and Latino progress, particularly the fraction of blacks who went on to college.

This is not the thinking that prevails among many analysts today.[26] Their counterargument is that the civil rights victories of the 1950s and 1960s and subsequent affirmative action programs made it possible for an upper-middle tier of blacks and Latinos to achieve economic and social parity with whites – to become like whites – because their relatively higher social class allowed them to take advantage of greater access to universities. But the movement could not create the conditions necessary for the majority of blacks and Latinos to be assimilated. For whatever reason – either more than a century of subordination and separation or inherent cultural incompatibility with white middle-class values of competition and accumulation – a high proportion of minorities were unable to take advantage of higher education and equal opportunity. They were immobilized economically by their own condition, suspended in a debilitating world of poverty, malnutrition, structureless adult–child relations, and violence.

In the 1980s, the federal government, pointing to the "failures" of expensive educational and social interventions, began cutting back drastically on its role in education. Essentially, the Reagan Department of Education argued that states and localities had to deal with education, and that it was up to individuals and their families to make do with what was available and to put pressure on school districts to be more effective. Higher efficiency with existing resources and higher state-level standards became the main guidelines for educational reform.

The corresponding argument on college entry is that low achievement in secondary school is the primary determinant of minority college attendance and completion. The average black or Latino high school completer is not able to do as well as a white completer on literacy or numeracy tests.[27] Reports from William Bennett's Department of Education in the late 1980s emphasized this difference and the lower socioeconomic class of the average black high school graduate. They never made a direct connection between college attendance and changes in blacks' achievement or family background, but "by implication, these reports provide an account of change over time in black college attendance rates that emphasizes black–white differences in achievement."[28] The idea is that fewer minority youth go to college because they are unqualified to do college work. This means that more federal grants and college scholarships for minority high school graduates have little effect on college enrollment.

There is no question that black and Latino reading and math scores are lower than whites'. The scores are so low that they raise serious questions about the quality of minority (and white) education even after fifty years of progress; and they merit national concern. But lower absolute minority achievement levels do not explain the stagnation in college enrollment rates among minorities. The average school achievement of minorities has increased dramatically, absolutely and relative to whites, as have their high school completion rates, although the achievement gap is still large and majority high school dropout rates still high.

In the past, as more minorities completed high school, the percentage going to college went up simultaneously, especially after 1965, when getting into college and finding a good job seemed much more hopeful. The likelihood of minority – especially black – college enrollment relative to white enrollment stopped climbing and began to fall in the late 1970s, *just as minority – especially black – high school achievement scores began rising rapidly relative to those of whites.* Both the earlier increase and later decline in the relative likelihood of blacks' attending college were also unaffected by corrections for family income, region, sex distribution, or other demographic factors.[29] Quite contrary to the individual-responsibility argument, this supports the claim that *neither* high school achievement nor the social class composition of high school graduating classes was a factor in the 1980s downturn in college enrollment.

A much more likely reason for the decrease in the growth of college enrollment rates for both blacks and Latinos is the slowdown in financial aid and the shift from grants to loans at a time of increasing poverty among minority families. "From 1980–81 to 1985–86, the total federal, state, and college 'package' of financial aid declined 3 percent after controlling for changes in the consumer price index, but the real financial situation became worse than that because the costs of attending a state college or university rose faster than the general cost of living."[30] Not only did the real value of financial aid decline significantly, the financial aid package changed from 80 percent outright grants in 1975–6 to 50 percent loans in 1985–6.

Recent research suggests that increases in the net cost of attending college and reductions in federal student aid have a negative effect on enrollment for white students from *low-income* families.[31] This is a "price effect" – the effect of a change in price for a given level of income on a consumption decision. But there were also income effects in the 1980s. Although the researchers could not test whether black or Latino students are affected to a greater or lesser degree than whites, it is likely that the reduction in the financial aid package in the 1980s hit minorities more than whites because (1) a higher fraction of potential minority college students come from low-income families, and (2) minority incomes fell from already low levels in the 1980s, especially between 1979 and 1982. The percentage of black high school graduates coming from families with incomes of less than $10,000 (in 1985 dollars) rose from 27 percent in 1968–73 to 35 percent in 1980–5. This compares with an almost constant 9 to 10 percent of white high school graduates with families having that low an income level.[32] The absolute proportion of Latino graduates from low-income families was probably lower than that of blacks, but not by much, and the changes were proportional and in the same direction, given the parallel changes in the overall distribution of incomes among Latinos during that period. One argument is that minority lower-income families are less likely to borrow than white families because minorities' employment is less secure and they have fewer assets. So even with the high rates of return of investing in college education, they would be reluctant to incur additional debt.[33]

With more high school graduates from poor, minority families competing for less funding in real terms, the chances of getting any kind of funding have gone down, and the chances of getting an outright grant have declined by more than half in real terms.

But there are other arguments. Remember that the stagnation in minority college enrollment is all the more significant because of the rapidly increasing payoff of college education and college completion for minorities in the 1980s. Yet in addition to the perceived enormous rise in the cost of attending college – less financing being sought by more poor minority families – the size of the college premium may also be perceived to be much smaller by minorities than we have reported. For one thing, the rising premium of a college education is less the result of rising real incomes for college graduates than of falling real incomes for high school graduates and the even more rapid fall in real incomes of high school dropouts. These declines in real incomes of young high-school-educated minorities were somewhat greater than for whites. So even though the premium of completing higher levels of education did go up for minorities, the average real incomes of younger minority college graduates at best grew very slowly in the late 1970s and 1980s. The minority community may not view this kind of "perverse" increase in premium in the same way they viewed the more positive increase in the late 1960s and early 1970s.

For another thing, the way we measure the payoff of a college education over a high school education assumes that the two groups of students are of equal ability. There is no evidence that the difference in ability increased in the 1980s between those blacks and Latinos who graduated from college and those who graduated from high school yet did not go on. But because of the anti–affirmative action climate in the Reagan years the risk of investing in college as perceived by a black or Latino with relatively low achievement may have increased. Many now finishing high school may have a much more pessimistic view about their chances of getting a good job in the present climate. Perhaps this explains the large increase in black high school male and female seniors who plan to enter the armed forces.[34] If the perceived risk of reaping a good return on investing in college is related to high school achievement, raising minority achievement could increase college enrollment substantially, even if the financial resources available do not grow, or even if financial aid is available mainly as loans.

From where many policy analysts stand, raising minority achievement in high school is the *only* way to raise college enrollment. Their approach is hardly psychological. It rests on a notion of equal economic outcomes only for those of equal ability. But the experience from the 1960s and 1970s suggests that a clear climate of commitment to improving minorities' opportunities evokes a highly positive response in the form of increasing minority college enrollment and graduation. The data on declining financial aid over the past ten years also support the idea that the amount and kind of public resources available to young people from poor minority families certainly affect how many invest in higher education. If minority incomes continue to stay low, higher-achieving high school graduates will still need financial help to go to college.

As college and college completion became the educational currency of value in the labor market in the 1980s, perceived barriers to college attendance, financial or otherwise, must have had a negative impact on minority performance in primary and secondary school. Here is how this works. Students who expect to go to college are required to take more math and language courses – and at a more advanced level – than non-college-track students. The more advanced a course is, the higher a student's performance on tests in that subject, even if the student doesn't do especially well in the course. In fact, studying more advanced subject matter is a key factor in explaining school performance as measured by national tests.[35] So increasing expectations among teachers and students about black opportunities to enroll in a four-year college could have a major impact on pupil performance in the precollege grades.

This does not mean that present policy makers are wrong to point to the low achievement levels of minority high school graduates. Where they err is in citing those statistics to justify falling college enrollment levels rather than using every possible means to raise enrollment, including more financial grants, continued affirmative action, and serious reforms in public primary and secondary schools aimed at helping low-income minorities do better.

8

Politics and black job opportunities: I

African-Americans' economic gains have always depended on the jobs and wages available to them. With greater global competition and new technology in the 1970s and 1980s, the structure of job opportunities changed. That change undoubtedly made black gains more difficult. Americans with high-level skills profited more than the less educated from the new structure. Globalization sped up deindustrialization, destroying a main source of black (male) upward mobility. And the new high-wage jobs in services and manufacturing required more education and more technical education than most blacks had.

Is this explanation for the decline of black fortunes since the mid-1970s supported by the evidence on job and wage changes? Only partly. Heightened global competition and the information revolution in the 1970s and 1980s do not by themselves explain why the private sector responded to these new economic forces the way it did, or why the relative incomes of lower-end jobs fell more rapidly than those at the higher end. Nor do they explain why the pattern was accentuated for minorities.

To complete the picture, we need to look at the response by the other major player in the job market – government. Government income policies, which had remained the same for almost two generations, also changed after 1973. These radically new policies had a role in shaping wage patterns. Although they were partly a response to the same forces of global competition that struck private business, they were also a result of distinct political choices with drastically different ramifications for different groups of economic actors.

A full explanation of the decline in black incomes in this period should include Carter and Reagan administration macroeconomic policies geared to increase corporate profits at the expense of wages. It should include the increase in unemployment rates used by the Reagan administration to slow inflation in the early 1980s, Reagan antilabor policies and actions, a turning away from compensatory education, urban redevelopment, and other social programs in the 1980s, and a distinct reversal of civil rights ideology during that decade. These were features of government policy that had not existed, in combination, since pre-Depression days. They reflected a particular policy response to new market conditions, but they were not the only, or necessarily the best, means available to produce sustained economic growth, and certainly not to create greater equity.

How does the federal government's management of economic growth affect black jobs and pretax incomes? To begin with, government intervention in the economy is a fact of life, no matter how much conservatives would like it to be otherwise. It uses its money creation and fiscal power to stimulate or cool economic growth. Since it taxes and spends, it can stimulate some sectors such as high technology, the military, and construction through tax credits and direct subsidies, and penalize others, such as major polluters or old-line industries in politically less blessed regions.

Government fiscal and monetary policy can also help or hurt various groups of workers. Blacks are mainly wage workers and, because of their history of slavery and economic segregation, are likely even today to be employed in the lower, more economically vulnerable strata of the job structure. A "tight" labor market policy that emphasizes high growth rates, low unemployment rates, and full production capacity means that a large number of less-educated blacks – who are the first to be unemployed when the economy weakens – will have jobs. A tighter labor market policy also means that wages for lower-skilled jobs will tend to be pushed up as employers bid for harder-to-find unemployed workers. Of course, the wages of those in higher-skilled jobs may be pushed up even more, since they are in relatively scarcer supply, and this may lead to a higher rate of inflation and higher nominal interest rates. This is the principal argument against a tight labor market policy.

A policy of fuller employment is not the only way that government economic management affects blacks' (and almost everyone else's) incomes. Government macroeconomic policies can influence whether economic growth is led by exports or by the production of domestic consumption goods. This was not a major issue in the thirty years after

World War II because U.S. producers so dominated world markets and because the U.S. domestic market was so much larger than all other markets combined. But things have changed. Whether the United States exports more commercial aircraft or not can have a substantial effect on today's growth rates and particularly on the growth of high-end, skill-intensive manufacturing, where most U.S. nonagricultural exports are concentrated. A smaller proportion of blacks work in export industries than in domestic-market-oriented industries. Therefore, an export orientation could leave them worse off.

That is not the end of the story. Through taxation and spending, the federal government controls almost one-fourth of our national product, and state and local governments control about 10 to 12 percent more. Taxation decisions obviously affect different groups' post-tax incomes. But just as important, government spending decisions affect their pre-tax incomes. Spending is not just an issue of direct subsidies to farmers, welfare payment to low-income mothers, social security payments to seniors, or veterans' benefits. When government decides to spend more on military hardware, it helps some groups of workers – in this case, highly skilled engineers and machinists, who tend to be white and male – much more than others. When it decides to spend more on health care, urban redevelopment, or education, it tends to benefit a different set of workers – in this case, more likely women and minorities.

A shift in spending from military subcontracting to government investment in human and physical infrastructure also tends to increase direct government employment. Although government subcontractors in private industry are closely scrutinized for equal-opportunity hiring and for the relative wages paid to black workers, subcontractors never seem to be as effective in hiring minorities and women as is government itself. This is partly the result of the kinds of jobs available in military production compared with education, health, transportation, and urban redevelopment. But it is also due to government hiring and pay practices, which have led the way in reducing race and gender discrimination.[1]

The federal government's treatment of business–labor relations is also crucial to the overall increase in wages during periods of economic expansion. Governments in Austria, Sweden, and Japan that rely on national agreements between business and labor on real wage increases in order to fashion macroeconomic growth and inflation targets tend to set real wage increases in line with agreed-on productivity gains.[2] Germany and other members of the European Economic Community also have tended to allow real wages to rise steadily and have expected productivity increases to match them during the post–World War II period.

So did the United States until 1973. In Europe and Japan, rising real wages are still an integral part of government macroeconomic policy. But U.S. government and business opted in the crisis of the 1970s to regain competitiveness through a wage containment and reduction strategy.[3] In the Reagan years, this turned into a conscious, active antilabor position. Among other things, it consisted of union busting and holding down minimum wages. A large number of both unskilled and skilled workers immigrating into the United States were ready to work hard for lower pay than native-born Americans – and so contributed to keeping the lid on wages. Some economists claim, with good reason, that wage containment was largely responsible for stagnant productivity and increased income inequality.[4]

Let us look at the possible impact on black incomes of four of the most important of these government macroeconomic policies: (1) anti-inflation, (2) labor wages, (3) spending, and (4) immigration.

BLACK INCOMES AND ANTI-INFLATION POLICY

In the 1950s and early 1960s, the U.S. economy was able to achieve high growth rates with almost no inflation. Unemployment rates were low. That changed with the Vietnam-fueled economic expansion of the 1960s. Inflation rates increased in the late 1960s and early 1970s, and jumped again with the oil price increase in 1973. The average overall economic growth rate fell and average unemployment rates rose. The process was called "stagflation." With the second oil price hike in 1979, inflation jumped once more – this time to a level that obsessed Americans politically (Table 8.1).

The shock of high inflation rates after decades of growth with stable prices made the Federal Reserve Board (with White House approval) tend toward tighter monetary policy. Low inflation rates became more important politically than high unemployment rates. The 1981–2 Federal Reserve inflation "shock treatment" of raising real (corrected for inflation) interest rates to historically high levels curbed inflation but also raised unemployment to 14 percent by late 1982.[5] It took until 1986 for unemployment to fall back to 6 percent, still higher than during the Carter expansion, and until 1987 for rates to fall to a more "normal" unemployment level of 5.4 percent. Thus, it took almost four years of recovery to

Table 8.1. *Gross national product growth, inflation, and unemployment rates, 1960–91 (percent)*

Year	Annual growth of GNP	Average annual inflation	Average annual unemployment	
			White	Black
1961–8	4.5	2.0	4.3	9.2
1969–76	2.2	6.3	5.3	10.4 (10.0)
1977–80	3.0	9.7	5.7	13.4 (12.4)
1981–8	2.8	4.6	6.5	15.5 (14.1)
1989–91	0.0	4.8	5.1	11.7 (10.4)

Note: Inflation rate is measured by changes in the consumer price index. From 1961 to 1968, the unemployment rate refers to "black and other." Figures in parentheses refer to "black and other." White unemployment figures include Latinos.
Source: Economic Report of the President, 1991, Tables B-2, B-39, and B-58.

reach reasonably low levels of unemployment. Even then, rates for black men and women were higher than they had been in the 1970s. Poverty rates rose sharply, and blacks' incomes fell relative to whites' as lower-skilled and part-time workers' wages were hit hard by the downturn. Figure 8.1 shows median income changes by race and the length of time it took for recovery to take place.[6]

The Reagan strategy produced reasonable economic growth rates with relatively low inflation for five years in the mid-1980s. Yet it achieved growth with little benefit for low- and middle-income workers. Income growth was high-end-biased. High unemployment rates were partly to blame; only when they fell in the mid-1980s did the incomes of the poor begin to rise.

Wage policy was also one of the major factors that defined both the capacity of the economy to grow and the distribution of the benefits of growth. The focus on maintaining low wages as the key to low inflation and large profits – hence economic growth – allowed business to avoid the productivity-increasing investments needed to raise profits in an environment where wages were expected to rise and inflation to stay reasonably low. Both the Carter and Reagan administrations attempted to induce business to invest more by making it easier for them to achieve large profits. The 1986 Tax Reform Act ended most of the tax incentives to business, but antilabor policies designed to "zap labor," to use Bennett Harrison and Barry Bluestone's phrase, continued under the Bush administration.

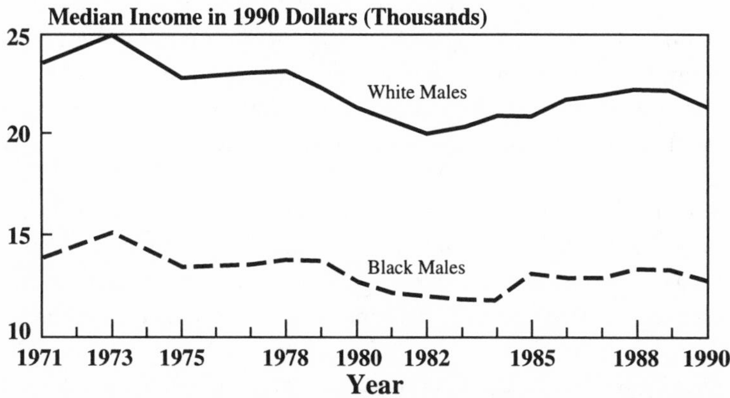

Figure 8.1. Median income, all male workers with income, by race, 1971–90. From Council of Economic Advisors, *Economic Report to the President, 1992,* Table B-27.

Strategies that pushed down wage demands and lowered taxes on capital gains lowered investment in new plant and equipment – exactly the opposite effect intended. Instead of investing in higher labor productivity and larger company profits over the long term, business poured money into real estate speculation and financial schemes that aimed at short-term profits with little implications for productivity. *Net* annual private investment (gross investment minus capital depreciation) and profit rates in the early and middle 1980s were actually lower than in the 1970s despite all the efforts to help business. Worse, businesses' capital infrastructure was hardly poised to respond to the next round of increased demand.

BLACK INCOMES AND GOVERNMENT WAGE POLICY

Government in the 1980s succeeded in helping business keep real wages from growing as rapidly as they did in the expansions of the 1960s and early 1970s by means of a three-pronged strategy: supporting business through an aggressively hard-line anti–organized labor scheme, using tight money policy to help keep unemployment rates relatively high, and greatly reducing the real (corrected for inflation) minimum wage.

Higher unemployment rates and minimum-wage policy affect the wages of lower-skilled workers more than higher-skilled ones, and antilabor policies affect lower- and middle-level wages. In the recession of the early 1980s, a large number of unemployed, younger and middle-age production and clerical workers were thrown into the labor market. The combination of these policies had a greater effect on lower- and middle-level jobs than on higher-level jobs, where unemployment rates are low to start with and labor organizing had little impact on wages in earlier decades.

Blacks tended to be hurt more than whites by these policies, because blacks are overrepresented in low- and middle-income jobs compared with high-income jobs (see Table 5.2). Blacks were also more likely to be unemployed or made to work part time because, on average, they had less seniority than whites.

Typically, business argues that higher-paying professional, managerial, and technical jobs are crucial to a firm's operation (especially in the information economy), so that wages in those jobs have to be raised in order to recruit the best workers and keep the firm profitable. Who performs those jobs is crucial, but their wages represent a small part of the firm's payroll. At the other end of the skill spectrum, the argument goes, wages have to be kept low in order to justify hiring workers. During the 1980s, the miracle of U.S. "job creation" was contrasted far and wide with "Eurosclerosis" – no job growth and higher unemployment rates. Wage "flexibility" (the ability to reduce real wages in middle- and lower-skilled jobs and replace old with new workers) got the credit for the miracle. The difference was that productivity and wages were rising more quickly in Europe (and Japan) than in the United States and that European (and Japanese) businesses were investing more in new capital equipment and worker training in order to be competitive at higher wages (Figure 8.2). In addition, during the 1980s, incomes at the high end went up much faster in the United States than in Europe (or Japan).

The antilabor message

In the 1970s companies had already been relocating plants to nonunion states or states unfriendly to unions as part of a strategy to lower wages. These same states, mostly in the South and Southwest, offered lucrative tax breaks to draw companies away from the high-tax, unionized Northeast and Upper Midwest.[7] Companies had also begun subcontracting to nonunion shops for a host of manufacturing and service tasks. Even if a company was not unionized, as in Silicon Valley, subcontracting to the "underground" economy was a way to avoid paying the growing costs of worker

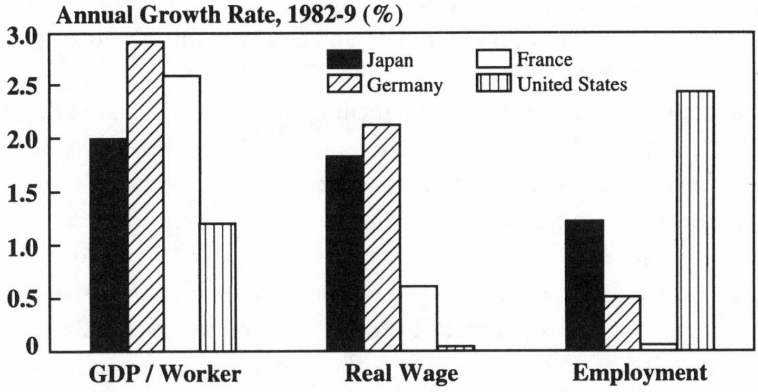

Figure 8.2. Economic performance measured by annual growth rate of gross domestic product (GDP), by country, 1982–9. From International Labour Office, *Statistical Yearbook, 1992* (Geneva: ILO, 1993), Tables 3A and 15.

benefits.[8] A new generation of sweatshop firms flourished not only in the garment industry, but in the high-technology sector. Temporary-worker agencies also flourished. Many companies hired temporary workers on a permanent basis in order to lower the rising costs of social benefits.[9]

These patterns became accentuated in the 1980s expansion, but were accompanied by a strong new official antiunion message from the government. The Reagan administration used a strike by government workers – the professional air traffic controllers organization (PATCO) – in 1983 to bring the message home. When the air controllers walked off their jobs to protest primarily working conditions (not wages), the administration invoked an antistrike clause for government workers to fire all the strikers. Most of them lost their jobs permanently when the government hired a new group of air controllers. The administration's action was carried out even though it increased the danger of air travel and even though most analysts agreed that the PATCO demands were justified in terms of airport safety.

There were other aspects of Reagan antiunion policy. A five-year lag developed in the response of the National Labor Relations Board (NLRB) to complaints by unions regarding unfair labor practices, even as complaints registered with the NLRB increased.

The strength of the government's antilabor message conveyed by the PATCO action and the NLRB delays was not lost on private employers. Caught in a profit squeeze in the late 1960s and early 1970s, management had already begun to launch its assault on the cost of labor. Supported by government in the 1980s, managers intensified their strategy of "globalization of production, the hollowing of the firm, outright union busting, and revised labor–management relations that included demands for the lowering of wages, the proliferation of part-time schedules . . . and the increased subcontracting of work."[10]

The strategy was typified by a series of labor–management conflicts at the Greyhound Bus Company, beginning in the early 1980s. After a long strike in 1983, the Amalgamated Transit Union (ATU) drivers were forced to give back 15 percent of their wages and benefits in order to be reemployed by the company. In 1985, the company insisted on renegotiating the contract, which still had a year to run. Threatening ATU drivers with replacement by nonunion workers, management demanded and got a package of concessions that essentially eliminated the union as a bargaining unit, lowered wages again, and gave the company the right to contract out many of the former union jobs. Two years later, Greyhound sold out to a Dallas-based entrepreneur, Fred Currey, who rehired Greyhound workers at half their already much lowered wages. Currey then bought what was left of Trailways Bus Company, forming a monopoly over passenger bus transportation. Through all this, the Reagan government looked on approvingly.[11]

The anti–organized labor message had only an indirect effect on blacks as a group, but for those who had gained access to union jobs and higher wages in the 1950s and 1960s, it was an important one. It pressed down their hard-fought, newly won middle-class status as part of the better-paid segment of the working class. Its symbolism when combined with the growth of low-paying alternatives to unionized jobs and the expansion of professional work was clear: government was no longer interested in the social mobility of the less-educated working class. To most blacks, that meant relegation to poverty and near poverty for their working lives.

Minimum-wage policy

As part of the overall low-wage policy followed since the mid-1970s, minimum wages lost ground rapidly as a policy tool to raise the incomes of workers in low-end jobs. The argument on minimum wage that won the day was that it would cost jobs, especially jobs for young people (although, because of decreasing real wages at the low end, most minimum-wage jobs are now held by adults). There is, in fact, very mixed evidence that higher minimum wages do cost jobs. It could well be that a higher legal floor on wages would have a positive effect on productivity and, in the longer run, increase jobs,[12] or it may be that in order to produce large increases in employment in today's highly competitive world economy, it really is necessary to keep wages from growing quickly. In a recent study, for example, David Card showed that the 1990 legal minimum-wage increase from $3.50 to $4.25 per hour had no significant impact on youth employment in low-income jobs. This was due partly to existing higher minimum-wage laws in many northern and western states. But even in California, where the minimum wage increased in the late 1980s, the effect on unemployment seems to have been small.[13] These results suggest that there is more than one side to the story of minimum-wage effects on employment.

Minimum-wage legislation was such that, adjusted for inflation, minimum wages fell from their high in 1968 of $6.26 (in 1991 dollars) to $5.50 in the mid-1970s and then sharply down in the 1980s. When no new legislation was passed during the entire eight years of the Reagan administration, the wage dropped to a low of $3.67 by 1989 (in 1991 dollars). This meant a decline of 27 percent (Table 8.2) and, in terms of purchasing power, pushed the floor lower than it had been in 1950. Even after increases in 1990 and 1991, the present minimum wage in real value of purchasing power is only about what it was forty years ago.

The impact on average black incomes of the declining real value of minimum wages depends partly on what is assumed about the way minimum-wage legislation affects the wages and employment of low-end workers – especially native-born low-end workers who may be more likely to take no job at all rather than work for such low pay. If lower real minimum wages pull down the wage offers to presently employed workers working at or above the minimum, then they do have the effect of lowering the average wages of the employed. If the minimum wage is too low to induce anyone but the very young and new immigrants to work at such jobs, lowering it farther may even have little effect on the employment of the less-skilled native-born. Black male adult unemployment rates moved down considerably but slowly in the 1980s expansion, falling from a recession high of 18.1 percent in 1983 to 14.2 percent in 1984 to a still-high 10 percent in 1989. Unemployment rates of black male youth (16 to 19 years old), once recovered from the 1980–2 recession, also did not do especially well during the expansion. They recovered from

Table 8.2. *Real minimum wages, 1950–91 (in 1991 dollars)*

Year	Minimum wage
1950	4.24
1956	5.08
1961	5.24
1967	5.71
1968	6.26
1974	5.52
1976	5.50
1979	5.44
1981	5.02
1989	3.67
1990	3.96
1991	4.25

Source: Statistical Abstract of the United States, 1992. Table 682, p. 418, adjusted using consumer price index in *Economic Report of the President,* 1991, Table B-58.

48.8 percent in 1983 to 42.7 percent in 1984 but then to only 31.9 percent in the next five years.

What role did falling real minimum wages have in creating jobs for blacks in the 1980s, or, to put it another way, what would have happened to black employment growth in the 1980s if real minimum wages had been rising, as they were in the 1960s? Have world economic conditions changed so much that it is no longer possible to have employment growth without keeping wages low? The Japanese have both increasing wages and employment growth (see Figure 8.2), but this may be due to a level of cooperation between employers, organized labor, and government that is impossible to attain in the United States. It may also be due to well-thought-out macroeconomic policy, which may be the way that Europeans might reduce current high levels of unemployment while keeping wages high. If the United States cannot create employment without low wages, we face the social dilemma of deciding whether it is better to raise low wages at the expense of some jobs or to provide jobs, even at low wages, to more workers. Neither solution is politically sustainable in the present social context.

BLACK INCOMES AND GOVERNMENT SPENDING

Federal government spending changed after the 1960s, and this had a big impact on the income growth of *higher-educated* blacks. The pressure to decrease spending as deficits grew accentuated in the late 1970s and made lower spending the centerpiece of Republican rhetoric throughout the 1980s. In practice, spending "reduction" was translated mainly into spending *shift* – in the late 1970s, from military to social spending and, in the 1980s, from social to military spending. From 1976 to 1981 (the last Carter budget), "national defense" fell from 24 to 23 of the federal budget and social spending stayed constant at 55 percent. But from 1981 to 1987, national defense rose to 28 percent of the budget and social spending fell to 50 percent. Translated in constant 1987 dollars, this means that the federal government was spending $26 billion more on national defense in the 1981 budget than in the 1976 budget, whereas social spending went up by $66 billion. The opposite happened in the Reagan years. Military spending went up by $90 billion between 1981 and 1987, and social spending, only $44 billion. Within military spending, money also shifted from support for personnel to support for developing and building new weapons.

If African-Americans were distributed proportionately across employment sectors in the same way as whites, shifts in government spending might affect higher- and lower-skilled blacks differently but not affect blacks as a whole compared with whites. That is not the case. Blacks are disproportionately represented in the soldiering part of the military and underrepresented in the hardware production part. They constitute a high fraction of those whose wages are paid with government funds directed to cities and have a proportional representation in the health care and education sectors. This is no accident. Wherever government is a *direct* employer, as in military service, urban services, health care, and education, blacks are proportionately or more than proportionately hired. These are also more labor-intensive and more service-intensive industries than, for example, aerospace and the higher-tech manufacturing associated with military prime contracts. Even so, the defense industry has one of the lowest rates of employing women and minorities, even in the private sector.[14]

Reducing direct government employment

Employment in the public sector was a traditional source of upward mobility for excluded minorities well before the days of "big government" began in World War II. The Irish and Italians used city patronage in the early part of this century to push their own into higher-paying positions at the same time that they were discriminated against in the private sector. Blacks began to use the same route in southern governments during Reconstruction until the process was brought to an abrupt halt by white reaction in the 1870s. But in the 1920s and 1930s, expanding black education in the South again provided an opportunity for blacks to move up by teaching in public schools. In 1940, 25 percent of black male and 75 percent of black female professionals nation-wide were teachers.

The federal response to the civil rights movement increased social spending in the cities and for the poor. This produced a sharp rise in public-sector employment of blacks, especially higher-educated blacks. By 1970, one-half of black male college graduates and more than 60 percent of black college-educated women were public employees, compared with 35 percent of white men and about 50 percent of white women. Most worked for state and local governments. Although 18 percent of the labor force in 1970 were government employees, 26 percent of African-Americans worked for the public sector.

Not only did government provide a disproportionate number of jobs to blacks, it paid them more than did private-sector employers. Government – especially the federal government – discriminated less. Black male full-time federal workers in 1970 got 85 percent of the income of white workers of the same age and education, and black female workers earned more than white female workers.[15] Since direct government employment is mainly a boon to the more highly educated, it was in that group that blacks received the largest benefits from the public-sector expansion in the 1960s and early 1970s. Most of the gains relative to whites that blacks made in the late 1960s and early 1970s were among the higher-educated, and at least part of that was due to increased public employment.[16]

Government employment growth slowed in the 1970s, then slowed sharply in the 1980s as financial pressures mounted on federal, state, and local governments. The slowdown put more downward pressure on higher-educated black incomes than it did on whites' incomes – for the two reasons discussed: a higher fraction of blacks were employed by government than whites, and blacks were paid significantly more in government jobs relative to the private sector than whites were (Table 8.3).

Federal employment reductions received the most publicity, but federal employment has always been a small fraction of the total public work

Table 8.3. *Public-sector employment and salary premium, by gender and race, 1950–88 (percent)*

	1950	1960	1970	1980	1988
Black males					
% employed in public sector	12.4	19.2	22.8	25.1	25.3
Public-sector salary premium	14.1	10.4	9.0	0.0	0.0
White males					
% employed in public sector	11.3	12.6	15.2	15.6	14.0
Public-sector salary premium	-7.4	-10.9	-10.3	-13.0	-11.4
Black females					
% employed in public sector	15.2	19.5	31.6	34.9	29.9
Public-sector salary premium	35.6	23.0	9.6	10.7	6.7
White females					
% employed in public sector	18.9	20.0	21.0	21.8	19.6
Public-sector salary premium	20.0	16.6	11.7	6.9	0.0

Note: Premiums estimated from regression equations of logarithm of income as a function of age, education, region and industry worked in, civil status, time worked per year, full-time workers. Employment figures for census year; income figures for preceding year.
Source: U.S. Census; 1988 Current Population Survey.

force – about 16 percent in the 1980s. The big impact came from cuts in federal programs at the local level and in federal transfers to the states. State and local government employment, which had grown at almost a 5 percent annual rate in the 1960s, slowed to less than 3 percent in the 1970s and slowed even more to 1.3 percent in the 1980s. The federal work force remained constant at about 2.9 million from 1980 to 1991.

But the cut in public employment was not the only change that put downward pressure on (higher-educated) blacks' incomes relative to whites'. Federal government in the 1970s and 1980s paid blacks income premiums that were steadily lower than private-sector incomes. This was not mainly the result of a rise in private-sector incomes for blacks but rather of a relative decline in public-sector pay. The public salary "premium" in Table 8.3 is estimated accounting for differences in age, region, education, and marital status. This premium for black males was 14 percent in 1949, 10 percent in 1959, 9 percent in 1969, and then zero by 1979. But white males continued to receive significantly less for public- than for private-sector work, correcting for education, age, and other variables – 7 percent in 1949, 11 percent in 1959, 10 percent in 1969, 13 percent in 1979, and 11 percent in 1987. The combination of lower salaries paid to whites and higher salaries to blacks made the difference between white and black incomes about 20 percent less in the public sector than in the private sector from 1949 to 1969. This difference declined to about 13 percent in 1979, and 11 percent in 1987, due entirely to lower pay for whites.

Black women's salaries were also closer to white women's salaries in public jobs than they were in private jobs. In this case, the income premium paid by the public sector to black women was 36 percent in 1949, but as discrimination declined in private jobs in the 1960s and 1970s and the equalization role of the public sector disappeared in the 1970s and 1980s, this premium fell to 10 percent in the 1970s and 7 percent in the 1980s. The premium also fell for white women, from 20 percent in 1949 to 7 percent by 1979 and to zero in 1987. Because black women had made some large gains overall relative to white women in the 1960s and 1970s, there was little relative advantage for black women to work in the public sector until the 1980s.

Table 8.4 shows the pattern in the 1970s and 1980s for three main groups employed in public-sector work – those with some college, those with a college degree, and those with graduate training. The income ratios in the public sector compared with the overall ratios in Table 8.4 show that public-sector salaries for blacks were much closer to whites' salaries than were private-sector salaries for blacks. For example, in 1959, 25- to 34-year-old full-time black male college graduates working in the public sector earned 84 percent of white salaries compared with 67 percent of white salaries in the labor market as a whole. The public-sector salary ratio fluctuated, but stayed about 12 percentage points ahead of the overall ratio even in the 1980s. At other levels of

Table 8.4. *Black–white public-sector median income ratios, full-time workers, 25 to 34 years old, by gender and level of education, 1959–89 (percent)*

	1959	1969	1979	1989
Male				
Some college	87	89	76	77
College complete	84	79	94	84
Graduate school	86	—	102	76
Female				
Some college	91	92	93	102
College complete	71	92	99	104
Graduate school	90	75	93	98

Source: U.S. Census; Current Population Survey samples, 1970, 1974, 1980, 1986, 1990.

college education, however, public-sector pay for black males did not stay ahead in the 1980s. For black women, incomes paid in the public sector not only stayed ahead of those in the private sector, but went up in the 1980s compared with those for white women. It became even more advantageous for black women to take public-sector jobs in the 1980s.

Funding to cities

Traditionally, the federal government has played the role of equalizing differences among regions and income groups. Before and during World War II, cities were both the dynamic poles of the industrial economy and the places where most middle-class Americans lived and worked. Although many of the poor lived there too, cities had an ample property tax base. Further, beginning in the 1930s, even though localities were given a great deal of discretion in dealing with the delivery of services, most of the financial responsibility for the poor was taken over by the federal government through safety net programs such as Social Security, unemployment insurance, and Aid to Families with Dependent Children. During and immediately after World War II, cities boomed under this arrangement.

By the 1960s, however, things had changed. The middle class had moved to the suburbs, leaving behind the poor. Worse, middle-class workers still used the city for employment, so cities with lowered tax bases had to provide just as much transportation and other services but did not have the revenue to sustain them. The race riots between 1965 and 1968 brought these contradictions home.

The political reaction was an enormously expanded federal role in trying to rebuild the cities. Federal spending on urban programs increased from 2 percent of all outlays in 1960 to almost 12 percent by the mid-1970s. Since overall federal spending was increasing rapidly during this period, this represented a "gigantic and unprecedented increase in federal transfer payments to cities and their needy residents. There was a vast expansion in programs that were locally run (if often federally administered) for housing, health care, street and highway building and repair, employment and training, and other municipal services."[17] For example, in New York City, federal aid rose from $120 million in 1961 to $2.5 billion by the late 1970s – one-fifth of the total municipal budget.[18]

The effect of this federal infusion on black incomes was direct and positive, largely because of the underlying "neighborhood" policy, which guided the distribution of funds and the local employment in community organization that this generated. The Model Cities Law required the formation of neighborhood advisory boards for the allocation of federal funds. The Community Action programs mandated "maximum feasible participation" at the neighborhood level. The Department of Housing and Urban Development produced nearly a hundred categorical programs designed for economic development and political and social empowerment at the neighborhood level. "The federal government hoped not only to appease minorities' demand for political participation, but also to increase the capacity of local governments as the cornerstones for addressing localized problems."[19] All this created the financial basis for community organizations within cities where none existed before. Community organizations required personnel. These were local, and since many of the cities concerned had large black populations, they were usually black. Many of the young, black, college-educated government employees of the 1970s got their start in urban community-based programs.

The community programs made some inroads against poverty and urban decay and provided community services. They were inefficiently run, transferred little power to poor people in neighborhoods, and helped economic development only minimally, but they did employ community organizers and gave some political focus to neighborhoods. They also supplied a legitimate upward mobility path for smart young blacks that required education and was an alternative to crime. Most important for black incomes, the money went directly into the neighborhoods and employed blacks themselves.

But ultimately, the programs could not be sustained politically. White backlash against the radical black power politics that seemed to be fostered by such neighborhood-based funding already began in the late 1960s and early 1970s.[20] White politicians reacted with anger to the failure of so many of the programs. They were run by inexperienced people, competed with city hall, and made a great deal of political noise but without much to show for it. They were also dominated by vocal minorities whose political capital had run out.[21]

Although spending for social programs in general slowed down under fiscal pressure in the late 1970s, cities continued to get substantial federal aid during the Carter administration. It was not until the Reagan revolution that the ax descended. Many of the cuts in social spending in the 1980s came via shifts in financial responsibility for social programs from the federal government to the states, cities, and nonprofit sector. Urban development grants were cut the most:

> The administration successfully scaled back the Urban Development Action Grant (UDAG) program by two-thirds, from a high of $675 million in 1981 to only $216 million in 1988 – an even more drastic cut when inflation is factored in – and then did away with the UDAG program altogether. Since the peak in the 1970s, federal aid for low- and moderate-income housing has been drastically cut. For example, in 1980, HUD's housing program budget was $55.7 billion; by 1987 this had been reduced to $15.2 billion.[22]

Many cities were already plagued by structural economic woes: as telecommunications technology improved and the locus of economic activity shifted to financial and business services and "clean" manufacturing, many firms moved out of urban centers into the suburbs, further reducing local urban tax bases. Cutting federal resources only made things much worse. It inevitably placed even greater financial stress on states and localities with large minority populations, as the costs of maintaining infrastructure, education, health care, and the justice system increased but the willingness of suburban whites to pay for those investments and services declined. White middle-class incomes were rising but hardly fast enough for them to feel sufficiently generous politically to help pay for the problems of minority communities in the decaying urban centers.

The impact of the cuts on blacks – especially young, low-income urban blacks – was large. As community organizations and a federal financial presence disappeared, anarchy replaced them. The lack of a systematic housing program for low-income individuals increased homelessness. This made other social services, such as schools, health services, and the criminal justice system, much harder and more expensive to manage. As we have already seen, urban minority schools got more funding in the 1980s, but conditions deteriorated more rapidly than the funds increased. The same could be said for hospitals and clinics. The elimination of community organizations and housing programs, as inefficiently as they were run, also made it even more difficult to attract and hold businesses in the ghettos. The cut in public funds had a large negative effect on legitimate business in general. The result was a sharp absolute decline in black incomes in the lowest quintile during the 1980s, even while the top 30 percent of black family incomes were increasing.

IMMIGRATION POLICY AND BLACK OPPORTUNITIES

Government immigration policy also affected lower- and middle-income growth in the 1980s. Immigrants became an important group of new workers and fed into the low-income jobs being created in services and low-end manufacturing. The legal setting for this change came in the 1960s, well before restructuring and as a response to very different political conditions. The 1965 Immigration Act decisively affected legal immigration to the United States by ending national origin as a criterion for preferential admission and replacing it with family reunification and occupational skills. The elimination of national origins criteria shifted immigration from European countries to the Third World.[23] By the early 1980s, Latin American and Asian immigrants began to represent a significant fraction of new entrants to the labor force.

Among the Mexican-origin Latino population alone, there were 10 percent more foreign-born in the 1980 U.S. labor force than in 1970 (36 vs. 26 percent). This translates into a *reported* number of 540,000 more foreign-born Mexicanos in the United States in 1980 than in 1970. Among younger age groups, the figures are more startling: 40 percent of the approximately 700,000 25- to 34-year-old Mexican-origin males in the 1980 census reported that they were foreign-born. This compares with 25 percent foreign-born among about 320,000 Mexican-origin males reported in the 1970 census, suggesting a net immigration in this younger male age group of 200,000 in ten years. If we add the large number of illegals who probably were not counted in the census, immigrants in the 1970s could have doubled the number of Mexican-origin young males in the U.S. labor force over only one decade.[24]

Does this mean that the restructured economy of the 1980s is becoming like the economy at the turn of the century? Yes and no. As large as the numbers associated with post-1965 immigration are, they are less than the massive number of immigrants who arrived here in the late nineteenth century and early part of this century. Immigrants in the 1970s and 1980s resembled the pre–World War I waves in that they settled in a few urban areas, sticking together in their ethnic enclaves. They tended to be employed in industries located in those areas that, on the whole, used relatively unskilled and low-wage labor: auto parts, restaurant services, the garment industry, textiles, construction, electronics, and food processing. This type of employment and the organization of many of these firms are similar to an earlier phase of economic development. But at the other end of the spectrum, a different class of immigrants – uncommon in the earlier wave – is filling professional jobs in engineering, medicine, nursing, and other high-end work. Increasingly they are making possible the expansion of high-end, high-productivity manufacturing and services. They are also reducing the pressure to college-educate the low-income native-born to fill these jobs.

The slow growth of minority male operatives' and laborers' incomes probably reflects downward pressures on wages by immigrant workers moving into those kinds of jobs, although it is difficult to estimate such effects. If new firms or new jobs within existing firms were not created in the absence of such labor, the impact on nonimmigrant workers would be nil.[25] But to the extent that industries substitute or even threaten to substitute immigrant for nonimmigrant workers, wages are held down. Immigration policy may be yielding a large payoff in higher than otherwise growth rates, but certain low-income groups may bear the wage cost of that policy.

Our estimates of income changes in the 1970s for native- and foreign-born Mexican-origin workers suggest that there is a "pulldown" effect of immigration on the native-born.[26] The mean income of foreign-born Mexican males fell sharply relative to that of white males during the decade. Incomes of the native-born also fell, though much less so. A decline in the average age or education of native-born Mexican-origin workers compared with that of whites could explain the fall in their relative incomes, but analysis shows that it does not. Native-born Mexicans, it seems, were pulled into lower-paying jobs along with their immigrant compatriots.

Labor Department claims notwithstanding, the large immigration may also have cost low-skilled blacks jobs. To Jack Miles, who wrote a particularly candid analysis of the 1992 Los Angeles riots, the conflict was as much a black–brown confrontation as a black–white one.[27] The large influx of Mexican immigrants into the LA area has made them the low-end service and manufacturing workers of preference. According to Miles, whites feel more "comfortable" and "safer" hiring Mexicans than blacks, especially black males.

This is a highly subjective analysis and misses the main point: both blacks and Latinos living in the riot-torn areas are desperately poor, both struggling for limited resources. The poverty rate in the hardest-hit area – South Central Los Angeles – was 33 percent in 1989, and almost 45 percent for young people under 18.[28] Miles's analysis also assumes that the effect on black employment is direct (whites prefer Mexican immigrants to blacks applying for the same job) rather than indirect – blacks may not be applying for the very low-wage jobs being accepted by immigrants.[29] Paul Ong, an urban planner at UCLA, agrees that the problem blacks have in getting jobs in Los Angeles is the result not only of a higher level of black segregation but of their unwillingness to take the very low-income jobs replacing the industrial jobs they used to have even ten or fifteen years ago.[30]

Post-1973 immigration policy is naturally divisive among groups at the lower end of the income structure. Immigrants are always resented, even in an immigrant society such as ours. Its divisiveness can be reduced by income policies that stress education and training for higher-wage work both of immigrants and of the native-born most likely to be competing with immigrant labor. This is how Germany is attempting to integrate workers from the former East Germany into the new German economy. The policy is expensive in the short run, but in the longer run it makes possible a high wage expansion of the economy by increasing the supply of skilled labor.

SOME CONCLUDING REMARKS

In a society that believes in individual initiative and the free-market economy, it is difficult to accept that government plays an important role in labor markets. But it does, and when economic conditions changed in the

1970s, government was under both fiscal and political pressure to change its labor market policy. The Reagan *political* victory and how the Reagan administration interpreted that victory made a big material difference mainly for lower-income blacks, but also for the young college-educated, who had in the past been disproportionately employed in public-sector jobs. So whatever happened in the private economy – globalization, the increased demand for high skills, the deindustrialization of the American heartland, the downward pressure on wages – government policies under Carter, and especially Reagan and Bush, exacerbated the negative effects of those changes on low-income Americans.

This did not have to be the case. The governments of other industrial countries implemented policies in this same period in response to the same increases in global competition and technological changes that had different income distributional effects on their populations and were no less successful in stimulating economic growth. It is true that many more jobs were created in the U.S. economy. But many of them were low income, and a high proportion did not go to the workers who already lived in this country in 1975. So the great increase in jobs neither improved the deteriorating social conditions of our cities nor raised the incomes of the poor.

Government macroeconomic policy response to economic change may have had just as important an impact on relative black incomes in this period as the change itself. When all the policies go in one direction, as they did in the 1980s, groups that did well under a different set of policies are bound to get hurt. And they did. Many who supported the changed government role argued that the previous policies were costly, ineffective, and "unnatural." Costly and ineffective they may have appeared until the full cost of the military and banking system subsidies that replaced them came to light. Public programs for minorities and the poor are no more "unnatural" in our modern postindustrial age than any other public–private economic partnership that is meant to have a positive effect on the society as a whole.

9

Politics and black job opportunities: II

Politics has influenced labor market conditions for minorities directly through mandated affirmative action in private labor markets. The single biggest drop (about half of the total) in black wage discrimination occurred between 1959 and 1973, and it came about both from federal legislative action in the early 1960s and from a Supreme Court that gave the legislation broad interpretation. This was the result of direct federal intervention in schools and labor markets. All of the evidence suggests that it had a lasting effect on the market's definition of equity.

What role does law play in wage discrimination in capitalist markets? How do laws change, and what is their subsequent impact on minority wages? The relation between political-legal action and markets is not obvious. More traditional defenders of markets as efficient resource allocators claim that political interference in labor markets – such as affirmative action – has only a negative effect on those it is intended to help.[1] But this ignores the crucial role that the political-legal system had in the treatment of minorities by the market for a hundred years before the 1964 Civil Rights Act. Once that role is accepted, logic argues that in the 1960s and 1970s government might have been able to undo some of the negative effects of the past. How much the political-legal system can undo, given the enormous changes over that century, and how much must be left to individual "choices" by blacks adjusting to new conditions, will be known only when government takes a clear course toward overcoming the past.

DEMOCRACY, MARKETS, AND DISCRIMINATION

Gunnar Myrdal's insights into the condition of blacks in the 1940s showed that racism in a democratic capitalist society is a complex social and psychological phenomenon. Democracy, as it developed in the eighteenth century, was a philosophical ideal based on human dignity and individual rights. According to the U.S. Constitution, race or ethnicity does not alter an individual's rights or access to citizenship (but, of course, slaves, native Americans, and women were originally not accorded political rights). At one level, U.S. constitutional democracy lay the foundation for fighting racism at all levels of society. Myrdal argued that this was more than just a legal base. As an abstraction, it expressed common feelings about justice, equality, and human progress.

Yet democracy is more than an abstraction. In practice, it is the rule of the majority, and a majority can choose to deny a minority its rights. In that situation, common feelings of prejudice and justifications for discrimination and unequal treatment can translate democracy's philosophical ideals into political power plays with disastrous economic and social consequences for less powerful groups. U.S. history is full of such power plays. Some – during the Reconstruction period after the Civil War – worked to decrease discrimination, but most were used by some groups capitalizing on the fears and insecurities expressed in racism to gain economic and political power at minorities' expense. Native Americans' land rights were systematically taken from them. Mexican residents' rights in the Southwest were transformed by the loss of the Mexican War in 1846–8. And once northern politicians and industrialists had reached a compromise in 1876 with the southern oligarchy to return its control of the South's political economy, racism was legitimized *by law* at the highest levels of government.

A good argument can be made that laws segregating whites and minorities were of political, not market, origin. There is a fundamental conflict between racism and the ideal of a capitalist free market. In theory, discrimination cannot exist in a free market, because it would always be profitable for an employer to bid away a discriminated-against worker from a lower-paying firm.[2] But once discrimination is sanctioned by the political system, and if it represents widely held political preferences by the majority, there is a social and political cost of going against the norm. Nonracist employers pay a higher social (and probably economic) price for bidding away minority workers than for going along with the politically established convention. And racist employers profit from minority exploitation because discriminated-against workers are not bid away.[3] Racist economic behavior has to be politically and legally sanctioned (or at least not condemned) by government institutions for discrimination to work in a competitive market. For much of U.S. history, state and federal governments were more than willing to provide such sanctions, ignoring both democratic and market ideals. The *practice* of capitalism and democracy incorporated racism and segregation; private labor markets and public resource allocation, whether they fit market theory or not, internalized discriminatory behavior.

LEGITIMIZED RACISM AS DENATIONALIZATION

Even after black slaves were freed and made full U.S. citizens under the Fourteenth Amendment, their citizenship rights (and those of other minorities of color) remained a source of constant struggle for more than a century. True, much of this struggle was defined by deep-seated racism in the South and by North–South white politics, but it was also sanctioned by prevailing attitudes toward nonwhites outside the South and political and economic expediency in northern power centers.

The legal process of taking citizenship rights away from minorities and legally separating them physically from whites in private and public institutions during this period was analogous to *denationalization*. Denationalization did not create racism or segregation. Racial barriers against non-European immigrants in factories and farms, in local communities, and in labor organizations already existed. But in order to function, they had to be legally sanctioned by the courts and by elected state and national governments. By defining part of the U.S. population as legally different from the majority, government could put it outside the national community and outside the norms of equal protection. Denationalization eliminated the need to confront uncomfortable economic and social issues at a time when the nation was rebuilding itself after the devastation of a long, bloody civil war and when it faced intensive labor conflict.

Between 1890 and 1901, constitutional conventions were held in the southern states to disenfranchise their African-American populations. The results were poll taxes, literacy requirements, and "grandfather clauses" that allowed only those to register whose father or grandfather was eligible to vote in 1867. All were used to keep blacks from voting.

Disenfranchisement led to unequal access to public resources. Local Jim Crow laws separated minorities from whites at public facilities.

Any serious reading of this history of black denationalization makes clear that it would have been impossible to pass such legislation at the state and local levels in the South without northern compliance. The fact that the Supreme Court had upheld infringement of black civil rights in a series of cases between 1873 and the early 1890s gave the signal to southerners that northern liberals wanted no power over the resolution of racial issues. In *Plessy v. Ferguson* (1896), the Court, upholding a Louisiana law requiring separate but equal accommodations for Negroes and whites in railroad cars, argued that separate public facilities could be equal.

The World War I economy drew blacks and Latinos into northern and western cities. Even though the move to urban areas increased minority wages and job opportunities, it did not renationalize minorities politically or territorially. It meant living in ghettos and even more formal segregation than in rural areas.[4] And *legalized* territorial segregation, in turn, had implications for discrimination in the workplace.

The evidence for these implications comes from the South. Jim Crow laws were not adopted there until the turn of the century, then usually after blacks had already been disenfranchised. The laws seem paradoxical in that for more than thirty years between the abolition of slavery and the passing of such laws, the social control of black labor had been left to sharecropping and other forms of peonage. The races appear to have mixed fairly freely in the post-Reconstruction South, even though there were racial antagonism, lynchings, and other forms of brutality against blacks. But Jim Crow laws in the South, as in the North, were legislated primarily in cities. Jim Crow was the result of industrial working conditions and urban living conditions; it was the natural extension of white supremacy in the close conditions of industrial urban life. Formal segregation also helped keep wages low in the factories – with Jim Crow, employers gave white workers status and kept them orderly by subjecting black workers to conditions that stressed white superiority.[5]

THE ECONOMIC IMPACT OF DENATIONALIZATION

Denationalization did not simply limit the participation of minorities in political life or constrain their equal legal protection. It had significant economic effects, both short and long term. In an extreme form, it demonstrated the necessary ties between citizenship rights and economic power in the marketplace.

First, segregation in the South, where almost all blacks lived in the nineteenth century, gradually deskilled blacks who had provided most of the region's antibellum and Reconstruction craft work. Caught between white employers and poorly paid white labor, blacks were effectively blocked for three generations from doing skilled industrial work. Denationalization guaranteed that minorities would remain available as low-paid, unskilled laborers, first in the South and then in the industrial North, and it protected white workers from competition from black skilled labor. In the North and West, denationalized black immigrants from the South and Latinos from Mexico were almost exclusively limited to unskilled jobs until well into the 1940s.

Second, as public resources were systematically withheld from minority schools, minority youth fell educationally farther behind their white counterparts. Even when blacks got schooling, it was of much lower quality than whites'. The combination worked well to keep black and Latinos less schooled and less able to claim equal wages even when they could get jobs that demanded more skills.

Third, denationalization had a profound, long-term impact on these outsiders' definition of themselves. If there was any integration of these groups, it was in the labor market. But there, without political rights and with limited access to formal education, they suffered severe job discrimination and ill treatment. With few exceptions, labor market integration meant low-end, manual work in agriculture and manufacturing. As a result, when minorities worked for whites, they generally received an unavoidable message of powerlessness and incompetence delivered in various forms. They were systematically kept out of skilled jobs and targeted for low-skilled work. Their wages were consistently lower for the same jobs and their jobs were the least secure and the first to be eliminated in recessions.

THE ASIAN EXCEPTION

Some minority groups were able to achieve relative economic success despite prejudice and the government intervention that legalized it. But these groups were exceptional. Japanese immigrants, for example, were able to extricate themselves from dependence on white employment and capital. They did well in the Southwest's agriculture and commerce despite discrimination. They developed islands of economic production that traded goods rather than labor to the surrounding white society. They turned inward, drew on their own community's credit institutions, and tried to be as self-reliant as possible. But even the Japanese, with their cohesive community and agricultural and commercial skills, lost out to white economic interests and the racist legislation supporting them. California's Alien Land Laws passed in 1913 and 1920 made it extremely difficult even for U.S.-born Japanese to buy or lease agricultural land. Restriction on Japanese immigration in 1908 was followed by the Immigration Act of 1924, which banned all further entry to the United States. The final blow came in 1942, when Japanese were rounded up, their property was sold at bargain prices, and they were hustled off to internment camps for the duration of the war.

Japanese success in the face of denationalization is often invoked to argue that discrimination, racism, and government policies are not overriding factors in minorities' poor economic performance. Discrimination, that argument goes, can actually stimulate hardworking immigrants to do better. Rather than accept low-level positions in white-run farms and in their factories, the Japanese were able, even in the context of extreme prejudice, to continue to accumulate wealth and further their children's education.

But there is no reason to believe that other, much less successful minorities did not also try hard to do better and to succeed despite denationalization. And there is no evidence that their lack of success can be attributed to lack of effort. So why did they fail and those Japanese who did not emigrate to Japan do reasonably well? Two factors provide the best explanation: the Japanese population was never allowed to become large enough for the Japanese to provide an essential source of cheap labor; and those who were successful had brought a crucial resource with them from Asia: *entrepreneurial experience.* According to Alejandro Portes, author of *Latin Journey:*

> Immigrants who have been merchants or factory owners in their country of origin are better prepared to find economic opportunities, put available capital to productive use, and even to generate it through pooled savings and rotating credit. This class of immigrants is not content to live off wages. They search for opportunities to establish their own businesses . . . and to apply the know-how brought from their own country.[6]

Being an entrepreneur in a racist environment was not easy, but ethnic capitalism and small numbers of people concentrated in certain cities enabled groups like the Japanese, Chinese, and Jews to develop enclaves of economic activity that were relatively autonomous from the prevailing hostility around them. The most important aspect of this autonomy was the absence of racism in employer–labor relations. Minority enclave capitalists exploited their compatriot workers as much as or more than white employers, but their workers were not relegated to low-level jobs just because they were minorities. On the contrary, because these firms existed in a hostile environment, the racist message was reversed: we minorities have to stick together, work harder, and produce more. And if we are successful, we will all be successful together.[7]

Other groups, without this class of entrepreneurs among them, could work hard but would still fare badly. They were not able to develop separate capitalist enclaves and therefore depended on whites for jobs and farm credit. And because they were important sources of cheap labor in the regions where they lived, keeping their wages low was important economically to white employers. This suggests that legal denationalization produced its most detrimental effects when minorities depended on whites for jobs and credit. If minorities had to come to whites to survive economically, they had little choice but to submit to the negative image white society had developed for them. Whites, in turn, developed this image of minorities as a justification for economic discrimination and unequal political treatment. It may have helped the majority rationalize the legal and political system's radical departures from the ideals of American democratic society.

Because of the nature of their insertion in the economy, minorities such as the blacks and Mexican immigrants who worked on farms and in factories faced the full force of denationalization. Even if they never accepted the script that white society had written for them, they were not able to develop *economic* alternatives that would allow them to get the capital and education needed to write a different script. The only possibility left was to fight for political equality and equal access to public resources as full-fledged Americans. That process of *renationalization* meant changing government policy toward blacks and Latinos as workers and citizens.

REDEFINING CITIZENSHIP

Just as the legal system was crucial in taking away minorities' citizenship rights, blacks and Latinos made their legal redefinition a major political struggle for much of their history in the United States. The strategy had a painful logic: the labor market and the government had relegated them to a denationalized status; regaining citizenship meant demanding constitutional rights that had already been given to white males. On the basis of the inherent ideology of constitutional democracy and the experience of Reconstruction, minorities knew they had at least some chance of winning those rights. Americans are highly conscious of the law and, like citizens of most other democratic, advanced industrialized capitalist societies, believe that their private actions can and should be shaped by the collective will. The degree to which the collective will should be imposed on individuals is a matter of controversy, but controversy to be settled through legally constituted political institutions.

By the 1930s, black organizations had recognized that the ice of discrimination had to be broken from the top, and with the economic upheaval of the Great Depression and Roosevelt's election, some who were sympathetic to the Negro cause came to national political power. The sympathizers were successfully pressured to take on the issue of discrimination in jobs, although the administration's philosophy was that full employment alone would go far to "solve" the Negro problem. Within such constraints, the administration's antidiscrimination moves were limited to those areas where the federal government could intervene with the least likelihood of court challenges – black employment quotas on Department of the Interior public projects and investigations by the newly created Fair Employment Practices Commission (FEPC) of employment discrimination in defense plants. It took the threat of an embarrassing march on Washington by blacks just when Roosevelt was mobilizing American support for a war in Europe to get him to create the FEPC, but it did produce a response – and results. Minority employment in defense plants rose significantly during the war. More important, the ice was broken. Not only did minorities make economic gains, they had tasted victory and a modicum of political power. The Roosevelt administration had sanctioned blank entrance into the American working class. With such sanction, the renationalization process began.

After the war, the arena of minority pressure shifted from jobs to political rights. President Truman disbanded the FEPC but integrated the armed forces. The Democratic Party risked losing the presidential election by adopting a civil rights plank at its 1948 convention. Dixiecrats walked out, but Truman won anyway. The signal was clear: racial integration was not politically disastrous for those who espoused it. Other messages were coming to the United States from abroad. Segregation was internationally embarrassing. How could this country fight a war against Hitler's racism and lead the "free" world against Communism but condone racism at home?

This was the setting for the landmark Supreme Court decision *Brown v. Board of Education of Topeka, Kansas.* The majority opinion, led by the new chief justice, Earl Warren, argued that *Plessy v. Ferguson*'s separate and equal was unconstitutional. For the South and the Eisenhower administration, "conservative" Warren's leadership on this issue was a shock, but it should not have been. California's courts had already struck down school desegregation in 1946 in a Latino-instigated case during Warren's governorship. The Warren court also understood that, with its leadership of the Western democracies in the Cold War, the United States needed the *Brown* decision. It affirmed a new political reality: a nation that stood for democratic ideals worldwide could no longer afford to allow the contradiction of its own denationalization policies. Georgetown law professor Girardeau Spann appears to be on target when he suggests that *Brown* was largely a response to *white* needs in a new era.[8]

But *Brown* must also be judged as a great victory for minorities in their long struggle for renationalization. The Court may have been responding to broader American needs for a better international image. Yet it necessarily legitimated minority civil rights activism to regain citizenship status denied since the late nineteenth century. It officially admitted that the United States had different classes of citizens and argued that this differentiation was no longer acceptable. Whether stimulated by foreign criticism or not, or whether it was decades late or not, *Brown* meant that the *politics* of inclusion was forever changed. The Warren court had sanctioned minority demands that they be treated legally the same as whites. From that point on, minorities were able to confront the economic and social reality of society through political action, as renationalized citizens, with a totally different level of political legitimacy than they had at any time since Reconstruction.[9]

True, *Brown* did not directly change minorities' economic positions. Integrated and equal did not in itself mean economic equality or even better access to skilled jobs. This should not be surprising. Political rights in a democratic capital society are a necessary but not sufficient condition for economic power. And in this case the Court was concerned only with political rights and their implications for access to public resources and to "publicly accessible" private establishments. The Court was not concerned with *initiating* changes in labor market rules in favor of greater equality, nor should it ever be expected to. Yet *Brown* solidified blacks' claim to U.S. citizenship and full membership in the working class. Equal schooling symbolized the right to social mobility in the same way it had been granted to European immigrants a half-century before.

It took fifteen years for the courts and Congress to force states and localities to comply with the *Brown* decision. It also took massive civil rights marches, armed troops, and a series of presidential interventions. As in any war over territory, those who had it did not want to give it up, especially when their ownership had been legally sanctioned for more than three generations. But relinquish it they did. The courts and eventually Congress acted to expand minority political inclusion. In 1955, the Supreme Court urged the states to comply with *Brown* "with all deliberate speed." In 1957, Congress passed the first of several Civil Rights Acts. It created the Commission on Civil Rights to study the barriers to minority voter registration. A civil rights division was added to the Justice Department. In 1960, Congress passed a bill appointing registration and voting referees to monitor election procedures. In 1964, the Twenty-Fourth Amendment to the Constitution banned poll taxes, and in 1965, Congress enacted the Voting Rights Act. Three years later, in *Green v. Newkin County,* the Supreme Court told the states that they had had fourteen years to integrate facilities (schools were the major unresolved issue), and now they had to show progress "at once."

In those same fifteen years, minorities mobilized as they never had before. They forced their way through the legal opening that *Brown* had provided. In the South, blacks assaulted the institutions created under the protection of *Plessy v. Ferguson.* The international embarrassment that the Warren court had tried to avoid was intensified by southern resistance, police dogs reminiscent of Nazi concentration camps attacking demonstrators, and the sight of black schoolchildren flanked by lines of rifle-bearing National Guard troops. The more the embarrassment, the more the civil rights movement flourished and the more rapid was the political and legal action to renationalize minorities.

The struggle for political rights had wider implications. *Brown* and the civil rights movement led to a resurrection of executive and congressional action on affirmative action in the labor market. President Truman had not renewed the FEPC after the war, and it was not until the end of the Eisenhower era that a commission headed by Vice-President Nixon, examining job discrimination, reported that such discrimination was still entrenched in the U.S. labor market. One of the earliest actions of the Kennedy administration was to reinstitute affirmative action on federal contracts (1961). In the Civil Rights Act, initiated by Kennedy, completed under Johnson, and passed by Congress in 1964, discrimination in the workplace was outlawed. The act also created the Equal Employment Opportunity Commission (EEOC) with the power to hear complaints and enforce the antidiscrimination provisions of the act. A year later, an executive order strengthened antidiscrimination provisions in federal contracts. Later, the Nixon administration, with Labor Secretary George Shultz taking the lead, continued to move on job discrimination by going after racial barriers in labor unions. Shultz's Philadelphia Plan, initiated in 1969 and finally winning in the courts, forced labor unions to meet the same conditions as employers in eliminating discrimination. And in 1972, another executive order again strengthened antidiscrimination provisions in federal contracts and added quotas and timetables for business to meet those provisions.

This pattern of court decisions and legislation after the initial executive-level ice breaking in the 1940s suggests important differences between actions on renationalization – those reinstating *citizenship rights* – and actions on employment discrimination. The Supreme Court took the "lead" on citizenship in response to a changing international and domestic climate, and Congress followed. But it was the executive and the executive-led Congress that moved on changing labor market practices. The courts only reacted to such legislation, interpreting it in accord with varying notions of what markets are allowed to do in democratic societies based on citizenship rights.[10]

Those who claim that the courts are inherently conservative in interpreting equal opportunity and equal treatment in labor markets are correct. The courts are particularly conservative in interpreting legislation that redresses past wrongs. Workers' legal rights in labor markets confront the very essence of market relations based on contracts freely entered into by what the Constitution (and the social contract underlying it) assumes are equal and free-willed individuals. The link between citizenship rights in a democratic society and worker rights in capitalist markets does not flow naturally from courts' interpretation of laws that established citizenship rights alone. If anything, the Constitution protects markets from government interference. Action on workers' rights is therefore a *political* matter that requires new laws redefining the relationship between capital and labor and bringing minority workers – as workers, not citizens – into a new relationship with employers and majority white labor. It is such legislation that is subject to court interpretation and such interpretations that can be overridden by further legislation.

Given this political-legal reality of democratic capitalist societies, initial action on employment and wages has had to come through the executive and the Congress. The best that can happen in the courts is that they interpret such government interference in markets as an extension of citizenship rights. If the courts are sympathetic, less political action is required to produce desired legislation. Unsympathetic courts require more political action. Yet judicial antipathy also has a positive side. Decisions unfavorable to minorities can work to mobilize them politically to advance their rights. And in the present context, political rights having been won, the focus of mobilization would be directed at extending citizen rights into economic markets.

THE ECONOMIC GAINS OF AFFIRMATIVE ACTION

Blacks made large relative income gains in the 1960s. These were not as large as in the 1940s, but they were just as impressive, since they started from much higher levels. And more than in the 1940s, the powerful events of the decade, including the civil rights struggle, Title VII, and federal intervention in labor markets, focused attention on discrimination against minorities.

Were these gains mainly the result of a government-induced change in labor market demand for minority labor? Did enforced affirmative action in the late 1960s and 1970s have a major effect on blacks' and Latinos' relative wages?

In an early study about this period, Richard Freeman tested for several possible influences on black incomes as a whole and on the incomes of black college graduates, all from 1964 to 1973.[11] According to his data, median incomes of nonwhite males in the labor force were 57 percent of white males' in 1963; by 1969, they had risen to 66 percent, and by 1973, to 68 percent. He claimed that the big gains for both black men and women began in 1966, the year the initial impact of the 1964 Civil Rights Act could be measured, and that federal intervention was the single most important explanation for income equalization during this period. Even controlling for growth in gross national product or for black education, the EEOC had a persistent, significant effect on income for all blacks, including those with a college education.

But not everyone agrees that federal intervention in labor markets was responsible for increased minority incomes in the 1960s. Economists James Smith and Finis Welch argue that secular changes – especially improved black education (because of desegregation) and migration from South to North and from rural to urban areas – are far more important than government antidiscrimination policy in explaining changes in blacks' relative income. According to them, "The racial gap narrowed as rapidly, at least for experienced workers, in the twenty years before 1960 (and before affirmative action) as the 20 years afterward. This suggests that the *slowly evolving historical forces* . . . – education and migration – were the primary determinants of the long-term economic improvement. At best, affirmative action has marginally altered black wage gains around this long-term trend" (italics added).[12]

A key argument for Smith and Welch against the affirmative action case is that this increase in payoff was the result of improved black schooling. Some of their own results contradict their claims: they document larger income gains in the 1960s and 1970s than in the preceding decade for some black workers who had completed their education much earlier in the 1940s and 1950s, and larger gains, in some cases, than for blacks who had completed their education later.[13] Many of the black male gains in the 1940s that Smith and Welch attribute to education were the result of a more equal income distribution that disproportionately helped blacks. Yet David Card and Alan Krueger's research on improved black schooling in the South does at least partially support Smith and Welch's claim, even though it still means that government intervention (in education rather than labor markets), not individual effort, was responsible for blacks' economic gains. Improvements in school quality appear to explain about one-fourth of the gains in relative income made by black men between 1960 and 1980.

Even so, why didn't improvements in black schooling show up in higher relative black incomes in the 1950s, and why didn't later desegregation in the 1960s and 1970s result in significant changes in black incomes in the 1980s? Few southern blacks with improved desegregated schooling would have reached the labor market before the late 1970s, when the relative income increases were petering out.[14]

Smith and Welch do admit that affirmative action had something to do with the increase in black incomes. But they attribute this to a "wage bubble" that they claim resulted from the need to hire an unusual number of minority workers – mostly college-educated – in the late 1960s to comply with EEOC requirements. They also claim that the bubble burst in the five years after 1971–2. But in this case as well, their data are not consistent: they show that it burst only for entry-level wages for college graduates and that more experienced workers had steady or rising relative incomes until 1979.

A number of new studies now support Freeman's position that the Civil Rights Act and subsequent enforcement of affirmative action had a major impact on blacks' relative wages. One, by economists Richard Butler, James Heckman, and Brook Payner of the South Carolina textile industry, concludes that the EEOC was a major factor in increasing the demand even for less-educated black workers in the 1960s. Another, by Heckman and law professor John Donohue, suggests that most of the relative income gains made by blacks during this period took place in the South and that it was precisely the South that was the early target of Title VII legislation.[15] The Card and Krueger research shows that even with the effect of better black schooling, most of the gains in 1960–80 were due to the impact of legislation. Sociologists Thomas DiPrete and David Grusky argue that gains in occupational attainment for minorities in the 1970s and 1980s were largely the result of "direct political interventions by federal agencies."[16] Put together, these studies establish the case for Title VII's having had an important effect on the U.S. labor market, especially in the South, where discrimination was greatest. In the words of *A Common Destiny,* "Major legal changes have occurred in seniority rules, hiring and promotion practices, and even in what constitutes labor market discrimination and have had wide-reaching effects on blacks' relative position in the labor market."[17]

Our simulation analysis adds one more voice to the chorus. It suggests than about 35 to 65 percent of the gain in the relative income of black males in 1959–73 and 50 percent of the gain for full-time Latino males in 1959–69 can be attributed to a direct reduction in pay discrimination.[18] For full-time black male workers (the group specifically analyzed by Smith and Welch), the percentage of the explainable gain due to a decline in wage discrimination (65 percent) is the highest among all the groups analyzed. For minority women as well, a high fraction of their gain relative to white men is explained by a decline in wage discrimination, especially for black women and especially in the 1970s.[19]

The sum of this empirical work suggests that political-legal intervention not only takes away, it can give back. And it can do so not only by equalizing different groups' education and training but by direct government intervention in labor markets sanctioned by the courts.

THE COST OF AFFIRMATIVE ACTION IN LABOR MARKETS

If affirmative action in labor markets works to equalize incomes, does it have a cost to the economy? Does it correct outright discrimination – to make sure that a black with qualifications equal to those of a white gets the same shot at a higher-paying job – or does it correct historical discrimination – to make sure that employers hire more blacks for jobs from which they have been historically excluded even though they are presently less qualified than whites? Under the first assumption, there would be a net gain to the economy, since formerly excluded workers capable of higher productivity would now be able to produce up to their capacity. Average productivity would rise and so would black incomes. Under the second assumption, blacks' incomes would rise but their productivity would not, and there would be a cost to the economy of paying blacks more than they were capable of producing.

The debate on this point is highly political and revolves around the meaning of "qualified." Individual-responsibility advocates argue that blacks who take an achievement test when applying for a job score much lower than their white counterparts. Yet because of affirmative action, blacks' test scores are ranked on a separate scale that gives them a sizable, positive "correction" relative to whites. There is no question that allegations about lower black test scores are true. About 2 percent of employers use achievement tests developed by the Labor Department for screening prospective employees, and in that sample blacks score much lower than whites applying for the same job. Under the affirmative action "correction" to such test scores, blacks get hired even when they test considerably worse than whites. The average hired black worker tests more than one-half standard deviation lower than his or her white counterpart.

But what does the test score difference mean in terms of job performance? This is the source of the controversy. Individual-responsibility proponents claim that the score difference reflects lower productivity. A number of studies purport to show that the achievement score differences for blacks hired under affirmative action represent anywhere from 2 to 10 percent less productivity on the job for each standard deviation of test score difference.

Yet such studies are highly problematic. First, none measures actual productivity; instead, they use supervisor ratings. Are supervisor ratings a good measure of productivity? They probably represent *some* measure of productivity, but they also probably have a large error component in the measurement of actual productivity. There is no way of knowing what that error is, because no study has matched supervisor rating with actual productivity. If ratings of black productivity compared with white were biased even a few percentage points, the alleged differences in productivity linked to lower black test scores in these studies would be wiped out.

Second, even assuming that supervisor ratings are accurate measures of productivity differences, it takes huge differences in employment test scores to produce small differences in supervisor ratings. This suggests that the tests are not a very reliable measure of supervisor ratings. In an earlier chapter, I showed that very large black gains relative to white gains in academic achievement test scores over the past fifteen years have shown up, at best, in slightly higher relative incomes for young blacks entering the labor force. This is analogous to the large differences on employment test scores reflecting only small differences in supervisor ratings: achievement test scores for those *with a given amount of schooling and training* may not tell us much about either income or productivity. The payoff to individuals of scoring high on achievement tests is mainly that it gets them farther in school, which then translates into access to better jobs and higher income.

When all is said and done, those who argue that affirmative action has led to lower average productivity in the U.S. economy have not made their case. Employment test scores are just not a very convincing measure of productivity, even though those who make the argument using test score data are totally convinced that lower black achievement scores must be reflected in lower job performance.[20]

AFFIRMATIVE ACTION UNDER ASSAULT: THE REAGAN YEARS

The Reagan administration came to power on the coattails of white reaction to "liberal" movements, so it was no surprise that civil rights enforcement agencies within the executive branch were rapidly transformed. The most telling changes came in the Civil Rights Commission, whose role as investigator of voting irregularities and other infringements on "citizenship" was altered by a new philosophy that minorities of color suffered no different citizenship problems than anyone else; in the Justice Department, with the naming of William Bradford Reynolds, whose views were openly hostile to the civil rights movement, to head the Civil Rights Division; and in the EEOC, whose mandate changed from aggressive enforcement of affirmative action to following the lead of Reynolds's division.

These changes were made in response to white backlash, mainly against affirmative action in labor markets. The Reagan victory suggested that civil rights had lost its moral appeal – that it had gone too far in the eyes of the "silent (white) majority." And the New Coalition did not count on minority votes, aside from the anti-Castro Cuban population in Florida. The South was now solidly in the Republican column, and Reagan brought back many of the blue-collar whites in northern cities who were disillusioned with inflation, falling real wages, Iran, and affirmative action. The Supreme Court had also given an indication that political times had changed. The *Bakke* decision, arguing that medical schools were reverse-discriminating against whites by choosing minority students with lower academic rankings, did not attack affirmative action across the board, but it did draw clear limits. When there were indicators available to measure merit, selection had to conform to those indicators.

The naming of William Bradford Reynolds and the assault on affirmative action was consistent with two facets of Reagan politics: overtly, appealing to Americans' deep-seated belief in the free market and, covertly, playing to heightened white resentment of minorities' economic gains in the difficult 1970s. There was no attempt in the 1980s to turn the clock back on citizenship rights, where the courts had been able to solidify minority gains – if anything, the decade saw the election of hundreds of new black and Latino legislators at the municipal and state levels. Jesse Jackson became the first black presidential candidate to win Democratic primaries. The Reagan target was the labor market, and this is where the new politics was designed to have its most serious impact.

The administration's strategy hinged on restoring a clear separation of political and economic rights. These had been intentionally blurred by Title VII of the 1964 Civil Rights Act, subsequent congressional amendments, and liberal interpretations of Title VII by the Supreme Court. In those interpretations, the statute had been consistently viewed as "remedial," which meant legally that it was targeted to meet a specific problem, but, as interpreted, meant the extension of constitutional rights into the worker–worker and worker–employer relationship:

> It is important to bear in mind that Title VII is a remedial statute designed to eradicate certain invidious employment practices. The evils against which it is

aimed are defined broadly: "to fail . . . to hire or to discharge . . . or *otherwise to discriminate* . . . with respect to . . . compensation, terms, conditions, or privileges of employment," and "to limit, segregate, or classify . . . *in any way* which would deprive *or tend to deprive* any individual of employment opportunities *or otherwise adversely affect his status.*"[21]

In *Griggs v. Duke Power Co.* (1971), the Court established that this included using testing or screening that was not specifically task-related and that had the effect of continuing to exclude previously excluded groups (the "disparate impact theory"). In *McDonnell Douglas Corp. v. Green* (1973), the Court went further to argue that prima facie evidence of discrimination was all that was necessary to prove employer intent. The Court also upheld the possibility of using quotas and goals to remedy discrimination, even after the *Bakke* case. In *United Steelworkers of America v. Weber* (1979), the Court allowed for numerical remedies "when the employer itself undertakes voluntary remediation of discriminatory patterns."[22]

The Reagan Justice Department went after this broad interpretation of Title VII in a series of cases. It challenged numerical remedies (following on the negative *Bakke* decision), who could benefit from numerical relief (only the victims themselves or nonvictims as well), and the constitutionality of race-conscious relief under the equal protection guarantees of the Fourteenth and Fifth Amendments (e.g., in *United States v. Paradise* [1987]). But except for cases involving layoffs, mainly because these depended on challenging the seniority system, the Court until 1988 generally upheld the earlier, broader interpretation. "Contrary to expectations," Eleanor Holmes Norton writes, "the Burger Court will be remembered as the judicial architect of a strong and broad interpretation of the employment discrimination statutes."[23]

With new Reagan appointments, all this changed. The Rehnquist court (including the addition of Justice Scalia) made a series of decisions in 1988 that legally revised affirmative action. In *Richmond v. Croson,* Thurgood Marshall writes, the Court made it "extraordinarily hard for any state or city to fashion a race-conscious remedial program that will survive [the Court's] constitutional scrutiny. Indeed, the Court went so far as to express its doubts that the effects of past racial discrimination are still felt in the city of Richmond, and in society as a whole."[24] In *Ward's Cove v. Antonio,* the Court implicitly overruled the *Griggs* decision. Now, rather than employers defending such practices, it will be employees who have to prove that the tests and other screens used in hiring are unjustified and discriminatory. In the last year of the Reagan presidency, the new civil rights strategy had finally broken through the Supreme Court.

But long before the Court came around to the Reagan view, executive agencies, led by the Justice Department, had already succeeded in sidetracking Title VII enforcement after sixteen years of executive, bipartisan congressional, Supreme Court, and, eventually, business support.[25] The lead role of coordinating equal employment opportunity agencies in the federal government, conferred on an aggressively effective EEOC in the civil rights reorganization of 1978, was shifted during the Reagan administration to Reynolds's division at the Justice Department. When the EEOC and Justice clashed on jurisdictional issues in the early 1980s, the White House overruled the EEOC in favor of Justice. This was more than an in-house power struggle. Even under Reagan, the EEOC wanted to defend the use of race-conscious numerical remedies for past discrimination, but Justice insisted that such remedies could apply only to actual victims – that is, quotas as such were illegal because they covered a whole class of people, not just the person or people bringing the discrimination suit. The victim-only position continued to be refuted by the Court until 1989, when the Court took an even more stringent antiremedy view in *Paterson v. McLean Credit Union*. But the effect of giving responsibility for affirmative action to a hard-line anti–civil rights assistant attorney general such as Reynolds changed the signals going to private business and local and state public agencies about their hiring practices. A Reagan appointee to the chair of the EEOC, Clarence Thomas – later named to the Supreme Court – covertly eliminated goals and timetables at the beginning of the second Reagan term, then reinstated them in 1986 under pressure from Congress during his reconfirmation hearings.[26] Even so, under Thomas's chairmanship and pressure from Justice, the EEOC continued to send out contradictory signals on enforcing affirmative action. There were constant threats to make fundamental changes in the very bases of enforcement – disparate impact and statistical proof – focusing instead on victim-specific remedies and the elimination of quotas and proportional representation. The commission also began insisting on full relief for each victim instead of negotiated settlements. As a result, there was a precipitous drop in the number of complainants getting relief. The backlog of cases also rose rapidly. And the other agency in charge of enforcing compliance, the Office of Federal Contract Compliance Programs, was allowed to operate in a way that contradicted its own regulations and thus became totally ineffectual.[27]

The end product of such foot dragging and rule changing was a reduction in the pressure on private employers and federal contractors to enforce affirmative action. Although employers may have preferred goals and timetables, it was unclear throughout the 1980s and especially after 1984 whether these would continue, even when upheld by the Supreme Court. When the Court itself turned on affirmative action in its 1988–9 session, it only confirmed the wider political changes emanating from the executive branch – changes reinforced by Bush's nomination of Justice Souter to the Court. By 1988, Congress was the only branch of the federal government still committed to ending discrimination in labor markets, and congressional liberals reasserted themselves in 1991 by passing a new Civil Rights Act, which reversed some the restrictive decisions of 1988–9. Nevertheless, without enforcement at the executive level, the Civil Rights Act of 1991 remained only a legal document with no teeth. A more zealous enforcement strategy after the 1992 election would be required to see whether the new law and a new administration could make a difference.

DID WAGE DISCRIMINATION INCREASE UNDER THE REAGAN ASSAULT?

Changing the signals on civil rights in the 1980s slowed the decline in wage discrimination for minority men, and for black women relative to white, but not for minority and white women compared with men. What does this say about the role of legislation and the Supreme Court during this period?

First, it is remarkable how long into the Reagan decade it took to halt the civil rights momentum developed in the 1960s and 1970s. By continuing to interpret Title VII broadly, the Burger court was apparently able to maintain the general signal that affirmative action was still on. Wage discrimination continued to decline, especially for black men and white women employed full time. Employers had developed habits around the quota system, preferring stability in hiring rules. Until the signals from the EEOC changed definitively in the mid-1980s, these habits also maintained the downward trend in wage discrimination.[28]

Second, the changes in the composition of the Court and the ultimate understanding that the new EEOC message was "permanent" did appear to contribute to an ultimate increase in wage discrimination against blacks at the end of the decade even as the economy continued to expand. President Bush's veto of the 1990 Civil Rights Act on the grounds of opposing its "racial quotas" also suggests that many employers came to favor doing away with quotas. Our estimates of wage discrimination for the end of the 1980s are hardly definitive, but they do indicate that the slower decline and ultimate increase in discrimination has a "dragging" effect on the wages of black men and women after 1985.

Third, the rapid rise in women's incomes and wages – especially white women's wages – relative to men's in the 1980s suggests that employers began to include women regularly in a host of jobs that they had not held before and were paying them higher wages despite declining enforcement of Title VII. Both changes meant that employers were acting in a less discriminatory fashion toward women, although wage and income differences between men and women remained very large, larger than those between white and minority men. In part, the shift has to be ascribed to the increasing political power of women in the 1980s and its indirect effect on the behavior of male employers. Market incentive to hire women provided by women's low wages and relatively high education in an increasingly information-oriented, business service economy interacted with women's newfound political clout to improve their labor market condition. Blacks had increasingly less marketable human capital characteristics and increasingly less political clout to stem the overriding of legal sanctions against discrimination.

In this zero-sum legal battleground of the Reagan–Bush era, it was logical that the women's political movement and the black political movement met at a turbulent and highly charged political-legal crossroads: the Clarence Thomas hearings. The Bush administration successfully confused the black movement in nominating for Thurgood Marshall's Supreme Court seat a conservative black who had served the Reagan–Bush political agenda faithfully. Thomas stood for black acceptance of the marketplace as neutral arbiter of African-Americans' success and failure in the economy – a virtual guarantee for freezing black progress. But because Thomas was black, he necessarily stood for black achievement regardless of his politics. This was intended to confuse blacks politically and allowed conservative white Senators, whether Democrats or Republicans, to vote for his confirmation without offending the black vote.

Anita Hill's testimony in this context successfully turned the confusing race issue surrounding Thomas into a much clearer gender issue. The specter of an all-male Judiciary Committee grilling a (black) woman about her sexual behavior incensed most women, whether black or white. Much to the surprise of the male senators involved, it produced an outpouring of female candidates for the Senate and Congress in the 1992 elections. It ironically also identified the Bush administration as "anti-women" much more than as antiblack, even while women's wages continued to increase relative to men's, including black men's, and white women continued to do better than black women throughout the Bush years.[29]

In terms of the composition of the Court, both blacks and women lost out in the Thomas hearings, but women at least came out of the loss with a clear political agenda and an enhanced movement. Blacks, in contrast, were left in even greater disarray.[30]

IS THE LAW IMPORTANT IN REDUCING DISCRIMINATION?

The Thomas hearings and the trial of four Los Angeles police officers accused of willfully beating Rodney King showed that, despite political retrenchment, the Supreme Court and the court system as a whole are important objects of political change for greater minority rights. For one thing, the Court remains one of two institutions (Congress being the second) charged with protecting constitutionally guaranteed rights and liberties. Thurgood Marshall argued that "those seeking to vindicate civil rights or equality rights must continue to press this Court for the enforcement of constitutional and statutory mandates."[31] He suggested that many in the civil rights movement came to think that the Court would automatically continue to support the rights won in the 1960s and 1970s – that these rights had been so repeatedly tested that they were part of the national political culture. But nothing is automatic when it comes to politics.

In the present situation, enforcement will require two simultaneous strategies: fighting for the "right" appointments when openings appear on the Court and turning to legislative bodies to force the Court's hand and to overturn Court rulings. The Court is inherently conservative on rulings that extend citizens' rights into labor markets. With the current composition of the Court, that conservatism seeks to move civil rights in economic life backward. The up side of the situation is that the Court's negative actions could mobilize minorities and enough whites politically, shifting action on labor market rights to Congress and the state legislatures, where it properly belongs. With mobilization, the push would be to move forward, and the Court would have to contend with the political ramifications of a hostile Congress. "By prevailing upon Congress . . . we can send a message to the Court – that the hyper-technical language games played by the Court last term . . . are simply not accurate ways to read Congress's broad intent in the civil rights area."[32]

A similar argument can be made for an executive branch that uses its Justice Department to enhance equalized protection under the law and strives to assure all communities that their rights are being protected by law enforcement agencies. The legal system is an expression of political values and norms, better known as ideology. Since the government's legal, educational, and economic apparatuses are linked so intimately to this ideology, political regimes must play a vital role in defining how the apparatuses separate blacks and other groups from, or incorporate them into, the mainstream. Ideology in the United States may reside in historical processes, but it is captured within and shaped by the presidency and the executive branch. African-Americans know this better than anyone. Their economic progress has been greatly influenced by what can only be called the "White House factor." It is to this aspect of politics that we now turn.

10

Black economic gains and ideology: the White House factor

Racial attitudes are individual, but their translation into economic outcomes is political. Politics – especially national politics – uses individual attitudes to construct broad economic and social policies. Whites may not like blacks (and vice versa) for various reasons; yet government sets the legal rules and the example by which the citizens of a nation – mainly those who do not think they have much in common – relate to one another. It also helps define the economic and social conditions in which diverse groups live. This political essence of race relations and racial economic inequality makes national government ideology crucial to the direction taken on race by institutions at all levels of society.

"Ideology" means the body of ideas reflecting the needs and aspirations of a society. Developing ideology is precisely what government must do and does: it organizes a vision, or "project," that reflects how a society wants to think about itself and how it can translate that self-image into concrete change. It is no accident that the main task of a presidential campaign is to develop a coherent, believable project with which voters can identify. Presidents and their parties have to stand for something clear and attractive. This national project sets the political tone for and usually guides the practice of presidential administrations.

From the 1930s until 1991 – the period we have been looking at in this book – two ideological frameworks for national projects have competed with each other: in one, government's role is to allow the marketplace to operate as freely as possible; in the other, government is needed to "correct" the market's most obvious social shortcomings. The race problem has had other, special political dimensions – whites' complex, deep-seated antagonisms and sense of superiority to blacks – but these have been heavily influenced by the ideological stance government has taken on economic strategy. If the market were just for all groups, regardless of race, it would be difficult to argue for government intervention to correct racial inequality. If the market were capable of social inequities, government would have good reason to step in with policies to change both the sources and practice of inequality.

Because of the unique social and political role that race has played in U.S. history, government ideology has been related to the politics of race itself. Historically, when an elected government advocated a philosophy that favored intervention in markets to soften unacceptably harsh outcomes, it was likely to intervene. But interventions that helped the working class as a whole did not necessarily reduce racial inequality. It took political action by blacks themselves to persuade those presidents who were philosophically interventionist to make ideological leadership on race part of their political strategies. And once presidents like Harry Truman and John Kennedy took the lead on race, they had an impact not only on racial inequality, but on the terms of the larger political debate. The Democratic and Republican parties changed after World War II, mainly because of race. Since economic interventionist presidents were more likely to act on inequality, the competing political strategies of the two parties inevitably (and correctly) linked the race issue to economic ideology.

Whatever the economic structural changes facing the nation – rapid industrialization, then globalization and deindustrialization – government action in education, macroeconomic policy, income policy, and job equalization go far in explaining what happens to blacks compared with whites during periods of change. Why did blacks make such large gains in the 1940s, 1960s, and early 1970s, and stop gaining in the 1950s and 1980s? Although they are all important, access to manufacturing jobs, better education, more equal income distribution, and less wage discrimination are not the only explanations. Blacks got work in higher-paying industries because *government* acted to equalize their access to those higher-paying jobs, in either the private or the public sector. *Government* provided education more equal to that of whites, so blacks were able to perform higher-skilled jobs and use that education. *Government* promoted more equal income distribution through incomes policies. *Government* passed laws and implemented them to reduce wage discrimination based on race. When all these processes came together, blacks did extraordinarily well; when the processes slowed, so did minorities' economic progress.

In this chapter, I claim that national leadership based on an ideological vision and the willingness to act on it brought education, jobs, and antidiscrimination enforcement together to make the 1940s and 1960s especially favorable for minorities and impeded those same factors in the 1950s and 1980s so as to make those decades especially unfavorable for minorities. The historical evidence suggests that in each of these time periods national leadership helped create a particular political climate for education, job creation, higher wages, and civil rights – what I call the "White House factor." I say "suggests" because it is difficult to prove empirically that politics makes a difference when other important changes occurring simultaneously go far in explaining why minorities did better relative to whites in the 1940s and 1960s and worse in the 1980s. Yet politics, and particularly national politics, seems to have been the catalyst for these changes.

At the same time, there is little doubt that difficulties in the local or the national economy influence the willingness of the white middle class to allocate public funds for policies that will bring blacks and other low-income minorities greater equality in this or the next generation. In a democracy, political figures are subject to constraints on where they can or cannot lead in the race issue. But in large part these constraints become important politically when an opposing political party is willing to exploit racial antagonisms and the public finance issues related to them for its own purposes. Indeed, this symbiosis between growing reaction to government poverty programs by key sectors of the northern white working class in the 1970s is crucial for understanding why racial politics took the turn it did in the 1980s. Yet it was only in the framework of a Republican Party leadership willing to use race to push a broader economic ideology favoring the wealthy and large corporations that working-class white backlash had any political meaning.

The idea of an underlying catalyst – ideological, political, and related to national leadership – is suggested by two different ways of looking at the four decades: (1) the impact of simultaneous economic and educational growth on minorities' relative income in the 1950s and 1980s was not similar to that in the other periods; and (2) national governments and their policies in the 1940s and 1960s were, in their practice, much more concerned with economic equity than were governments in the 1950s and 1980s.

WHY THE ECONOMIC AND EDUCATIONAL ARGUMENTS ARE NOT ENOUGH

Labor markets were "tight" in both the 1940s and 1960s, and minorities did much better as a result. When workers seeking employment find it easy to get jobs and employers find it difficult to fill them, black and Latino workers with poor education and training are pulled up into better-paying, higher-skilled work. They move from agricultural work into industry. They are less likely to be unemployed or employed part time. With fewer unemployed workers, wages in lower-skilled, lower-paid work go up more rapidly than wages in highly skilled jobs, since it is in these low-end jobs where replacing workers from the ranks of the unemployed becomes more difficult. All this favored minority workers relative to white workers in the 1940s and 1960s. It spurred large gains in minorities' relative income.

A full-employment economy is key to explaining such gains in the two periods. But the 1920s, 1950s, and much of the 1980s were also marked by relatively moderate unemployment and rising wages. From the best information we have, it appears that blacks did not make significant relative gains in the 1920s. Census data show that their gains were also negligible in the 1950s, although their economic situation improved in absolute terms almost as much as whites'. Just keeping up in the 1920s and 1950s was not enough to bring the vast majority of blacks into the mainstream of the consumer economy. Nor did blacks do relatively better in the 1980s despite the long growth period from 1983 to 1990.

In addition, both the 1940s and especially the 1960s were preceded by and were themselves marked by increases in minority education. Education in the South had been improving in quality, especially in the 1940s, but also as early as the 1920s.[1] The "supply-side" argument claims that education increases set the stage for minorities to fill better, higher-paying jobs previously closed to them. Younger blacks, some of them already growing up in the urban North but most still in the South, were beginning to get access to primary and secondary schooling in the 1930s and 1940s and, in the South, to gradually higher-paid teachers and smaller classrooms. These younger, more schooled workers replaced older, semiliterate, and illiterate job seekers in the labor force. At the same time, younger workers moved into industrial and service jobs that required schooling – jobs that their educated predecessors could not perform. And as the educational expansion and improvement continued, blacks continued to move up the occupational ladder.

An education explanation makes sense when new opportunities open up for minorities as their education increases and improves. Some proponents of the supply-side view argue that such opportunities did open up secularly in these four decades as a "natural," market-driven part and parcel of industrialization and growth, and that black males did consistently and steadily better during this period mainly because they developed better skills. The argument goes that demand was growing for all skills anyway, and it was increased education in a previous period that enabled working-age blacks to take advantage of economic growth. Others claim that not only the amount of education but the quality of that education and therefore the relative income payoff of more schooling, increased for black men relative to whites.

The main problem with all these claims is that they ignore other data showing stagnant (even declining) incomes for both black men and women compared with whites in the 1950s (and 1980s)[2] even while the years and quality of schooling for those coming into the labor force were catching up with whites. Nor are these claims consistent with most histories of the black condition in the 1950s, which describe highly restricted and glacially changing employment opportunities for minorities of color, especially those with higher education. At the end of the 1950s, according to economist Stephen Michaelson, the payoff to blacks of investing in college education was extremely low.[3] So few jobs were available for minority college graduates outside of teaching and preaching that going to college was largely a question of enhancing status *within* the minority community.

Once other things changed, however, more and better education kicked in to improve relative incomes. In the 1950s, the implementation of legal changes that made it possible a decade later for young blacks – especially those with a college education and those in the South – to get much better jobs and pay had not yet taken place. Until the law changed and the South was forced to desegregate, the payoff of education for blacks remained low.[4]

This leaves the question of whether raising the average level and quality of education in the 1980s and 1990s without improving opportunity in the labor market was enough. Judging from the high measured payoffs to blacks of a college education, increasing their access to college in the

1980s would have made a big difference in their relative incomes. Labor market opportunities went to waste because of the slowdown in the college graduation of young blacks. This makes sense because the 1964 Civil Rights Act and the EEOC created a situation in the 1970s and 1980s where blacks could get better jobs with better education.

The counterargument is that the political and ideological conditions of the 1980s made it much more likely that blacks would *not* go to college to take advantage of high potential payoffs. Federal grants for low-income populations were available but did not expand in real terms even though their family incomes fell. The support systems in colleges and universities that helped minorities do well enough to finish were also gone. High school counselors – because of changing ideology – may have been more likely to advise minorities to go into the military rather than to college. And in the ideological-political setting of the Reagan–Bush era, black high school graduates could have correctly perceived that there were relatively few good jobs available for black college graduates even though those that were available had high average incomes attached to them. In the "backlash 1980s," borrowing money to step into an unfriendly, high-risk college situation may not have seemed as rational for blacks as our data on payoffs make it appear.

This is where ideology and national leadership can make a difference. "Outsiders," such as blacks, long kept marginal to the mainstream, make decisions about their work lives based on a different set of perceptions than those who can count on acceptance based only on "normal" performance standards. The idea that the national leadership is on one's side, and that there is at least a disposition to improve the political-social atmosphere that conditions one's everyday life, changes the way that blacks and Latinos perceive the discrimination they will face and the opportunities they will have. This is difficult for whites to understand and accept. But many interviews with young blacks and Latinos – some with graduate school education and very good jobs – show that they almost universally view the work world as a hostile place where they face barriers and potential personal humiliation on a daily basis. They attribute much of this to the larger, national political context. It makes sense, then, that supportive national leadership itself can alter the aspirations and decisions of young minorities and, with executive decisions and new laws, can also alter the behavior of employers. Donohue and Heckman argue, for example, that the massive black emigration from South to North in the early 1960s dropped sharply after the passage of the Civil

Rights Act in 1964. Apparently, blacks felt that something had changed and the reason for leaving the South was on the way to being eliminated.[5] Politics can shape ideology regarding race issues, and ideological change can shape economic behavior.

This is what seemed to have happened in the 1940s and 1960s. Those decades were marked by a combination of minority militancy and the presence of national governments sensitive to minorities as political constituencies and as special, disadvantaged groups. These were governments that put much emphasis on using federal power to achieve greater equity, including intervention in labor markets and the expansion of federal employment. In addition, the United States was engaged in a war in the early 1940s and late 1960s. Not only does war increase the demand for labor, decreasing unemployment and raising wages, it requires mobilization and ideological unification, especially in terms of race and ethnicity.

Federal government policies also changed the rules of the game in minority hiring. Most of this change was direct: government, led by the federal government, began – mainly symbolically – by hiring blacks in the 1930s and, as government expanded, in the 1940s, 1950s, and especially the 1960s. Blacks (and much less so, Latinos) got a significant share of government jobs by the 1960s – jobs that were paid wages more equal to those of whites than in the private sector. Laws were passed that made discrimination illegal on government contracts, then in the private sector itself. The change was partly the result of the indirect impact of government leadership on the private sector. Federal government policies in the 1940s and 1960s and in much of the 1970s sent a signal to the private sector that things were different regarding minority hiring.

But the national leadership of those decades did more than that. Through a series of important symbolic actions, it conveyed to both minority and white communities that it was willing to change widely held views of minorities' place in American society. Its actions, like all politics, have to be judged in the context of the time. Some of them may seem insignificant by today's standards. But the main issues are how they were viewed by minority communities and what subtle messages of support and change they conveyed to both minorities and whites. The importance of these messages is clearer when they are compared with what went on in other periods, such as the 1950s and 1980s, when a different set of messages was being conveyed. In this spirit, let us compare, briefly, the New Deal and the Kennedy–Johnson administrations with the Eisenhower, Nixon, and Reagan years.

THE NEW DEAL AND IDEOLOGICAL CHANGE

The Roosevelt administration confronted racism in only muted tones during the 1930s and 1940s. But even so, it began to make the "Negro problem" an issue and, for the first time since Reconstruction, to include blacks in federal programs. Contractors employed by certain federal government departments were required to hire blacks in proportion to their representation in the labor market. There were important spokespeople for the black cause in the administration, such as Harold Ickes, secretary of the interior, Eleanor Roosevelt, and Robert Weaver, himself black.[6] The armed forces were not desegregated until after World War II, but black militancy and the Roosevelt administration response in the late 1930s and early 1940s opened the door a crack for blacks to get a fairer share of defense industry jobs. The changed rules were obviously aided by labor shortages, which made employers more inclined to hire minority labor for higher-paying jobs, but it was public intervention in shaping the employment climate that pushed them reluctantly toward less discrimination.

For all the human misery caused by the crisis of 1929–32, it did begin a process of bringing blacks into the American mainstream. This did not occur because of a change in Americans' attitudes toward race and people of color. Blacks continued to be segregated residentially and to be victimized by racist practices throughout the Depression and the 1940s. Whatever groundwork was laid in the 1930s for minority inclusion was the result of a massive political change. With Roosevelt's inauguration in 1933, Americans gave up on business-run government and turned the reins of the economy over to Washington. Decisions were made from the center, and with those decisions came a liberal philosophy that gave increased attention to workers, the old, and the poor. Because of the efforts of a few New Dealers, notably Harold Ickes and the people he hired, and of a number of black organizations and their leaders, blacks were specifically included in New Deal programs. This was a small step – too small for most black leaders. But it was a breakthrough. In Gunnar Myrdal's words:

> The New Deal has actually changed the whole configuration of the Negro problem. Particularly when looked upon from the practical and political viewpoints, the contrast between the present situation and the one prior to the New Deal is striking. . . . For almost the first time in the history of the nation, the state has done something substantial in a social way without excluding the Negro.[7]

Ickes's role was instrumental, especially in appointing blacks to high and visible government positions and in the power he wielded as head of the Public Works Administration (PWA) over hiring practices on government projects. On September 1, 1933, he issued an order prohibiting discrimination on all PWA projects and made sure that a nondiscrimination clause was included in every PWA contract. When this was found to be almost impossible to enforce, he instituted a labor quota system for skilled workers based on the 1930 occupational census. No contract could be approved unless employers provided proof of compliance. And when the plan proved successful, it was extended to unskilled workers, even in the face of opposition from white building trades unions. When Ickes's assistant, Robert Weaver, moved to the U.S. Housing Authority in 1937, he established a similar system there.[8] The quota did not affect many black workers, nor did it force the unions to accept black members, but it did show that it was possible for government to give some protection to black laborers, and it set a precedent for breaking down discrimination barriers on the job.

Not all New Dealers were anxious to follow Ickes's lead, and many resisted, making the Negro problem an issue. Roosevelt himself was more a benign bystander than an activist. He was well aware of the political costs in the South of being identified with blacks, and, for example, scrupulously avoided pushing for antilynching legislation. During the war, he never did desegregate the armed forces or fully meet black demands on access to defense jobs. Even so, Ickes and others were influential. By the end of the decade, almost every department in the federal government had a black adviser, and the number of black employees had increased substantially. In Ickes's view, for example, if blacks and whites were brought together in a common effort to improve working-class conditions, "their previous antagonism would dissipate; the 'Negro problem' would then be recognized as individual and not racial." And if blacks took advantage of the educational opportunities afforded them under the New Deal, they would be able to compete on more equal terms with whites.[9]

New Dealers were not oblivious to the underlying racism in American society; they simply thought that by bringing black and white workers together through federal leadership and funding, blacks would lose their sense of separateness and whites would accept blacks on a common class ground. The Depression, in the opinion of many in the Roosevelt administration, had created the possibility of uniting Americans in a new social order. In that order, there would be equality of opportunity and the weak would be protected against the strong. The spirit of togetherness and opportunity created by the welfare state would make possible the elimination of black–white differences. The race problem therefore had less to do with race than with the structural conditions in which the races lived. If a new structure were created, racism would gradually disappear.[10]

Most black leaders did not agree with this analysis. Although they viewed federal programs as a positive step, the programs necessarily affected only a small percentage of the huge number of blacks living in destitute conditions. In the early 1940s, conflicts between the liberals inside and activists outside erupted over segregation in the armed forces and job discrimination in defense industries. When A. Philip Randolph, head of the Sleeping Car Porters Union, organized the March on Washington Movement in 1941, black and white liberals inside the administration tried to head off the march. Ultimately, they got FDR to give in to Randolph on defense hiring: "After several conferences, the president said that if Randolph would call off the march, he would issue an order 'with teeth in it,' prohibiting discrimination in employment in defense industries and in the government."[11] On the eve of the proposed march, the president issued Executive Order 8802, which said that "there should be no discrimination in the employment of workers in defense industries or Government because of race, creed, color, or national origin. . . . And it is the duty of employers and of labor organizations . . . to provide for the full and equitable participation of all workers in defense industries, without discrimination because of race, creed, color, or national origin."[12] The Fair Employment Practices Committee (FEPC) was set up to investigate complaints of discrimination in violation of the order. Although the committee had no power to institute punishment and did not like to recommend contract cancellation, it helped blacks in their quest for fairer treatment. Employers and trade unions did not like appearing at the FEPC's hearings or the unfavorable publicity such an appearance created. The existence of the order and the FEPC tended to delegitimize discrimination, especially in the "pull together" climate of the war effort.

Most blacks went along with the New Deal even before 1941 and gave overwhelming electoral support to the Democrats despite the minimal economic gains they made before World War II. This made sense. The New Dealers were in Washington, holding the reins of the most powerful U.S. government that anyone could remember. And for the first time since blacks could remember, the federal government recognized the Negro minority as an integral part of the American people. It began to include them in the national territory as Americans, not just as former slave African-Americans. Government programs gave small but significant relief to the degradation and separation of African-American life. Although some, such as W. E. B. Du Bois, argued that real inclusion could not occur without the development of a powerful economic black community, most saw greater inclusion even on white liberal terms as a plus.

In retrospect, blacks were right to support the New Deal, despite all the dependency on white Washington power it may have created in the black community. The greater income equality pushed by New Dealers did eventually benefit blacks, as did their small efforts to reduce discrimination. John Hope Franklin argues that "despite serious criticisms leveled against the FEPC and other agencies of the government that tried to eliminate discriminatory policies, their activities showed clearly that the federal government could do much to modify racial employment practices."[13]

If nothing else, blacks had finally come to be included in the official ideology of national progress. They had been able to push themselves onto the national agenda, and it had paid off in large economic gains. Those inside the Roosevelt administration had much to do with that ideological inclusion, even if it was not exactly what black leaders wanted. Roosevelt had gone farther than anyone since Reconstruction, and it set the ideological tone for Truman and later Democrats in the 1960s.

THE EISENHOWER YEARS

The New Deal and World War II had unleashed new aspirations for blacks and a refusal to go back to the old conditions. It had set in motion a dynamic that produced important changes during the 1950s in some southern states such as Texas that had large black (and Latino) populations. Nationally, de jure Jim Crow began to be systematically broken down and destroyed by the legal and political actions of minorities themselves. This did not end segregation, but it opened the door for minorities to white institutions and destroyed the *legal* basis for separation between minorities of color and whites. The victories of the 1950s set the stage for a growing black middle class to join the American mainstream.

In addition to the leaders who had fought it out in the 1930s and 1940s, there was a whole new generation of blacks who would not accept racial degradation. They faced a nation that was still racist, but also a judicial system packed with FDR- and Truman-appointed liberals and a northern wing of the Democratic Party ready to confront southern conservatives. These were the pluses. On the negative side, McCarthyism and a wave of anti-Communism made civil rights organizing or any other kind of organizing much more difficult. The union movement, which was just beginning to open up to minorities, was severely constrained by Taft-Hartley.

Historian William Manchester, describing the early 1950s, writes that "Negroes still did not exist as people for mainstream America. In popular entertainment they were more like pets. Stepin Fetchit, Hattie McDaniel, Butterfly McQueen, and Eddie Anderson – these were good for the nudge and the guffaw but they weren't looked upon as human beings."[14] The Joseph McCarthy era, the days of the House Un-American Activities Committee, generated a spate of militant conservative groups. Their initial targets were the radical (Communist) New Dealers in government and the universities. But blacks and Mexicans were also defined as undermining the purity of the national culture. By branding minority leaders as Reds and "outside agitators," anti-Communism and American purity conveniently became one issue of defending the national (white) territory against foreign intervention.

In this context, the Eisenhower presidency could have made a real difference for continued minority gains. Despite their marginality to mainstream society, blacks in the early 1950s could view the future as promising. The Korean War tightened the labor market and provided continued mobility into skilled work. Blacks were gradually becoming full-fledged members of the working class. In Korea, they fought alongside whites for the first time ever. The Truman administration extended and deepened New Deal policies regarding equal rights. Black earnings relative to the earnings of white workers, both men and women, rose to their highest historical levels, thanks in part to the more equal treatment of low-income Americans in the economy and less racial discrimination in jobs. Although reliable data are not available for intercensal years,[15] it appears that black incomes reached a high relative to whites' in 1952.

Legal decisions and the subsequent rise of the civil rights movement in the South gave the Eisenhower administration the opportunity to lengthen minorities' economic strides of the 1940s and early 1950s substantially. But the president took the opposite tack. His was a business-oriented administration full of rock-ribbed conservatives for whom Jim Crow was less a matter of political support for segregationists than something unnatural and politically annoying in the workings of the market. Much higher on the agenda was extending U.S. economic power around the world and combating Communism. Blacks had to shout to get attention in this political atmosphere, and shout they did. The 1950s eventually became a battleground between the legacy of New Deal reformism and this resurgence of traditional conservatism.

The administration chose to drag its feet in favor of conservatism. Minorities won an important civil rights victory in the Supreme Court in 1954 with *Brown v. Board of Education,* but only mixed economic gains relative to their white counterparts. At least part of this economic result has to be blamed on the Eisenhower administration. It did its best to hold back the forces of change being unleashed by the civil rights movement. The administration did not consider the black fight for equality morally wrong. Rather, it was "disruptive" to more gradual, orderly processes of change. Wage discrimination tended to increase after 1952, not decrease.[16]

The role of the presidency in the 1950s is typified by Eisenhower's reaction to the Supreme Court's overturning of the "separate but equal" principle in *Brown.* As expected, the Court's decision unleashed a storm of violent reaction. Seventeen southern and border states and the District of Columbia had school segregation written into their constitutions. Now they were told they would have to desegregate. The new chief justice, Earl Warren – the same Earl Warren who, as Republican governor of California, had presided over the desegregation of that state's schools after *Mendez v. Westminister* – was vilified in the South. Legislatures in Virginia and the Black Belt passed complex measures designed to lead to long judicial battles and circumvent the Supreme Court's ruling. At the local level, whites revived the Ku Klux Klan and White Citizens' Councils. They vowed to defend the racial status quo.

Eisenhower did not agree with the Warren decision on political grounds, believing that integration could not be legislated but would have to come about through gradual economic and social development. Even so, he ordered all District of Columbia schools integrated at once and ended segregation on all navy bases. He also appointed a few blacks to White House posts. But these were clearly reluctant acts and clearly indicated a go-slow attitude. Eisenhower was more interested politically in sending a signal to southern schools and businesses that he was not supporting such radical moves, so little integration took place and the effects on education and hiring were minimal. The national leadership stood for obeying the law, but not advancing it. Eisenhower predicted, with consternation, that the Court's decision would lead to social disintegration in the South. He was right.

The Court decision and black organizing ultimately did have an impact on Congress and the Eisenhower agencies. The Montgomery bus boycott and Little Rock not only thrust Rosa Parks, Martin Luther King, Jr., and Orval Faubus into the national spotlight; they made civil rights and racism political issues. In a world where dozens of new countries inhabited by people of color were gaining independence and the United States was competing with Communism for hearts and minds, the nation's international image was suffering. Racism and segregation were an embarrassment. The United States was the greatest economic power on earth, brimming with consumer goods, sure that its democratic system was an ideal to be emulated, yet blacks had to fight to get seats on white-run buses or to go to white schools. But the Eisenhower administration never intended to take an active part in what was going on. It had to be dragged into acting on desegregation and then only enough to preserve its image.

THE KENNEDY–JOHNSON ERA

John Kennedy won the presidency on the basis of large black turnouts in key states, but he initially underestimated the expectations that blacks had of his administration and, to an even greater extent, the depth of the race problem. His priorities were a summit with Krushchev and putting a man on the moon. The first freedom rides in the spring of 1961 were more a source of potential embarrassment to the administration than a catalyst for action.[17] Liberals of the early 1960s, according to historian Manchester, believed that strong leadership and a fundamental sense of decency in the American people would overcome ignorance and bigotry. It was just a question of time – of carefully and systematically implementing the law and bringing about inevitable change. But blacks and Latinos did not want to wait. They "expected their white sympathizers to understand . . . that to the new Negro [and Latino] freedom for his people was more important than any issue in Vienna – or in Vietnam, or Cuba, or outer space."[18]

Once the freedom rides began and, the following year, James Meredith tried to enroll at the University of Mississippi and, in 1963, black students enrolled at the University of Alabama, the Kennedy administration weighed in on the side of civil rights with all the power at its disposal. There was no question that it would uphold federal law, even if it meant incurring southern white hatred. On June 10, 1963, Kennedy called on Congress to "enact a broad, sweeping civil rights bill committing it to the premise 'that race has no place in American life or law.' "[19] And although he was opposed to the march on Washington called by A. Philip Randolph twenty years after he had first proposed it, the march became the high point of the decade for those blacks who thought that their grievances could be redressed by working within the system. Kennedy met with the leaders of the march and was impressed by their fervor and dignity. More than anything, he made a major *ideological* commitment to correcting years of segregation and economic inequality.

With a sympathetic administration in Washington, the civil rights movement had an important and sustained impact on minorities' incomes. The Civil Rights Act, pushed hard by the Kennedy administration and finally passed in 1964, had much to do with the sharp rise in professional and managerial jobs for minorities and in their relative income that began in 1965–6 and continued until the recession of 1974–5, and even (at a slower pace) until the end of the 1970s.[20]

By 1965, however, the issue had turned from what black New York Congressman Adam Clayton Powell called the civil rights phase of the black revolution to the "gut issue of who gets the money."[21] Michael Harrington's *The Other America* was about poverty, not civil rights. Lyndon Johnson, under Daniel Patrick Moynihan's influence, had also made the leap from civil rights to economic equality in his policy thinking by mid-1965.[22] The race riots in ghettos across the nation between 1965 and 1968 were not explicitly about Jim Crow; they confronted the appalling economic conditions of minorities in the midst of plenty.

At first there was much hope that legislation could also resolve the money issue. Johnson was intent on completing the New Deal agenda and attempted to do just that with his "Great Society" program. The Eighty-ninth Congress passed eighty-nine major administration bills, including those creating Medicare and the Office of Economic Opportunity, designed to eradicate poverty and equalize opportunity for minorities of color. But civil rights legislation probably had a greater impact on minority economics than did antipoverty legislation, although the direct government employment part of the Equal Economic Opportunity legislation seems to have had important effects on the job mobility of higher-educated blacks.

Poverty was a much more complex issue than legal rights. The approach to it was never coherent, and allocating public money to the working-age poor quickly became unpopular with white voters and with the white intellectuals who dreamed up the legislation. The very change from civil rights to money transfers created many more difficulties than it solved. It was couched in a brand of minority militancy that scared whites, and it explicitly meant redistributing income from the majority white population to people of color. The debate over why the antipoverty legislation did not work continues to the present, but since other sustained income-maintenance programs such as Social Security were successful in lowering the poverty levels of their target groups, there is every reason to believe that a politically supported effort aimed at improving the lot of the working-age poor could also work. The main unanswered questions are how to mobilize sustained political support for such assistance and where and how to apply it. When political support ran out for income transfers in the 1970s, it was just a question of time before such programs would dwindle away.

The Johnson administration's efforts to improve the economic situation of minorities also failed because of a sluggish economy after 1973. But just as the success of earlier efforts at equalization was linked to national politics, so the "failure" of affirmative action and the War on Poverty cannot be extracted from the same context. Attempts to create greater equality did not fail only or even mainly because of economic problems or global restructuring. Equality itself became a useful political issue for the "new Republicanism" and was exploited as such.

THE POLITICS OF BACKLASH

If the 1960s were a period of great economic gains for blacks and other minorities, they were also the years when the New Deal coalition that had helped minorities make those gains unraveled and the nation entered an economic crisis. In the face of that crisis, two economic models, based on different ideologies, squared off. The so-called free-market approach won. But that was less a tribute to its economic problem-solving power than to the political organizers backing it. They were able to pull together a new coalition while traditional Democrats failed to come to grips politically with the new economic realities.

Backlash against affirmative action and poverty programs was a building block of the new politics. So were antiunionism, low inflation, and, implicitly, slow or no growth in real wages and greater income inequality.[23] The last two should have been very unpopular with the mass of American voters, but when presented as a precondition of economic competitiveness, economic growth, and lower tax rates, they lost their negative edge. Conservatives were also successful in making "welfare" spending a symbol of New Deal economic policy. They blended minorities of color and welfare into inseparable images and, to boot, expanded the minority identity to include crime and violence. As inflation rose and real wages fell, economic insecurity increased in the white working class, and these images became sharper and more acceptable. Insecurity and fear fueled the success of conservative politics, which in turn played to rising popular feelings among whites against social spending, taxes, and affirmative action. Such feelings did not develop overnight. And they would not have been nearly as important politically if a large bloc of southern white voters, still pitted against black advancement, had not formed the key element in a resurrected national conservative ideology. They were the base, and those white northern voters who shared their ideology were added to it.

In the words of Thomas and Mary Edsall:

> Race and taxes . . . functioned to force the attention of the public on the costs of federal policies and programs. Those costs were often first experienced in terms of loss – the loss of control over school services, union apprenticeship programs, hiring, promotions, neighborhoods, public safety, and even over sexual morals and a stable social order. . . . Opposition to busing, to affirmative action, to quotas, and to housing integration have given a segment of the traditionally Democratic white electorate ideological common ground with business and the affluent in shared opposition to the federal regulatory apparatus.[24]

The New Coalition

A fundamental change occurred in twentieth-century American politics when Richard Nixon was elected in 1968. Despite George Wallace's third-party candidacy, Nixon won five southern states (Florida, Kentucky, South Carolina, Tennessee, and Virginia) and all but one electoral vote in a sixth (North Carolina). Wallace won five others. The significance of Nixon's showing in the South was that it continued the region's political break with the Democratic Party, which had been brewing since the 1948 Democratic convention. With help from South Carolina's Strom Thurmond, Nixon had built on Barry Goldwater's relatively strong performance in the South even in the 1964 Democratic landslide. The shift of southern white voters to the Republicans was based on one issue – civil rights. In Richard Nixon, these voters had the first Republican president beholden to the South for his victory. In John Mitchell, Nixon's chief political adviser, they had at once an attorney general sympathetic to their stand against federal radical integrationism and a strategist who saw the Republican future wedded to the South's electoral votes.

Between 1968 and 1972 Nixon and Mitchell showed that it was possible to win elections without black votes and without the votes of white liberals who championed civil rights and equal opportunity. In 1968, there were other issues on the agenda, so Nixon's victory represented much more than his stand on the civil rights issue. In many ways, the victory was an illogical outcome of a turbulent year. If a Democratic candidate such as Robert Kennedy, distanced from Johnson's war, had survived the campaign, Nixon and the South might have had a different political history, and the politics of inequality a different outcome. But win Nixon did, and he won with a message of ambivalence about pursuing school integration in those states that had not yet complied. Southerners read him loud and clear: they expected help from a Nixon presidency in slowing down and even halting the desegregation juggernaut. He was ready to accommodate them, not so much because of personal beliefs (he was neither a segregationist nor particularly a racist) or his economic philosophy (he acted like a Keynesian throughout his seven years as president) as because of political expediency. He agreed with Mitchell that the South was the key to reelection in 1972. Implicitly, he was to show that the Democrats' New Deal coalition of 1960 and 1964, putting together minorities of color with the traditional Democratic base of the northern white working class, was running out of steam, both ideologically and demographically.

Events in the Nixon administration were to show two other things. First, it takes real presidential commitment to turn social motion around, and it was not clear that Nixon wanted to do more than give the South some symbols of his commitment, mainly to win the Wallace vote in 1972. The schizophrenic attitude toward civil rights of Nixon and his team was reflected in his appointments. He named a close California friend, Robert Finch, who was distinctly pro–civil rights, to head the Department of Health, Education, and Welfare, and Finch named two even more liberal Republicans, Leon Panetta as director of civil rights in HEW and Jack Veneman as undersecretary, to head the civil rights team in that department. James Farmer, a prominent black, was also named to play an important role in HEW. Daniel Patrick Moynihan, a Democrat and Harvard political scientist who was not particularly liked by black activists because of his 1965 black family report to Lyndon Johnson but still completely committed to fighting poverty, was named as one of two White House staffers heading up domestic policy formation (the other was Arthur Burns).

Second, the events showed that if a president wants to reverse motion, other factors have to fall into line, and they did not in the late 1960s and early 1970s. There was still support for civil rights *and* equal opportunity in Congress, dominated by liberal Democrats and many liberal Republicans. There were the courts, still dominated by New Deal Democrats and Warren-type Republicans, who took desegregation seriously. And there was the civil rights movement, in the process of splitting into two camps of more traditional integrationists and younger separationists, but still able to push hard politically for greater equality between minorities and whites.

Nixon himself came down heavily against the pro–civil rights forces within his own administration during its first two years. He did so first by insisting on delays in federal funding cutoffs to southern school districts that had been mandated by court orders to desegregate, pushing to allow these districts more time to develop desegregation plans. Although there was no chance that this would result in any change in desegregation policy (e.g., Nixon's promised "freedom of choice" by the local community) – a policy that had already been decided in the courts – Nixon's action gave the *impression* that he was doing his best to reverse civil rights legislation, and he was. Ultimately, school districts in the South had to desegregate anyway, but the struggle between Mitchell and HEW, with Finch caving in because of his loyalty to the president, led to Panetta's forced resignation in February 1970.[25]

When Abe Fortas had to resign from the Supreme Court in April 1969 because of a financial scandal, Nixon nominated Judge Clement Haynsworth, Jr., a strict constructionist from South Carolina. The Senate rejected Haynsworth, primarily because of his civil rights and labor record. Seventeen Republicans voted against Haynsworth. Nixon responded by nominating G. Harold Carswell, another constructionist and, again, a southerner. But Carswell was also rejected, more because he was only marginally qualified to sit on the Court. Nixon was humiliated, but he used his defeat to endear himself to the South:

> I understand the bitter feelings of millions of Americans who live in the South about the act of regional discrimination that took place in the Senate yesterday [April 8, 1970]. They have my assurance that the day will come when men like Judges Carswell and Haynsworth can and will sit on the high Court.[26]

Within a few days, Nixon had nominated Harry Blackmun, a strict constructionist but a Minnesotan. Blackmun was confirmed easily. Nixon had gotten his strict constructionist and, in defeat, had won a major victory in his southern strategy.

Once Nixon endeared himself to the South with these symbols, he let go on civil rights and allowed events to take their course. Despite his early foot dragging on school desegregation, it was forced to proceed anyway. The president turned around and asked Congress for $1.5 billion in May 1970 to help school districts that desegregated. Although the bill did not pass the Senate, a similar bill passed into law in 1972. The Nixon appointee for commissioner of the Internal Revenue Service, Randolph Thrower, revoked the tax exemption of white private academies popping up around the South as a means of avoiding desegregation. Despite southern ire, the ruling was upheld and the Justice Department sent lawyers to the South to make sure that desegregation was carried out.

Under Secretary of Labor George Shultz, the administration's policies could even be called pro-minority on the labor and economic side of the ledger, and this helped minorities expand economic gains made since the mid-1960s. For example, Shultz proposed the Philadelphia Plan in 1969, which "set up a quota system to compel half a dozen hard-hat construction unions to train black youth as apprentices, with full union membership at the end of their training program, on federal construction programs."[27] Although the unions fought the plan, the courts upheld it, and it was implemented. This was consistent with Republicans' antiunion bias. But in the late 1960s, antiunion bias did not translate into the kind of union-busting wage policies that hit labor in the 1980s – for a very simple reason: Republicans still had to convince northern white workers that they should leave the Democratic Party, and unions were still popular and relatively strong. Nixon was willing to increase unemployment rates somewhat to slow inflation but was committed to avoiding any economic policy that would bring on a recession. He expected to slow down the overheated economy and reduce inflation, but still have economic growth and *rising* real wages. Even later wage–price controls, which labor considered biased toward business, did not slow the large real-wage increases of 1971–2. While showing that Republicans stood for growth and not recession, Nixon could win over northern workers with social issues, namely the antipathy to expanding welfare rolls. This was the race problem as it appeared to northern working-class taxpayers. "Just such antagonisms of class and race, rubbed raw by Republican oratory, were one reason why conservative Republicans, such as Ronald Reagan of California, had made serious inroads into the vote of the white workingman in 1966. To Nixon's strategists, the welfare issue was a possible lever for the emergence of the Republicans as the majority party by the end of the 1970s."[28]

But the irony of the early Nixon years was that Daniel Patrick Moynihan was the framer of this welfare reform. He was able to convince the president to propose a family income maintenance policy, widely practiced by European governments. In Moynihan's view, the supply-side education and training programs of Johnson's War on Poverty did not and would not eliminate poverty. Since 1965, he had argued that the years of discrimination and separation heaped on top of the wrenching change from rural to urban society had done serious damage to the black family. Moynihan saw the way out in making federal assistance *family-based* and raising low-income family consumption through direct income transfers.[29] After George Shultz added work requirements and work incentives to the package to assuage white working-class sensibilities about handouts, Nixon was ready to present welfare reform to the nation. Although the package failed in Congress, attacked by both Left and Right, the fact that the president would even consider such a proposal, as well as sponsor a huge conference on hunger at the end of 1969, suggests how much the liberal agenda still influenced even a conservative Republican president in the late 1960s and early 1970s.

In the longer run, the *politics,* not the economics, of the Nixon administration undid minority economic gains. Once Nixon and Mitchell developed the New Coalition based on different aspects of the race issue, being tough on civil rights and poverty was more a losing than a winning position even for Democrats. The progress of desegregation in the South contributed to this process: civil rights turned north into highly segregated eastern and midwestern cities. There it affected the core of the Democratic white working-class base. So the symbolic acts of 1969 and 1970 had little immediate effect on minorities in the context of the social momentum of that time. But by the end of the 1970s, the political alignment that those symbolic acts helped build brought to power Republicans who could reverse the course of the 1960s.

The conservative victory

The brilliance and logic of Mitchell's southern strategy became fully clear in 1980, when Ronald Reagan beat a sitting Democratic president from the South. Although Jimmy Carter was not a liberal in the traditional sense, he had supported civil rights legislation and named a large number of blacks to high-level positions in his administration. This is not what lost Carter the election, but it did count against him in his politically crucial own backyard. Reagan, in contrast, did not have any civil rights baggage. Like Nixon in 1972, he was able to appeal ideologically to the conservative white South, his Sun Belt corporate backers, and Wallace's white backlash working class in northern cities – all at the same time.

Because of economic chaos in the late 1970s – especially the major plant closings in the steel and auto industries – and the resulting growth of white backlash against civil rights in the North, Reagan and Nixon differed on the degree to which they could and were willing to move against labor and against the poor. Between July 1979 and July 1980, more than 600,000 workers were laid off in primary metals, fabricated metals, and motor vehicles and equipment industries, most in Democratic Party strongholds in the Upper Midwest. This, along with inflation, declining real incomes, and increasing tax burdens, turned key groups of working-class Democrats against the interventionist model.[30]

In the name of restoring the nation's economic health, Reagan was able to use an activist free-market government ideology to redistribute national income to the already rich, dismember organized labor, and remove the last affirmative action, poverty program, and compensatory education underpinnings from the gains of the 1960s and 1970s. The results were predictable. Real wages rose slowly even during the expansion that followed the major recession of 1981–2, poverty increased, minority education stagnated, affirmative action entered a go-slow phase, and it took the entire decade for minority relative incomes to get back almost where they started. Profits skyrocketed, the rich flourished, and money became king.[31] Reagan policies hurt most blacks economically in ways unheard of under Nixon.

All this did not seem to be a formula for political success, but it was. Most voters found stability in neoconservatism. Key groups of white voters had become disillusioned with "welfare for the poor" and other social programs that did not seem to benefit them. The "conservative egalitarianism" pushed by the Republicans, with its emphasis on equal results for equal work and equal ability, appealed to whites who had "made it on their own," unlike blacks, who seemed to them reliant on affirmative action and other government interventions.[32] This appeal worked for most of the decade until it became clear that working-class whites were hardly benefiting from the program. Like the 1920s, the Reagan 1980s were a return to "normalcy" after a period of turbulence. But normalcy in the 1980s meant playing to unabashed white middle-class materialism and abandoning a tenuous commitment to racial equality. For minorities, this implied an end to a different normalcy, one that increased their possibility of entering the mainstream of society.

Most of the effects of Reagan's macroeconomic policies were class-intensive because they were aimed at keeping down the price of labor and controlling inflation. Reagan policies that kept wages low were even worse for minorities, since low-income earners were hit especially hard during the early Reagan years and such a high percentage of minority wage earners have low incomes. In this sense, William Julius Wilson is right in claiming that the ideological-economic issue in the 1980s was class, not race.

A major piece of the hidden political agenda was, in fact, race. Civil rights issues were crucial under both the Reagan and Bush administrations for providing the political underpinning to class-intensive economic policies. Reaganomics included tax and social spending cuts that were popular because they appeared to be (and were) hurting minorities (the stereotypical welfare recipients) more than whites. George Bush used a black prison inmate as a symbol of Democrats' "liberal" views on crime – a white working- and middle-class issue – to win the 1988 election. Bush also made a point of vetoing the 1990 Civil Rights Act on the basis of its affirmative action, "quota" clauses. All these were important, politically symbolic acts. But as symbols, they represented much broader and deeper policies that had a real impact on blacks' economic progress.

Public policy analyst David Ellwood shows how medical services and Social Security benefits continued to rise in the late 1970s and early 1980s for the elderly and disabled, but benefits for all others, except for medical protection, declined.[33] There was a clear and rapid flight away from support for the poor, beginning under Carter but reaching its full expression in the Reagan years. The largest budget cuts in the 1980s were made in ten social programs – for example, the Comprehensive Employment and Training Act program (moved entirely into state budgets), work incentives, child nutrition, food stamps, and legal services – most of which subsidize the working poor. In six of the ten, close to 50 percent or more of the program's participants were blacks or Latinos.[34] The Bush administration continued these policies and even intensified reductions in some programs.

Such cuts in social services to the poor effectively destroyed the community infrastructure built up in urban ghettos during the War on Poverty. Whatever criticism can be leveled at these infrastructural institutions, they did serve, along with churches, as the only cohesive force in rapidly disintegrating urban poverty environments.

And as part of their overall effort to "deregulate" the market, conservative Republicans pushed for and got an effective end to affirmative action in labor markets. They argued that present generations should not have to pay for the racial oppression of past generations – hence the class action basis for the EEOC's legal cases against employers in the 1960s and 1970s should be transformed into individual cases of discrimination, applied to all races and ethnic groups, men as well as women. The administration sought to disallow the use of simple statistical evidence of discriminatory hiring patterns and insisted that intent to discriminate must be proven. Reflecting this shift, the lead agency on affirmative action during the Reagan years was the Justice Department instead of the EEOC. Assistant Secretary Bradford Reynolds, openly hostile to affirmative action, was put in charge of civil rights at Justice.[35] Under Reynolds, the department even tried to impose its anti–affirmative action views on local and state governments. It told "more than 51 cities, counties, school districts, and state agencies to stop using numerical goals in the hiring of women, blacks, and Latinos."[36]

Was the overall strategy politically successful? On the whole, yes. It solidified Republicans' hold over the South and turned many working-class white Democrats resentful of affirmative action into independents. Democratic politicians saw the handwriting on the wall and did little to resist Reagan's reforms. But despite disorganized Democratic opposition, Republicans could not turn their ideological advantage on race into longer-term economic rewards for the majority of white Americans. Reagan and Bush economic policies were too one-sided – too favorable for a few and unfavorable for the many. As the costs of laissez-faire economics mounted, new forms of government intervention looked better – even necessary – in order to make the U.S. economy competitive in the new global context. With the end of the cold war, military spending as a major element of industrial policy – one consistent with Republican free-enterprise rhetoric – also began to decline, constraining Reaganomics even more.

When Bill Clinton came up with an interventionist project that made sense, he won the presidency over a Republican laissez-faire ideology that had seemed invincible only eight months before. Race seemed not to be an issue in the campaign. But it was, even in the deteriorating economic environment. Blacks voted overwhelmingly for Clinton, and whites voted marginally for Bush. The vote reflected the continuing fear among many whites that Clinton would restore welfare spending for the poor, and the continuing faith that blacks had in government intervention. Twelve years of conservative rule had a major impact on the ideology of racial inequality. Not only were race relations put on the back burner, but employers, teachers, social workers, and state and local governments all got the message that racial inequality was mainly blacks' problem, not one of government responsibility. The ultimate result was an ideological shift that forcefully and negatively affected minorities' ability to overcome entrenched discriminatory practices.

NATIONAL LEADERSHIP COUNTS

Not only did the Reagan and Bush administrations change the rhetoric and symbols of civil rights, they implemented economic and social policies that they knew would be costly for the poor and, in that sense, would affect blacks and Latinos more than others. One can imagine that they did this believing sincerely that an economy freed from government intervention would produce higher economic growth rates and provide more stimulus to the poor to improve their situation by themselves, without waiting for handouts.[37] In the long run, they could argue, their policies would make blacks and Latinos better off than interventionist government programs. But the point is that one of the ways of selling the "free market" (including its antilabor ideology) to the white working class was to tie it in with an abandonment of civil rights and antipoverty policies. The accompanying political symbolism conveyed a message to both minorities and whites that was likely to have much greater negative effects than a free market would have positive effects. Indeed, I argue, the net effect has been negative.

There is still the question of causality. Does national leadership make the difference here, or does national leadership simply reflect the people's will? Probably some of both. No doubt, there was a white backlash in the

1970s, and it emerged from white fears about minorities and about the economic crisis, as well as from disillusionment with government social programs.[38] Exploiting the backlash, the Republican Party came to power nationally in the 1980s with a new coalition. But by the end of President Reagan's second term, most Americans' concerns had turned to issues of social disintegration. The national leadership, had it wanted to, could have developed a mighty campaign against poverty and for early childhood education, a family policy, and investment in college education for the most needy. The campaign could have been launched in the context of a conservative agenda of improving productivity and reducing instability in the inner city. It did not do so. Rather, it continued to exploit backlash. It chose not to lead the American people down the road to greater equality despite widespread support in the electorate for doing *something* about the fallout from that poverty, if not about poverty itself.

This is just one example of leadership pulling the electorate and the nation's agenda in a particular direction. The Roosevelt, Truman, Kennedy, Johnson, and Carter administrations pulled them in the opposite direction, even though for most of their years in power, racial equality was far from a consensual issue. It did not help the Democratic Party's cause in the long run to do so, but it did change the lives of most blacks and Latinos and, indeed, most Americans for the better.

Now, after twelve years in the opposition, Democrats are back in power with new leadership. Racial inequality played virtually no role in the 1992 campaign, to blacks' chagrin and to most white Democrats' delight. By putting race to the side and focusing on the domestic economy, Bill Clinton was able to fracture the Republicans' tried-and-true New Coalition. But now in office, will his administration lead the American people to greater racial equality despite well-entrenched opposition even within the party? Can it be done without committing political suicide?

11

Is there any hope for greater equality?

After twelve years of the Republican brand of civil rights, African-Americans rejoiced at a change in the White House. Will this change in 1993 – or any other Democratic victory in the 1990s – put blacks back on the road to greater equality? What could a Democratic president do to make that happen, and what are the constraints that might keep him or her from taking any major actions on the race issue?

Candidate Clinton's populist economic message during the long and victorious campaign portrayed a nation that would recover its multicultural energy and build a more cooperative society from the bottom up. Clinton argued for greater economic equality as one of the *bases* for more balanced and sustainable economic growth. He talked about new types of social programs that would benefit middle- *and* lower-income Americans. And everywhere he went, he promised not only more jobs, but better jobs. Even though he did not specifically talk about race, that message sounded good to blacks and many whites – it represented the possibility that lower-income Americans would be paid attention to, that the nation's cities would be attended to, and that poverty and social disintegration would again receive the honest attention they deserved in a society as rich and innovative as ours. Almost half of America's voters wanted to believe not only that things could get better socially, but that Democrats were the logical ones to make it happen.

Inauguration week was a tribute to this message. It began at Monticello and on the steps of the Lincoln Memorial, where, flanked by a crowd of black and Latino entertainers, Clinton, his wife, Hillary, Vice-President-elect Al Gore, and his wife, Tipper, stood on the steps and sang "We Are the World." Moments later, James Edward Olmos, a Mexican-

American and star of *Stand and Deliver,* a film about the real-life story of a high school teacher who showed that disadvantaged Chicanos in East Los Angeles could pass advanced placement tests in calculus, introduced a nation-wide bell-ringing ceremony to celebrate the hope of "all the American people" in this new administration. Then on inauguration day itself, Maya Angelou, poet laureate and a black woman of great presence and dignity, told another version of the story:

> Lift up your faces, you have a piercing need
> For this bright morning dawning for you.
> History, despite its wrenching pain,
> Cannot be unlived, and if faced
> With courage, need not be lived again.
>
> Lift up your eyes upon
> This day breaking for you.
> Give birth again
> To the dream.[1]

At the end of these ceremonies, it seemed that the new administration was committed to nurturing a multicultural society and that it recognized the unequal treatment that many of those cultures had received in the past. This symbolic recognition alone had great importance, as did the list of appointments to key cabinet positions, which included Ron Brown, Mike Espy, Henry Cisneros, Harriet O'Leary, as well as the surgeon general, Joycelyn Elders, and several subcabinet members with considerable clout. The message that the administration was trying to be "representative" of the real America counted for minorities. It was a radically different message than that sent out in the 1980s.

African-Americans know that a new ideological approach is the bottom line of any real improvement in their economic situation. It changes the lay of the land, the conditions under which a whole host of smaller decisions inside and outside of government are made. It also gives African-Americans and other minority groups a larger political space for defining the direction of economic and social action. Their spokespeople in the government are no longer the Clarence Thomases and Linda Chavezes.

Yet moving past symbolism into concrete actions requires a well-orchestrated, coherent vision of how to achieve greater equality and greater unity in the context of a society that has become skeptical of government programs, a highly competitive world economy, and a citizenry running scared – of layoffs, crime, insecurity in old age, and a seemingly ever-shrinking paycheck. The new administration's program has not met this challenge head-on. Instead, it has developed a mixed strategy of conservative economic growth policy, progressive taxation (to shift the cost of government programs to the wealthy), and a social policy based on a combination of greater public-sector efficiency and somewhat greater equity in service delivery. The administration has consciously tried to keep race out of the political discussion and has seemed unwilling – or unprepared – to press home the alternative vision it used so effectively in the 1992 election to undo the Republican coalition. Do these strategies make sense in light of the kinds of constraints still existing even for a victorious Democratic Party in the post–cold war era? Or are the administration and the party missing an opportunity to reshape the political agenda?

WHAT WORKS TO REDUCE INEQUALITY?

The main arguments of this book are that economic inequality in the United States still has an important racial component and that a government with the will to reduce racial inequality can, by its general ideological stance toward race and by specific public policies, achieve that goal. When government has focused its power on racial and ethnic income differences and discrimination in the past, it has had a major impact on the economic conditions of blacks and other disadvantaged minorities. It can have a similar impact if policies combine investment in the education of disadvantaged children and minority college education with expansionary economics. It can have an impact if it combines pro-labor wage and training legislation with the implementation of existing antidiscrimination laws. Government can do all this.

Government has the capability to invest public funds in education and infrastructure in ways that are more favorable to low-income Americans and even more favorable to low-income minorities – focusing public investment on Head Start and on rebuilding cities and providing decent housing rather than on developing military hardware, and phasing out programs that subsidize the already wealthy while expanding programs that increase low-income workers' skills and access to jobs.

Government can affect access to credit for private investments. The two main investments that middle-class consumers make are those in housing and in their children's college education. Credit markets for these investments are exactly the ones that African-Americans have a harder time entering than whites and where government can play a crucial role directly or indirectly to increase access. Government can also favor investment in inner cities, either by reducing regulation on loans to businesses that go into inner cities or by providing direct incentives to such businesses.

Government can support macroeconomic policy that tends to lower general unemployment rates, again favoring the low-income and minority groups who are the most likely to be unemployed when the economy is slack.

Government has the legal power to equalize opportunity in labor markets when there is evidence that discrimination exists. Once the Civil Rights Act of 1965 was passed, the most important issues concerning government action became the act's interpretation by the Supreme Court and its implementation by the Equal Employment Opportunity Commission. Although the Court in the 1980s began to limit the earlier powers of the act, it is still possible for the Justice Department and the EEOC to use earlier standards of class-action failure-to-hire cases instead of the individual discrimination criteria used under Reagan and Bush and to speed up the handling of complaints.[2]

Government can set the standard on wages and employment: blacks were employed in high positions in government a generation before they reached similar positions in the private sector, and black–white wages in government work are more equal even today than in the private sector, which in the current labor market with its increased number of adults earning low wages would affect much more than just youth incomes. Government can raise minimum wages in the private sector. It can also be the employer of last resort, providing short-term employment for disadvantaged youth at reasonable wages.

Government can send an ideological signal that racial inequality as expressed in wage discrimination, political underrepresentation of minorities, poorer educational treatment for minorities, misleading stereotypes, as well as less individual responsibility for social discipline in minority communities are unacceptable. The great advances for many in the black community at the same time that other blacks face deteriorating social conditions make the politics of sending this signal much more complex than it was in the 1940s and the 1960s. It is especially difficult to develop a package that deals with the poverty/race problem at the same time that it covers a different set of issues for middle-class blacks.

However, the bottom line of any ideological strategy for reducing racial inequality is that the race issue must be on the table. It must be the subject of honest political discourse. This means overturning conservative policies of removing race from out-front political discussion. Overt discussion of racism in political circles has been stigmatized – indeed, many politicians are ready to deem taking racism on as an issue racist. The mainstream politics of race has been pushed into the realm of innuendo and subconscious fears. In this climate, how does government change the signal in order to face up to continued discrimination at the same time that it deals honestly with such issues as street violence, social disintegration, and welfare dependency?[3]

When government is able to combine economic, legal, and ideological actions, it has a ripple effect on inequality beyond the direct impact of the actions themselves. It styles the actions of employers and workers in the private sector as they adjust to changes in the "atmospheric pressure" of the social contract. This is precisely what happened in the 1940s and 1960s, and could happen again in the 1990s. But will it happen under the present strategy, or do we need something quite different?

LEGACIES AND LIMITS

Even were the new administration's domestic policies more organized, it would face an uphill fight in trying to reduce economic differences between blacks and whites. The reasons are obvious. Slow economic growth and stagnant real incomes for men have created a "lifeboat" atmosphere – the most deserving citizens are still viewed as those who make their own success. The vast majority of the white population does not believe that blacks are treated unfairly anymore. Southern conservative Democrats are wary of social programs that are aimed at reducing poverty in big cities. Together with Republicans, they control the Senate. The New Coalition created by John Mitchell has not really disappeared; for the moment, it has only lost a single battle in a long war.

This poses a perilous contradiction for progress on racial issues, similar to that faced by all Democrats since the early 1970s: the forces of traditional conservatism can easily line up against issues such as greater racial equality if given the opportunity. The negative intertwining of race with "tax and spend," "welfare state" economic policy remains a potentially highly successful conservative political card. Because most Americans are still very skeptical of government intervention in anything and have little faith in government fairness and efficiency, they could easily be swayed by the conservative "market" card used against any program that attempts to equalize opportunity or improve conditions in inner cities. There is absolutely no doubt that the card will be played and played repeatedly. The secret to preventing it from being played or to reducing its effectiveness is a successful economic growth policy – mainly more and better jobs for the white working class.

Conservatives are not just waiting for the Clinton administration to falter in promoting a new social program. They have done everything they can to block liberal appointees that would promote such a program. They are also pushing hard with their own alternatives for "solving" poverty, all based on privatizing and "automating" the social sector, beginning with public education. The premise underlying these efforts is already widely held in society and therefore has great appeal: government bureaucracy is the most inefficient way to deliver services to the poor. The logical conclusion is that government should get out of social service delivery, even while it may still have to finance such services. The most popular expression of this effort is school vouchers, but it is hardly limited to education. Conservatives are backing the earned income tax credit (although not a very large one, as the 1993 budget debate in the Senate showed), which would raise the standard tax deduction to reward the working poor; child-care tax credits rather than public day-care centers; the sale of public housing to tenants; rent vouchers to replace public housing subsidies; and the privatization of a whole host of public services, such as garbage collection, park maintenance, and prisons.[4]

School voucher initiatives were on the ballot in several states in November 1993, notably in California. Although they varied in content, their thrust was the same: give parents a voucher for an amount much less than the total cost per pupil in public schools and allow the voucher to be used in private schools as well as public schools willing to convert to "voucher schools." This, proponents claim, would give parents choices. It would introduce competition to the monopoly that public schools have on education. It would also improve education through such competition, increase efficiency, since private schools can deliver good education for less, and give the same ability to choose to low-income parents that is now implicitly available only to those with high incomes and able to afford good private education.

Although there is no evidence that private schools deliver good education for less, or that private education of good quality would be available to inner-city residents on even a moderate scale were vouchers made available, or that a large number of parents would transport their children to "better" private or public schools very far outside their neighborhoods, the argument has wide theoretical appeal to parents because public education has seemed to do so poorly in response to changing demographics, changing social conditions, and changing labor markets. Public education simply does not seem to be innovative in a world that is demanding more of teachers and administrators, and so is an easy target. Perhaps the most misleading claim by the voucher initiatives is that "marketizing" schooling alone will lead to improvements in educational delivery or will reduce poverty. Most educators well realize that a high proportion of private schools, even under much more favorable classroom conditions than exist in public schools, are not innovative. The proof of the pudding is that the performance of 48 percent of private school students is worse on nationwide NAEP tests than the public school median. And unfortunately, many of the more innovative approaches in public education nation-wide are little known even in the education community.[5]

However, the school voucher initiatives and the efforts to privatize other social programs are not really about improving public education or making services for the poor more efficient. They are about attacking the liberal notion that government can help make the country a better place, with the specific intention of delegitimizing the Democratic Party as the defender of that notion.

> Advocacy of school choice in this context is designed to demonstrate to voters of all income groups the qualitative difference between public schools and private and parochial schools, and to place the blame for those differences on the public-sector bureaucracies and unions now allied with the Democratic Party. . . . The ultimate goal of the conservative campaign is to persuade Americans that Democratic politicians behind an inefficient, recalcitrant bureaucratic state should be treated the same way that consumers would treat the proprietors of a badly-run business.[6]

Despite conservative claims that the poor are the most ardent backers of such initiatives, school vouchers, for example, have not received wide support from black or Latino organizations. The most vocal spokespeople for school vouchers are the same elite and upper middle class who have done particularly well in the free market and are the largest supporters of all measures that would reduce taxes or subsidize anything private. They are also least affected by the quality of public services since they rely on them much less than the poor. This leaves all of these initiatives open to counterattack from innovative proposals by public-service-oriented Democrats. The essence of these proposals has to be based on increasing the quality of public services at negligible cost.

Conservative ideological and organizational strength are not the only problems the new administration faces. It has also inherited a legacy of important divisions in its own party. President Clinton was elected with a "mandate" for change, but the election showed how potentially tenuous his base is. Clinton won the election because blacks, Latinos, and Anglo-Catholics and Jews gave him a high fraction of their votes. Anglo males gave George Bush a plurality and Anglo Protestant males gave him a fairly substantial plurality. And in electoral vote terms, if California's economic disaster and Perot's withdrawal in July had not given Clinton clear sailing in this fifty-four-electoral-vote state by early October, November's election would have been really close. Even among Clinton's plurality, there are strongly divided views on the kinds of programs Democrats should be pushing, divisions based largely on the traditional party constituencies – unions, blacks, and older New Deal liberals versus the "new alliance" of high-tech business people, younger professionals (especially women), and the white suburban middle class concerned about social disintegration, the environment, and a kinder, gentler America. The traditional Democratic base sees the need for expansionary economic policies to reduce unemployment, pro-labor regulatory legislation, an aggressive development strategy in urban areas, and increased and improved social spending for reducing poverty. The new alliance, such as it is, pushes increased trade, increased public investment, and efficiency in public intervention rather than expanded government intervention for reducing poverty.

THE CLINTON APPROACH

In this context, the new administration took one page out of George Bush's book and another from Franklin Roosevelt's. Bill Clinton tilted conservatively on economic growth policy but was New Dealish on the social aspects of economic policy and race. His economic package ended up relying on lower interest rates to achieve higher growth and increase good jobs, aiming to keep interest rates down and restore confidence in government by gradually reducing the budget deficit. This looked and behaved like a George Bush economic plan (with some key differences in tax policy), with the ironic result that Bush probably could not have gotten nearly as strong a deficit reduction package through Congress. Restoring confidence in government had a distinctly different purpose than it did in the Bush administration, but from a budget and jobs standpoint, both administrations tried to hold down government spending and employment.

In contrast, Clinton's approach to social policy and race is in the Roosevelt tradition. For Clinton, the issue of race is mainly an issue of *class*. This means that greater racial equality is to be achieved through steady economic growth and a redistribution of benefits from the rich to lower- and middle-income earners, primarily through tax and health care reform and by offering incentives to private business in key sectors (including inner cities) to create jobs. With greatly reduced spending freedom under deficit reduction, there may also be some public investment, especially in the form of training dislocated workers. The ideological component of this approach to racial inequality focuses on restoring faith in the public sector, on shifting welfare to workfare, on raising the discussion of *responsibility* in the black community, and on quietly (so quietly that after a full year in office, the administration had no director in place for the Civil Rights Division of the Justice Department) restoring more activist civil rights enforcement. Where is such a strategy likely to leave blacks in the 1990s?

The political effects of Clinton economics

The approach Clinton seemed to favor during the transition was to give the economy a shot in the arm with a stimulus package, reducing recessionary unemployment from the 7.5 percent of the late fall down to a 5.5 to 6.0 percent range (this would translate into about 2 million additional jobs), then pass an education/training legislative package combined with longer-term private investment stimuli and direct public investment in new technology (such as fast trains, electric cars, telecommunications, and environmental innovations) to ease the transition from a military economy (solving the medium-term problem) and to raise productivity and create faster job growth in the longer term. The Clinton health care reform would slow corporate America's fastest-growing component of costs, with a net positive effect on overall employment (even as health care jobs expanded in the medium run and then tapered off down the line). And the Clinton plan for the cities would create new kinds of employment and training for inner-city youth.

The approach was sound and, as a class approach to race, might have produced important changes consistent with the ways government can effectively intervene to raise black incomes relative to those of whites. It also could have held the Democratic Party together long enough to develop a new Democratic coalition. But from the outset, the president-elect responded more to the message of the financial community than to those who elected him. Financiers were far more concerned with the inflationary (long-term interest rate) effects of tighter labor markets and government spending than the positive employment/government revenue effects of stimulating the economy and increasing public investment in human resources. In their monetary model, which had been the mainstay of Bush's plan for recovery, the main stimulus to economic growth and employment would be lower long-term interest rates – that meant cutting the deficit first and raising public investment second. It also meant a longer, slower recovery. Clinton listened, naming Lloyd Bentsen as secretary of the treasury. His nomination was intended to calm bond markets, and it did. Long-term interest rates fell steadily in the first year of the administration. By inauguration day, an unsubtle change had taken place in the "Putting People First" program: Bill Clinton still believed in education, training, and other public investments as long-run solutions to the employment problem, but lower interest rates, not federal spending, had become the main vehicle to short- and medium-term job growth.

The new administration therefore gave up some important campaign promises early by proposing an already conservative budget package, at least in terms of spending and budget reduction. It then ended up giving away even more to conservative Democrats in the Senate. A macroeconomic policy with even some stimulus (through funding of infrastructure projects in the cities) would have increased growth more than a policy of just lowering interest rates. And holding back on the heavy brake applied by a sharp reduction in the federal deficit would have given the administration more leeway in expanding public investment.

Even so, the administration was able to keep its promised tax increases on very high income earners as part of the deficit reduction package, as well as an income tax credit for low-income taxpayers. This allowed for greater equity in the way post-tax income is distributed and implicitly – through more tax revenues – saved some social programs and made possible some expanded government investment. The income tax credit went far in helping low-income blacks (and all other low-income earners) by substantially raising their post-tax incomes (in some cases by several thousand dollars). The two tax measures were also the only equity elements (albeit important ones) that survived the budget struggle. Higher taxes were used mainly to cut the deficit rather than expand public investment or stimulate the economy in the short run. Beyond the earned income tax credit and making the rich rather than the middle class or the poor pay for deficit reduction, the Clinton budget was not favorable for blacks or the working class. Many congressional liberals had hoped for much more.

But the political fallout from the president's economic growth policy and budget strategy was much more negative. It revealed starkly that the president did not have control over his party and that the intraparty struggle that dominated the 1980s was far from resolved. In that atmosphere, blacks could only lose.

The struggle erupted over the North American Free Trade Agreement (NAFTA). Liberal Democrats in the House, burned on the budget, took their stand on NAFTA – an agreement of relatively little consequence for the economy in the short run, but one that had taken on enormous *political* significance in the slow recovery from the Bush recession. NAFTA seemed not only to threaten improvements in jobs for blacks and other low-income workers, but also to threaten further layoffs for skilled, unionized labor. Feeling excluded from the economic decision-making process in the White House, unions and other traditional Democrats took a high-stakes political stand on NAFTA. Despite all the rhetoric on both sides, the agreement itself became less an issue than the struggle for power and for ideological influence over economic policy.

During the campaign the unions agreed with Clinton's general argument that net domestic investment as generated by the free market during the 1980s was too low and that federal spending was highly concentrated in transfer payments and the military industry, both largely government consumption. If Clinton had taken on conservative Democratic opponents of that position in the Senate and had pushed harder for a stimulus with somewhat less deficit reduction, expanding trade through NAFTA would have seemed less troublesome to its primary opponents – the labor unions and other working-class groups, including blacks and Latinos. The traditional wing of the party could have been allowed to join in pushing the much more important parts of the Clinton program: crucial public investment in human resources, research and development, and infrastructure, such as improving roads, bridges, sewers, the nation's transportation system, environment, and telecommunications, all complementary to the expansion of private investment. As it was, the fight over economic policy leaves the party badly split – so split that the social policy agenda, crucial to economic improvement for blacks, will suffer.

Jobs and human capital

Despite the split among Democrats, racial inequality may still be reduced by administration-sponsored legislation on health care and education. Health care reform – the centerpiece of Bill Clinton's social (and long-term economic) policy – would give low- and middle-income working-class blacks a disproportionate increase in social benefits just because they comprise a disproportionate share of those not covered by some type of health insurance. Education reform could continue to improve black education more than white, as it has in the past twenty years, because increases in standards tend to lift the bottom of the distribution more than the middle or the top. Since the Clinton version of reform includes much more for Head Start and other early interventions, it would probably have an even greater impact on blacks than educational reform in the past. Bill Clinton can argue, with good reason, that the earned income tax credit plus health care reform plus educational reform may do more for blacks economically than any legislation since the Civil Rights Act – and will much more than offset any possible short-term negative effect from NAFTA.

Educational and modified health care reform legislation passed because they were ideologically the most well-defined pieces of the Clinton program (and probably the ones with the greatest consensus behind them). Although health care reform has a large equity component, both reforms made it through a conservative Senate mainly because they emphasized greater efficiency in delivering public services and raising productivity by improving human resources. Secretary of Labor Robert Reich argues in *The Work of Nations* that the main role of national states in the new global information economy is to create highly productive labor through high-quality educational and training systems. Healthy, trainable, and trained workers make private capital investment more productive, and hence attract it from all over the world. Recent growth models stress the primary role of "endogenous" technology – the result of qualified workers, technicians, scientists, and managers constantly innovating in the workplace and creating new knowledge that increases productivity.[7] Increasing the quality of the work force improves the possibility of developing new knowledge, which in turn increases productivity and growth.

The Clinton educational reform bills are the concrete expression of this philosophy. They propose *systemic* reform of the educational system, specifically raising enforceable high school standards that would increase what students have to know in order to graduate. Systemic reform also includes increasing preschool interventions, changing teacher training, and improving and enforcing changes in curricula all the way down to the primary grades. In other legislation, the administration will bring the college loan program back under direct control of the federal government. This will expand the amount of credit available to potential college students. The president proposed and Congress passed a largely symbolic public service program for college students that would enable them to fund a large portion of their college education by serving in the Police Corps or as teachers or in other public service capacities after graduation.

Another innovative part of the Clinton legislative package on education was the reform of vocational education, viewed as a major initiative in improving the transition of youth from school to work. This is the president's apprenticeship proposal, based in a vague way on the highly successful German dual-apprenticeship system, in which more than 60 percent of German youth enter apprenticeship programs in firms, which are paid for *by the firms,* while continuing to attend government vocational schools on a part-time basis and ultimately being state-certified as one type of skilled worker or another. The Clinton version is much more limited, aiming to induce more non-college-bound youth into career programs in high school, to keep them in school for at least one year beyond high school, and to provide them with job training in firms as they continue in school. The hope is that this will make them much more employable, more certifiably skilled, and more productive than under the present system.

Vocational educational reform is a valuable initiative, and in the best-scenario case it will induce states to propose realistic plans of integrating non-college-bound students into the workplace. As the reform is implemented, it should produce a new structure within the existing secondary/community college/postsecondary training system that would reduce the number of high school dropouts, increase career job access to reasonably well paying jobs, and promote employer–school cooperation. It could potentially reduce racial inequality.

However, the initiative's potential success could be severely constrained by the job market. States and local communities can build career programs, but the success of those programs depends on the existence and growth of good jobs with good wages and further training opportunities.[8] A better-educated work force will "create" better jobs only over the long haul, and the response by employers in the long haul is conditioned by other factors, such as the direct influence of rapid deficit reduction and the indirect influence of slow world economic growth on U.S. economic growth. Even the more successful school-to-work transition systems, as in Germany, are running into serious trouble in today's labor markets, for two reasons: more and more high school students want to go to universities, not into apprenticeship programs for skilled jobs, and only a few of the apprenticeship programs, such as in electronics, offer good job opportunities. These programs are filled by the better of the non-university-bound students, and the rest offer careers with much less promise.

The reform of vocational education could suffer because the large-scale spending needed for both public and private sides of the equation will not be forthcoming: on the public side, the most important part of the proposal is the tie between the high school career programs and postsecondary institutions. Apprenticeship programs have the best chance to succeed at the postsecondary level, where they at least already exist in some places. This means that, to work on a large scale, the apprenticeship portion of the initiative must be essentially a postsecondary program. As everyone who has worked on this legislation realizes, preparing youth for high-skill jobs and moving them into jobs through apprenticeships will take more than just getting them to finish high school.[9] This makes the costs much higher than the states can currently afford and is far different from the high school dropout antidote program the president envisions. On the private side, the program will ultimately depend on employers' willingness to hire youth as apprentices. This, in turn, means that employers not only will have to be hooked into the career programs in high schools and community colleges but will also have to be willing to allocate resources to employing and training young people in their firms on a large scale. German firms spent $50 billion on apprenticeships in 1990, an amount almost as large as the entire $60 billion public budget for all levels of education (including university).[10] Compare this with the estimates of the American Society for Training and Development according to which private employers in the United

States spend slightly more than $30 billion a year on *all* training (most of it going to management training) for a labor force more than three times as large as Germany's.[11] Without incentives for employers to increase training and without other incentives and direct public investment to increase employment possibilities (especially investment in the inner cities), the transition from school to work programs could fall on its face. Nor would such programs do much for one group that really needs them to work – inner-city black youth.

Avoiding race

On the ideological side, the Clinton administration has decided to focus on an efficiency approach to the public sector, an approach that includes Vice-President Gore's report on "reinventing government" and the proposals to improve health and education through "systemic reform." It attempts to meet the challenge of making the public sector more efficient in delivering services to everyone, including the poor, and of giving Americans a reason to have more confidence in Democrats as efficient managers of public funds. The approach represents at least some confrontation with conservative ideology at all levels of society and should be recognized as such. To the degree that the legislation involves popular support, it is also helping to build a new Democratic coalition around good public-service delivery by public–private partnerships.

An ideological approach to inequality based on efficiency and investment in human capital has a decided *class* bent, designed to bring white working-class voters back into the Democratic fold, while trying to give enough social and economic benefits to blacks (as predominantly working-class Americans) that they stick it out with the president politically over the long haul. It represents a careful approach to the race/poverty issue, perhaps necessary for the times. As former governor of a conservative southern state who lost an election in 1980 by not paying attention to the potential pitfalls a liberal faces in a conservative climate, President Clinton is sensitive (some say too sensitive) to the need to cover bases and to keep race out of the headlines.

But there is danger in pursuing too careful a policy on race. The administration has convinced many that "careful avoidance" is not just tactical, but based on a belief that race is not an issue in the 1990s. The embarrassments the administration suffered in appointing an assistant attorney general for civil rights during its first year in office show the

difficulties of that strategy. The president had initially appointed an intelligent, articulate black lawyer, Lani Guinier, who had written extensively about voting rights and had served in Jimmy Carter's administration. Guinier was supported by a broad spectrum of the black community. But conservatives discovered that she had taken a "controversial" position on electoral representation, one that would have guaranteed blacks (and other minorities) proportional representation in areas where blacks (and other minorities) lived. To some extent, this might also have increased the number of Republican seats in Congress. She quickly became too "radical" for the Clinton administration, anxious to avoid any unnecessary confrontation with the Senate during the crucial budget battle. He asked her to withdraw her nomination, and she did. That was in April 1993. Guinier's replacement, John Payton, faced the opposite problem: although a highly regarded Washington attorney and the counsel for the District of Columbia, in hearings before the Congressional Black Caucus in November, he was found to have no experience with legal aspects of voting rights and admitted to not voting in Washington, D.C., elections. He withdrew his name from nomination. It was not until the spring of 1994 that the post was finally filled by a well-respected Boston lawyer, Duval Patrick.

This is not to say that a class approach to race cannot work to make blacks better off economically and socially than they have been under Republican administrations. The delivery of after-tax income (through a tax credit), health care, and better education to working blacks and their children may even reduce racial inequality by enabling them to consume more. But it still does not solve the problems of wage discrimination and the lack of decent-paying jobs and upward mobility for those same people. It does not overcome the disintegration of the inner city, or reduce the job discrimination and financial and educational difficulties faced by young blacks getting college educations. It falls far short of even a moderately aggressive use of federal agencies to reduce discrimination by enforcing civil rights legislation and of the kind of ideological reconstruction needed to push the electorate toward resolving racial inequality. It still consciously avoids putting the race issue explicitly on the table through either a return to solid enforcement of civil rights legislation or a thorough discussion of what must be done to begin rebuilding family and community in inner cities. Hence, it not only avoids dealing with solutions to racial inequality, but runs the real risk of failing even to address

that (class) part of racial inequality associated with the disproportionate number of working blacks in lower-income groups.

The approach also risks degenerating into the conservative tactic of limiting race policy to anticrime legislation. It is all well and good to identify serious problems in the inner city, propose tough measures to fight crime, drugs, and the killing of youth by youth in shootouts, and ask blacks to take more responsibility for their own families and communities. President Clinton began to seize the initiative on moral rebuilding in the black family and community in his Memphis speech to black leaders in November 1993. Ideological leadership on family and community values is important. But if this is not balanced with a coherent discussion of discrimination, the decline of cities as economic centers, and the social problems associated with the physical and economic separation of the races, the race issue will continue to be reduced to one of overcoming black "failure." The social outcomes of that political strategy are all too well known – more blacks (and Latinos) in prison, even less social cohesion in minority families and communities, and further urban decline.

Most important, making race a class issue does not create the social and ideological conditions in which blacks and whites will work with and for each other to produce more at work and build a more stable community at home. And as long as the white working class can be easily wooed away by the race specter from its support for the Democratic agenda, Democrats will have few occupants in the White House. In that important sense, the current mix of policies not only does not meet the criteria spelled out in this book for a successful sustained attack on racial inequality, but is bad party politics. To correct both problems, a different strategy is needed.

TOWARD A MORE COHERENT STRATEGY ON RACE

What happens in Washington is largely a result of ideological battle – a struggle for the hearts and minds of the American public, a war of perceptions. Ronald Reagan came to Washington as a radical reformer at the far conservative end of the political spectrum, yet played public sentiment well and convinced the Democratic Congress that he had the public behind him. Reagan knew about ideology and was crystal clear about its use in governing. He chose his political battles carefully and through them solidified his ideological conception of the nation's future. Bill Clinton's ideology as it emerged in the campaign is much more centrist than Reagan's and much more logical given what the United States faces in this generation and the next. Government and the private sector must be in partnership, and the wealthy will have to bear their fair share of solving the(ir) excesses of the 1980s. American society is headed for some form of multiculturalism – it can be either on a road rife with conflict and negative implications for productivity and social safety, or, as the new president spelled it out in his inaugural speech, on a road of creative partnership among various ethnic groups, the stuff of American mythology. But for the president to get the public behind this conception and to pull Congress his way, he must put together a string of victories that as much build a *systematic ideological base* as push through a series of economic packages. This means carefully picking fights that establish what his administration stands for and carrying each fight to its logical end. He may lose some of these, but even the losing issues have to make an ideological point, make it well, and make his opponents look bad.

In retrospect, Lani Guinier's appearance in front of the Senate Judiciary Committee (the same committee that did in Anita Hill) could have been a perfect opportunity to make conservatives in Congress look like unreasonable mudslingers – could have made it clear that Clinton knew how to use an eloquent, politically sophisticated black woman to do his political infighting. No matter that Clinton did not agree with some of her writings. It was too late for that kind of intellectual subtlety. Her presence on television after her withdrawal showed that she would have made a strong case for civil rights and could well have won confirmation, scoring for African-Americans and for the administration. By withdrawing her appointment, Clinton hoped to win favor with the Senate so that it would pass his economic package, including the BTU tax. Instead, he sent a clear signal to both friends and enemies: the ideological high ground was still held by Reagan conservatives, and they could make the president look weak and ineffectual.

This does not bode well for the rest of the Clinton program, or for the Democratic Party. Democrats will not do well in the 1990s unless they are able to develop a popular ideological vision and make it the everyday currency of public discourse. Step by step, speech by speech, act by act, party leaders have to change America's conception of the problem and the solution. That implies being very creative politically in achieving greater income equality, in treating crime as a social and economic problem, in fighting special interests (such as the oil, gun, insurance, and tobacco lobbies), and in investing public funds in children and young people – all the antitheses of the conservative agenda. Shifting ideological ground allows the more mundane but just as important pieces of social reform legislation to emerge from Congress in a form that helps those who are now least able to find success in the marketplace. If the president does not do ideological battle around legislation and appointments – ideological battle specifically intended to shift the political ground under the conservatives (including those in his own party) – Democrats should be pessimistic about their chances for reshaping politics in the 1990s. African-Americans should be just as pessimistic about their chances for greater economic equality.

For both Democrats and blacks to be winners in the 1990s, the ideological discourse has to include race. This may be counterintuitive to current political thinking in all but a few factions of the Democratic Party. But it is the only way to move Democrats to new, out-front approaches to racial inequality that both uncover the misthinking of most conservative egalitarianism and deal honestly with the present reality of black life and black–white relations in the United States.

Such a discourse could also move the *problem* of racial inequality beyond equity in and of itself to a broader framework that links inequality to economic efficiency and growth. This link has two segments: First, America needs a coherent set of national policies in order to be competitive in the new global information economy. Coherence requires commonality of purpose; and commonality of purpose requires creating a sense of social and economic fairness. Second, the cost of maintaining social peace and social health has risen so rapidly that it now makes more sense than ever to reduce inequality in the resources invested in children in order to avoid the much higher spending on alienated, unhealthy, unproductive adults. A crucial part of such a strategy would be a new public policy focus on the crucial role of family and community values, initiated by the president in Memphis in November 1993. Government can be important in supporting such values, if people trust it to do so.

In an age when coherent *sustainable* national policies are needed to compete with other nations' coherent economic policies, the Reagan–Bush strategy systematically destroyed confidence in government and reduced its efficiency. The federal government became an institution to be picked on and picked over. No wonder that developing a sustainable national economic policy to deal with the challenges of the new competitive world was impossible in that environment. On the contrary, the selfishness of the "me decade" exacerbated a hostility to and distrust of government policies brewing since the mid-1970s and fostered increased competition among individuals and groups at the low-income end for dwindling tax dollars. It had effects beyond the federal government, at the state and local levels, and even in communities, universities, and schools. Cooperation and a sense of social responsibility were sacrificed on the altar of individual achievement. The Reagan–Bush strategy is analogous to a private company that focuses so hard on making short-term profit by exploiting existing resources and pitting workers against one another that it reduces the productivity of its workers and loses the long-run competition.

The 1990s present the challenge of restoring confidence in the efficiency and fairness of the government, and that means, among other things, restoring the process of reducing economic inequality between blacks and whites. Such confidence is needed to develop the kind of coherent domestic economic policy that will lead to long-term increases in worker productivity and higher levels of investment and savings – the fundamental elements of strong competition in the present global economic environment.

A different kind of strategy is needed – one that emphasizes cooperation, working together for common goals, and increasing individual worker and citizen security in return for higher productivity. This is the work-management model that has performed so well for companies such as Hewlett-Packard, for the Toyota–GM joint venture in Fremont, California, and for worker-owned firms such as Weirton Steel. Significant, sustained movement toward greater economic equality among racial and ethnic groups is needed to build this cooperation and the economic coherence that it would eventually produce.

Beyond restoring faith in government, a major problem facing all national governments in highly industrialized countries is the increasing cost of not allowing some groups to participate fully in the mainstream economy. The high social costs of poverty are an enormous drag on society. Even if much of the crime and social disintegration is compartmentalized in the ghettos of large cities, they have an impact on the lives of the middle class. The fastest-growing budget item in most states is spending on prisons. But the social cost of poverty is only partly borne by government. The middle class is a "hostage to worry" about crime, and spends more and more each year on guns, self-defense courses, and other paraphernalia related to warding off assailants.[12] Although the fear may be greater than the actual probability of assault, rape, robbery, or homicide, its cost to individuals is real. Furthermore, the "public's growing fear of crime is coming amid cutbacks in many police forces and the sense that the police may not be around when needed."[13] Indeed, only a small percentage of criminals is caught. All this means that whatever the costs of increasing crime, they are being privatized, and they are rising.

The rising social costs of poverty should be a convincing argument for the need to reduce racial inequality. About one-fourth of all the poor are black. If black and white men with the same education earned the same wages and experienced the same levels of unemployment, some of this poverty would be eliminated directly. But the indirect effect of eliminating discrimination on black families' poverty could be much larger, since at least some black men would be willing and able to head black families now headed by black women.[14] Reducing poverty then would have an even greater secondary impact, since children would grow up in better material conditions. Their performance in school would improve, they would go farther in school, would be more likely to get decent jobs, and would move out of poverty altogether.

By reducing what government ends up spending on the poor later in their lives, a strategy that aims at reducing poverty and improving the health and educational conditions of early childhood becomes an investment in greater national economic efficiency. The vicious circle of increasing social costs will gradually break. Down the road, as early-childhood investment reduces spending on adult social problems, more public funds will become available for general education and other activities that improve worker productivity and growth rates. And those funds will be used more efficiently because black and brown children from families with better education, more skills, and higher income will be easier to teach.

A strategy that hopes to win over the American electorate cannot politically take on either the issue of restoring faith in government or that of reducing crime and social disintegration without confronting race. But if addressed in a creative, honest way, greater equality can be a winning issue. It can translate into gains for whites and blacks and provide an ideological vision of the United States that is meaningful for both groups.

This vision was tested in the 1992 presidential campaign and it worked. All the campaign lacked was an honest, explicit discussion of race – an understandable omission in a come-from-behind victory. Yet now it is time to make up for that omission and move on to reshaping society. Any other strategy will be a losing one. It will leave the nation inexorably divided at a time when it must come together – at a time when technological change and corporate restructuring are not enough to achieve economic progress.

Appendix A

The analysis of inequality among gender/ethnic groups was based on a postulated earnings function for each group, in which annual income depends on industry and location of work, personal characteristics (civil status), and human capital characteristics (education and work experience), such that

$$\ln Y = \mu + b_1 I + b_2 P + b_3 R + b_4 M + b_5 L + b_6 IM + b_7 S + b_8 AT + b_9 \ln W + b_{10} \ln H + \epsilon \quad (1)$$

where Y = annual wage earnings and self-employment income,
I = a vector of dummy variables indicating industrial sector,
P = a binary variable indicating public-/private-sector employment,
R = a vector of dummy variables indicating geographic regions of residence,
M = a vector of dummy variables indicating marital status,
L = a vector of dummy variables indicating labor market experience,
IM = a binary variable indicating native- or foreign-born,
S = a vector of dummy variables indicating level of schooling,
AT = a binary variable indicating whether the individual is still attending school,
W = the number of weeks employed during the preceding year,
H = the number of hours per week employed during the preceding year,
μ = the intercept term,
$b_1 \ldots b_{10}$ = the coefficients or vectors of coefficients of the variables,
ϵ = the error term.

For each year, five regression models were estimated as subsets of the full-income model in equation (1). These models were then used as the basis for simulations to find the "attributes" effect (given the white male payoff [coefficient] of each attribute, what is the impact of the gap in attribute x associated with each ethnic/gender group compared with white males?) and the "price" effect (given white male attributes, what is the impact of the difference in payoff [coefficient] of attributes between each group and white males?). The five models can be represented as follows:

1. A human-capital equation in which log earnings is regressed on labor market experience and education:

$$\ln Y = \mu + b_5 L + b_6 IM + b_7 S + b_8 AT + \epsilon_1$$

2. A human-capital equation with time worked included:

$$\ln Y = \mu + b_5 L + b_6 IM + b_7 S + b_8 AT + b_9 \ln W + b_{10} + \epsilon_2$$

3. A "structure" equation in which log earnings is regressed on industrial sector, public employment, marital status, and region:

$$\ln Y = \mu + b_1 + b_2 P + b_3 R + b_4 M + \epsilon_3$$

4. A "structure" equation with time worked included:

$$\ln Y = \mu + b_1 I + b_2 P + b_3 R + b_4 M + b_9 \ln W + b_{10} \ln H + \epsilon_4$$

5. A combined-factors equation where log earnings is regressed on human capital and structure factor together, including time worked:

$$\ln Y = \mu + b_1 I + b_2 P + b_3 R + b_4 M + b_5 L + b_6 IM + b_7 S + b_8 AT + b_9 \ln W + b_{10} \ln H + \epsilon_5$$

The simulation model used to obtain the effect on relative black and Latino incomes of attribute differences between blacks and whites and Latinos and whites is represented in the following three ratios obtained from using the regression estimates of log income for each group, substituting, for example, white attributes in the regression equation for black incomes, and black attributes in the regression equation for white incomes. The three ratios are obtained in the case of each of the five equations above.

$$R_k = \frac{V_k Q_k}{V_r Q_r} = \left(\frac{\sum_{i=1}^{n} \mu + \sum_{j=1}^{m} b_{jk} x_{ijk}}{n}\right) - \left(\frac{\sum_{i=1}^{n} \mu + \sum_{j=1}^{m} b_{jr} x_{ijr}}{n}\right)$$

$$P_k = \frac{V_k Q_r}{V_r Q_r} + \left(\frac{\sum_{i=1}^{n} \mu + \sum_{j=1}^{m} b_{jk} x_{ijr}}{n}\right) - \left(\frac{\sum_{i=1}^{n} \mu + \sum_{j=1}^{m} b_{jr} x_{ijr}}{n}\right) \quad (2)$$

$$C_k = \frac{V_r Q_k}{V_r Q_r} = \left(\frac{\sum_{i=1}^{n} \mu + \sum_{j=1}^{m} b_{jr} x_{ijk}}{n}\right) - \left(\frac{\sum_{i=1}^{n} \mu + \sum_{j=1}^{m} b_{jr} x_{ijr}}{n}\right)$$

where R_k = the ratio of the estimate of group *k*'s log income to the estimate of the white male (*r*) log income;

V = the value of the group's attributes;

Q = the quantity of the group's attributes;

P_k = the "price effect" for group *k* – that is, the effect of the lower "value" of group *k*'s education, work experience, and structure variables and of time worked on group *k*'s income relative to white males' values for the same set of white male attributes;

C_k = the "attribute effect" for group *k* – that is, the effect of group *k*'s lower amount of education, experience, and time worked and "lower" structure attributes on group *k*'s income relative to white male attributes, given the white male "value" of these attributes;

b_{jk} = the estimated regression coefficient of the *j*th variable in the estimated regression equation for group *k*;

x_{ijk} = the value of variable *j* for individual *i* in group *k*.

Appendix B

The two matrices in this appendix specify the typology we developed for analyzing the changing job structure in the United States in the past thirty years. Jobs are divided into three types: low-paying (Job I), middle-paying (Job II), and high-paying (Job III). This three-way division enables us to chart changes in the number of new jobs created as well as changes in the "quality" of jobs (as measured by the wages they command) by ethnic group and gender.

The division into job types I, II, and III is based on an analysis of average incomes in various industry/occupation categories. There is wide variation within categories, but in general what is defined here as a low-paying, middle-paying, or high-paying industry/occupation is characterized by low, medium, or high mean relative incomes, respectively.

Occupations are defined as regular census occupations. Industries are defined as regular census industrial classifications except for the division of manufacturing into three categories – high-tech manufacturing, which includes three-digit industrial classifications (180, 181, 321, 322, 371, 372, and 341), defense manufacturing (three-digit classifications 292, 352, 362), and traditional manufacturing, which includes all other three-digit classifications 100–392 and the division of services into two categories – high services (three-digit categories 700–12, 721, 730, 732, 740, 742, 812–61, and 872–92) and low services (722, 731, 741, 750–802, and 862–71).

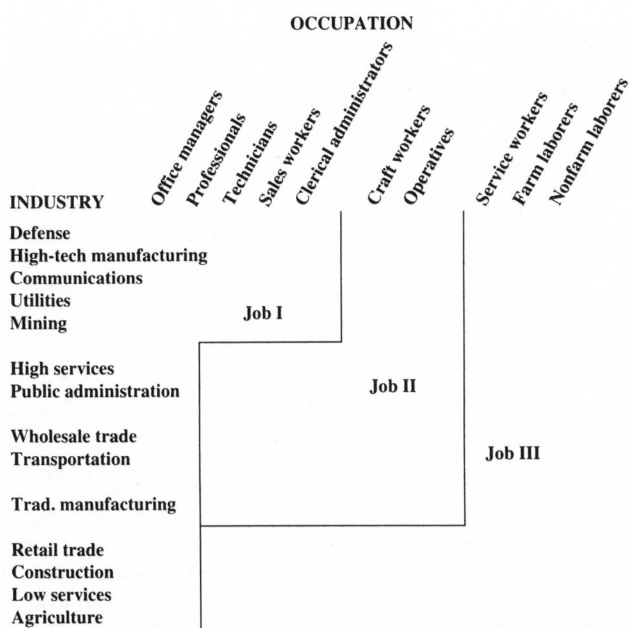

Matrix A.1 (men).

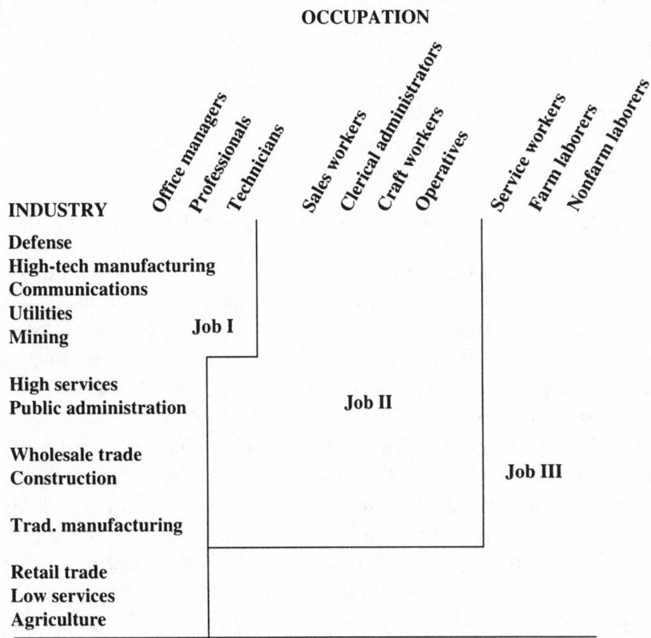

Matrix A.2 (women).

Notes

1. Introduction

1 See Nicholas Lemann's compelling account of this relationship in *The Promised Land* (New York: Knopf, 1991).
2 See Taylor Branch, *Parting the Waters* (New York: Simon & Schuster, 1988).
3 Although Nobel Prize–winning economist Gary Becker argued that discrimination could exist in markets because of white worker "tastes" for racial division of labor, Becker's analysis just adds a second structural condition to which markets quickly adjust: "worker tastes." For racial inequality to change, white worker tastes for inequality would have to change in addition to black versus white educational and experience characteristics. How do worker tastes change? Economists have little to say about this issue, but Becker and others would argue that government intervention would not generally reduce the taste for racial separation. See Gary Becker, *The Economics of Discrimination* (Chicago: University of Chicago Press, 1957).

2. The ups and downs of African-American fortunes

1 These gains and even later stagnation in black male incomes relative to those of whites may well be biased upward because of declining black male labor force participation rates relative to white rates, especially in the 1960s, and the usual exemption of black poor from census statistics. This bias has been discussed in a number of articles, among them William A. Darity, "Illusions of Black Economic Progress," *Review of Black Political Economy* (Winter 1980): 153–68; Charles Brown, "Black–White Earnings Ratios Since the Civil Rights Act of 1964: The Importance of Labor Market Dropouts," *Quarterly Journal of Economics,* 99, no. 1 (1984): 31–44; and James J. Heckman, "The Impact of Government on the Economic Status of Black Americans," in Steven Shulman and William Darity, Jr. (eds.), *The Question of Discrimination* (Middletown, Conn.: Wesleyan University Press, 1989), pp. 50–80.
2 The equalization slowdown in the 1950s began toward the end of the Korean War. Ironically (or coincidentally), the Supreme Court's decision in

Brown v. Board of Education, mandating equal access for blacks to public resources, occurred at about the same time. The impact of *Brown* is discussed in Chapter 7.

3 The existence of a high percentage of low-income blacks and Latinos makes it much more likely that a minority middle-class family would have low-income extended family members and therefore additional claims.

4 Bennett Harrison and Barry Bluestone, *The Great U-Turn* (New York: Basic Books, 1988).

5 Estimated changes in household income inequality are heavily influenced by the pattern of male income growth in the 1970s and 1980s and the *measure* used for income inequality. For example, males with lower incomes did badly in the late 1970s and early 1980s and slowly gained on males with middle incomes at the end of the 1980s as the labor market gradually became tighter. On the other hand, males in the highest income category held their own in the late 1970s, but made huge gains compared with everyone else in the 1980s expansion (1982–9). Thus, the measure of income inequality used in Figure 2.6 – the Gini coefficient – which compares the proportion of income earners with the cumulative proportion of total income earned and weighs changes at the high income end more than at the low end, shows increases in income inequality primarily during the 1982–9 expansion (see also, e.g., Frank Levy and Richard Murnane, "U.S. Earnings Levels and Earnings Inequality: A Review of Recent Trends and Proposed Explanations," *Journal of Economic Literature,* 30 [September 1992]: 1333–81). Another common measure, the log variance of income, however, gives more weight to changes at the lower end of the distribution. Income distribution measured by the log variance became much more unequal in the period of income decline at the low end (late 1970s) and less so in the 1980s expansion (see, e.g., Martin Carnoy, Hugh Daley, and Raul Hinojosa, *Latinos in a Changing U.S. Economy* [New York: Hunter College, Inter-University Program, Puerto Rican Center, 1990]).

6 The Gini coefficient puts higher weight on changes in incomes at the high end than at the low end. The results reported here are consistent with those of other studies. See Levy and Murnane, "U.S. Earnings Levels and Earnings Inequality."

7 The mean income of the top 20 percent of black families was 68 percent of the mean income of the top 20 percent of white families in 1979; in 1985, the figure was still 68 percent; in 1988, 69 percent; and in 1989, 67 percent. For the top 5 percent of black and white family incomes, the proportion was 63 percent in 1979, 65 percent in 1985, and 61 percent in 1989.

8 See Barbara Bergmann, *The Economic Emergence of Women* (New York: Basic Books, 1986); Barbara Reskin (ed.), *Sex Segregation in the Workplace: Trends, Explanations, Remedies* (Washington, D.C.: National Academy Press, 1984).

9 In the past, Latinas were much more likely to work in manufacturing than either blacks or whites. They were the Mexican cannery workers and the Puerto Rican women who labored in New York's factories. Like black women, they were domestics, waitresses, and kitchen workers, but by the

1960s these were atypical jobs for Latina workers (only 11 percent were employed in low-end services compared with 43 percent of blacks). Historically, Latinas – particularly Mexicanas – have had lower education than both black and white women; yet with the same level of education, they earned about the same pay as white women. So Latinas have had to face pay discrimination not as Latinas but as women.

10 Gerald Jaynes and Robin M. Williams, Jr. (eds.), *A Common Destiny* (Washington, D.C.: National Academy of Sciences, 1989), p. 314.

11 Although the data for Puerto Ricans are not divided in this way, it is evident from the high percentage of female-head-of-household, no-husband-present Puerto Rican families that, as with blacks, an important explanation for Puerto Rican poverty lies in family patterns. For Mexican-origin Latinos, in contrast, most poverty exists in two-parent families with low incomes.

12 The percentage of the Latino poor living in female-headed households, no husband present, has remained remarkably stable at 38 percent since the early 1970s.

13 See William Julius Wilson, *The Truly Disadvantaged* (Chicago: University of Chicago Press, 1987), chap. 3.

14 The corresponding figures for Cuban-origin Latinos (77 percent) and those for Central and South Americans (69 percent) are close to the Mexican average. Puerto Ricans are therefore a prominent outlier.

3. *The politics of explaining racial inequality*

1 These are not the only explanations: among others, a lack of adequate black intellectual and business role models for black youth to emulate and a lack of sufficient capital in the black community to make it more "self-sufficient."

2 See the *New York Times*, May 8, 1992.

3 See Arthur Jensen, *Educability and Group Differences* (New York: Harper & Row, 1973).

4 Thomas Sowell, *Race and Economics* (New York: David McKay, 1975); Sowell, *Markets and Minorities* (New York: Basic Books, 1981); Sowell, *The Economics and Politics of Race* (New York: Morrow, 1983).

5 The conservatives' position on school vouchers is typical of this wider anti-government stance and its link, in this case, to blacks' poor performance in school. Authors from Milton Friedman (with Rose Friedman in *Free to Choose: A Personal Statement* [New York: Harcourt Brace Jovanovich, 1980]) to John Chubb and Terry Moe (in *Politics, Markets, and America's Schools* [Washington, D.C.: The Brookings Institution, 1990]) explicitly contend that poorly performing (minority) students do better in privately managed education. In Chubb and Moe's terms, the efforts of the public sector to democratize schooling create a huge, ineffectual bureaucracy that hurts the chances of the very-low-income students it purports to be helping.

6 James Smith and Finis Welch, "Black Economic Progress after Myrdal," *Journal of Economic Literature*, 27 (June 1989): 519–64. For a direct re-

sponse to this view, see David Kiefer and Peter Philips, "Race and Human Capital: An Institutionalist Response," in Garth Magnum and Peter Philips (eds.), *Three Worlds of Labor Economics* (Armonk, NY: Sharpe, 1988), pp. 117–43. Kiefer and Philips contend that the major gains in blacks' relative earnings in the twentieth century were partly, if not largely, due to changes in the kinds of jobs available to them, not necessarily to the quantity or quality of education. They argue that the growth of urban industrial jobs was independent of reductions in the black–white education gap.

7 David Card and Alan B. Krueger, "School Quality and Black/White Relative Earnings: A Direct Assessment," *Quarterly Journal of Economics*, 107, no. 1 (February 1992): 151–200.

8 There are many problems with relating test scores to productivity, not least of which is the difficulty of measuring productivity. I discuss this at length in Chapter 4.

9 Kiefer and Philips, "Race and Human Capital," p. 118.

10 Thomas Sowell claims that "the past is a great unchangeable fact. Nothing is going to undo its sufferings and injustices, whatever their magnitude." See his "Are Quotas Good for Blacks?" *Commentary*, June 1978, p. 42.

11 See, e.g., Daniel Patrick Moynihan, "The Professors and the Poor," *On Understanding Poverty* (New York: Basic Books, 1969). Moynihan's writings provide plenty of ammunition for those who feel that earlier liberal intervention in the ghetto was wrongheaded. Moynihan argued that "no Negro was involved in any significant way" in planning the major antipoverty legislation of the 1960s – the Economic Opportunity Act of 1964 (pp. 14–15). In contrast, earlier and later antipoverty legislation, namely Social Security, Medicare, and Medicaid, all involving older Americans, was heavily influenced by organizations representing seniors. Since civil rights organizations had always focused public policy on discrimination and inequality – on structural barriers to equal treatment in the labor market – Moynihan reasoned that had blacks, Latinos, or low-income whites been involved in shaping the Economic Opportunity Act, they would have undoubtedly put more emphasis on good adult jobs and less on welfare and food stamps. Far from helping the poor do better economically, white intellectuals who ultimately influenced the War on Poverty created "a welfare bureaucracy . . . who sought to bring political activism and, in effect, discontent to the poor of the land, including, most visibly, the black poor of the decayed central cities of the North and West" (ibid., p. 16).

12 Daniel P. Moynihan, *The Negro Family: The Case for National Action* (Washington, D.C.: Department of Labor, March 1965).

13 Charles Murray, *Losing Ground* (New York: Basic Books, 1984).

14 Shelby Steele, *The Content of Our Character* (New York: St. Martin's Press, 1990), pp. 101, 107–8.

15 See ibid., p. 80.

16 The argument is directly opposite to the explicit ideology of civil rights organizations as defined by black and Latino leaders since at least the 1930s.

According to that ideology, the condition of minorities was the result of discriminatory low wages and lack of opportunity rooted in the "structure" of American society, not the result of minorities' culture or inherent lack of capability. However, it now seems to be shifting toward a more "realistic" view of the culture of poverty.

Liberals in the 1960s had, in fact, assumed that poor communities had to be organized at the base in order for the individuals living in them to be transformed. Policy focused on political-social organizing in poor urban communities to change their underlying conditions, and hence the conditions of poor individuals.

The individual-responsibility view rejects both characterizations, arguing that allowing market signals to govern choice and forcing (by eliminating welfare) the poor to accept market rules would produce the greatest likelihood of upward mobility.

17 Gunnar Myrdal, *An American Dilemma* (New York: Pantheon, 1944).

18 *Report of the National Advisory Commission on Civil Disorders* (New York: Bantam Books, 1968).

19 Becker, *The Economics of Discrimination.* Becker's analysis remained the benchmark well into the 1970s for economists studying discrimination, although many disagreed with it. See, e.g., Kenneth Arrow, "Models of Job Discrimination," in Anthony H. Pascal (ed.), *Racial Discrimination in Economic Life* (Lexington, Mass.: Lexington Books, 1972), pp. 83–102, and Orley Ashenfelter and Albert Rees (eds.), *Discrimination in Labor Markets* (Princeton, N.J.: Princeton University Press, 1973).

20 Michael Reich, *Racial Inequality* (Princeton, N.J.: Princeton University Press, 1982).

21 Charles Lawrence, "The Id, the Ego and Equal Protection: Reckoning with Unconscious Racism," *Stanford Law Review* 39 (1987): 317, 330. Quoted in Derrick Bell, *And We Are Not Saved* (New York: Basic Books, 1987), pp. 4–5.

22 See Bell, *And We Are Not Saved.*

23 Andrew Hacker, *Two Nations: Black and White, Separate, Hostile, Unequal* (New York: Ballantine Books, 1992), p. 29.

24 Reich, *Racial Inequality.* See also Michael Reich, "Postwar Racial Income Differences: Trends and Theories," in Magnum and Philips (eds.), *Three Worlds of Labor Economics.* Reich writes: "The improvement in the relative position of black men in the 1960s was not just the product of high rates of economic growth as James Tobin argued at the time. It was also directly connected to the sociopolitical movements pressuring for change in that decade. These movements did not succeed in creating a nonzero-sum game based on class rather than race conflict. As a result, little was left of these movements by the early 1970s" (p. 163).

25 William Julius Wilson, *The Declining Significance of Race: Blacks and Changing American Institutions* (Chicago: University of Chicago Press, 1978). Wilson upheld this notion in later works.

26 Wilson, *The Truly Disadvantaged.*
27 Barry Bluestone and Bennett Harrison, *The Deindustrialization of America* (New York: Basic Books, 1982).
28 Robert Reich, *The Work of Nations* (New York: Vintage Books, 1992), pp. 208–19.
29 Wilson, *The Truly Disadvantaged,* pp. 148, 150.
30 Ibid., p. 150.
31 See also David Ellwood, *Poor Support* (New York: Basic Books, 1988).
32 H. Edward Ransford, *Race and Class in American Society* (Cambridge, Mass.: Schenkman, 1977).
33 Ibid. The original conceptualization of class within caste is attributed to W. Lloyd Warner in Allison Davis, Burleigh Gardner, and Mary Gardner, *Deep South: A Social-Anthropological Study of Caste and Class* (Chicago: University of Chicago Press, 1941).
34 Michael Reich, "Postwar Racial Income Differences," p. 160.
35 Nicos Poulantzas, *Classes in Contemporary Capitalism* (London: New Left Books, 1975).
36 See Martin Carnoy, *The State and Political Theory* (Princeton, N.J.: Princeton University Press, 1984). See also Albert Hirschman, *The Passions and the Interests* (Princeton, N.J.: Princeton University Press, 1977).
37 See Christopher Jencks et al., *Inequality* (New York: Basic Books, 1978); Carnoy and Levin, *Schooling and Work in a Democratic State.*
38 David Gordon, Richard Edwards, and Michael Reich, *Segmented Work: Divided Workers* (New York: Cambridge University Press, 1982). Gordon, Edwards, and Reich call the institutional environment that surrounds the accumulation process the "social structure of accumulation." Their argument is that this environment is developed through conflicts between social movements (especially the labor movement) and employers that produce government coalitions which formalize new institutions governing employer–labor relations. It is these employer–labor relations that have the major impact on income inequality generally and racial inequality specifically.
39 Derek Bok, *The Cost of Talent* (New York: The Free Press, 1993), pp. 101–2; see also Graef S. Crystal, *In Search of Excess* (New York: Norton, 1991), and Steve Lohr, "Recession Puts a Harsh Spotlight on Hefty Pay of Top Executives," *New York Times,* January 20, 1992.
40 Reich, *The Work of Nations.*
41 Harrison and Bluestone, *The Great U-Turn.*
42 They also suggest that the distance between the minority middle class and the minority poor may have stopped widening by the mid-1980s, especially among younger minorities.
43 Samuel Bowles and Herbert Gintis, *Democracy and Capitalism* (New York: Basic Books, 1987).
44 Samuel Bowles and Herbert Gintis, *Schooling in Capitalist America* (New York: Basic Books, 1975).

4. *Are blacks to blame?*

1 Claude Steele, "Stigma: Race and the Schooling of Black Americans," *Atlantic Monthly,* April 1992, 68–78.

2 Even William Julius Wilson, author of the *The Truly Disadvantaged,* who does not believe in the individual-responsibility view, cites the Asian-American example to support his "end of racism" argument.

3 "No race that has anything to contribute to the markets of the world is long in any degree ostracized. It is important and right that all privileges of the law be ours, but it is vastly more important that we be prepared for the exercise of those privileges." Booker T. Washington, Address at the Cotton States and International Exposition, Atlanta, September 18, 1895, quoted in Julius Lester (ed.), *The Seventh Son,* vol. 1 (New York: Random House, 1971), p. 43.

4 W. E. B. Du Bois, *Dusk at Dawn,* quoted in Lester, *Seventh Son,* p. 44. Those leaders, according to Du Bois, could come only from the segment of the black community that had the kind of education enjoyed by white leadership. "It would not do," he argued, "to concentrate all effort on economic well-being and forget freedom and manhood and equality. Rather Negroes must live and eat and strive, and still hold unfaltering commerce with the stars."

5 Jonathan Kozol, *Savage Inequalities* (New York: Vantage, 1992).

6 These data are comparable to those for blacks and whites reported in Jaynes and Williams (eds.), *A Common Destiny,* pp. 335–6.

7 Latinos had no such system, although a number of public colleges in states such as Texas eventually became Latino higher education institutions because of the overwhelming numbers of Latinos who attend them.

8 But the proportion of all 18- to 24-year-olds enrolled was 27 percent for whites, 23 percent for blacks, and 20 percent for Latinos. See National Center for Educational Statistics, *The Digest of Educational Statistics, 1992* (Washington, D.C.: U.S. Department of Education, 1992), Table 173.

9 Ibid., Tables 170, 173. See also Jaynes and Williams (eds.), *A Common Destiny,* Figure 7-6.

10 An indicator of this slowdown is that the number of Latinos enrolled in four-year colleges increased by 43,000 in 1976–80 and only 29,000 in 1980–4. National Center for Educational Statistics, *The Digest of Educational Statistics, 1991* (Washington, D.C.: U.S. Department of Education), Table 146. The High School and Beyond survey shows that 7 percent of Latino 1980 high school seniors had received a bachelor's degree or more compared with 10 percent of black seniors and 21 percent of white seniors.

11 Steele, "Stigma," pp. 68–78. The proportion of black and Latino high school graduates, 25 to 34 years old, who had graduated from a four-year college stayed steady at 15 to 16 percent in the 1980s, compared with 29 to 30 percent of whites. But since an average 55 percent of recent white high school graduates, 40 percent of blacks, and 45 percent of Latinos enrolled in college, this means that of the 38 percent of white high school graduates who

enrolled in four-year colleges, about 75 percent graduated; of the 22 percent of blacks in four-year colleges, about 65 percent graduated; and of the 22 percent of Latino high school graduates in four-year colleges, about 65 percent graduated.

12 Beginning in 1950, the black male labor force gained one year of additional schooling for two decades, from 8 to 9 to 10 years in 1970, whereas whites gained about 0.8 year during that time. Thanks to the expansion of college education in the 1970s, blacks leaped up to 11.6 years by 1980 and whites added more than a year to 13 years. This trend slowed for both groups in the 1980s, but blacks continued to gain, reaching 12.4 years in 1990 compared with 13.3 years for whites.

13 We should not forget that, until after World War II, blacks were not even vocationally tested in most places because they were not considered comparable to whites. Early-twentieth-century educators, such as Frederick Terman, creator of the Stanford aptitude test (now known as Stanford–Binet), and Ellwood Cubberley considered blacks to be below the range of scores in the white classification scheme, and so not eligible for vocational testing. See Robert Newby and David Tyack, " 'Victims without Crimes': Some Historical Perspectives on Black Education," *Journal of Negro Education* (Fall 1971): 192–206.

14 See Richard Sennett and Jonathan Cobb, *The Hidden Injuries of Class* (New York: Random House, 1972); Martin Carnoy and Henry Levin, *Schooling and Work in the Democratic State* (Stanford, Calif.: Stanford University Press, 1985); and Steele, "Stigma," pp. 68–78.

15 The California State Department of Education estimates that the number of limited English proficiency students in California schools shot up in the early and middle 1970s, from 168,000 in 1972 to 290,000 in 1976. By 1990, the number had increased to 860,000. A large fraction of these were Latinos.

16 Marshall Smith and Jennifer O'Day, "Educational Equality: 1966 and Now," in Deborah Verstegen and James Q. Ward (eds.), *Spheres of Justice in Education* (New York: Harper Business, 1991), pp. 53–100.

17 Ibid., p. 77.

18 Ibid., pp. 80–4, and Ina Mullis and Lynn Jenkins, *The Reading Report Card, 1971–88* (Washington, D.C.: National Assessment of Educational Progress, Educational Testing Service, 1990).

19 Smith and O'Day, "Educational Equality," p. 82.

20 Jennifer A. O'Day and Marshall S. Smith, "Systemic School Reform and Educational Opportunity," in Susan Fuhrman (ed.), *Designing Coherent Education Policy: Improving the System* (San Francisco: Jossey-Bass, 1993), p. 257.

21 Mullis and Jenkins, *The Reading Report Card.*

22 See I. V. V. Mullis, J. A. Dossey, M. A. Foertsch, L. R. Jones, and C. A. Gentile, *Trends in Academic Progress: Achievement of U.S. Students, in Science, 1969–70 to 1990; Mathematics, 1973–1990; Reading, 1971–1990; and Writing, 1984–1990* (Report No. 21-T-01). Prepared by the Edu-

cational Testing Service for the National Center of Educational Statistics, U.S. Department of Education (Washington, D.C.: U.S. Government Printing Office, 1991).

23 Gary Becker, *Human Capital* (New York: Columbia University Press, 1964).

24 Smith and Welch, "Black Economic Progress After Myrdal."

25 The simulation analysis used to makes these estimates is described in Appendix A.

26 The education gap depicted in Table 4.5 is based on regression estimates where education, work experience, and foreign birth status are the independent variables and log of income is the dependent variable. This is known as the human-capital model. Other variables, such as sector worked in, region worked in, and civil status, are not controlled for.

27 In an addendum to Chapter 9 of the second edition of *The Economics of Discrimination* (Chicago: University of Chicago Press, 1971), Gary Becker discusses the importance of the income distribution effect in the 1940s: "Surely the presumed change in discrimination against Negroes is very different if their relative incomes rose because of their advance into skilled occupations than if they rose because relative earnings in unskilled occupations, where Negroes are heavily represented, rose" (p. 151).

28 Thus, sectoral shifts in the 1940s and 1950s seemed to have an even more powerful impact on minorities' relative economic position than did relative educational gains (see Chapter 5). See also Kiefer and Philips, "Race and Human Capital," Table 6.1, which supports this view.

29 See Jaynes and Williams (eds.), *A Common Destiny*, pp. 334–5, for this same point. The average number of years of schooling increased in the 1980s for different groups approximately as follows:

	1980	1988
White males	12.9	13.3
Latino males	11.1	11.8
Black males	11.5	12.4
White females	12.8	13.2
Latina females	11.5	12.2
Black females	12.1	12.7

30 David Card and Alan Krueger, "Does School Quality Matter? Returns to Education and the Characteristics of Public Schools in the United States," *Journal of Political Economy*, 100, no. 1 (February 1992): 1–40, and Card and Krueger, "School Quality and Black/White Relative Earnings," pp. 151–200.

31 Marlaine Lockheed and Adrian Verspoor, *Improving the Quality of Primary Education* (New York: Oxford University Press for the World Bank, 1991).

32 Card and Krueger, "Does School Quality Matter?"

33 Bowles and Gintis, *Schooling in Capitalist America,* show a small positive relationship. In a more recent review, John Bishop suggests that when the analysis includes only high school graduates who do not go on to college, there is no positive relation between performance in academic subjects and earnings. See John Bishop, "The Economic Consequences of Schooling and Learning," Working Paper 91, Cornell University, Center for Advanced Human Resource Studies, 1992.

34 Frank Levy and Richard Murnane, "Skills, Demography, and the Economy: Is There a Mismatch?" Paper presented at the Milken Institute's Conference on Labor Economics, Employment Policy, and Job Creation, Washington, D.C., November 10–13, 1993.

35 For the measure of economic performance of young men and women with various ethnic origins I used mean hourly wages of all individuals who reported earning income. This measure conforms to the one used by Murnane and Levy and should reflect changes in the market value of labor. The average hourly wages of all workers is more sensitive to business cycles than the average wage of full-time workers, but is more representative of the entire potential labor force of young high school graduates between 16 and 24 years of age than the full-time-worker sample. Nevertheless, the mean hourly wages of full-time young blacks and Latinos relative to those of whites show a pattern similar to that in Table 4.7.

36 Relative wages could also have risen because of decreasing participation by young blacks in the wage labor force – what economists call the "selection effect." Lower participation systematically prevents an increasing proportion of the least employable young blacks from earning any wages at all, and hence raises the relative wages of those remaining, biasing upward estimates of gains. The pattern of relative wages over time shown in Table 4.7 does not fit a steady upward drift due to selection bias, and well it should not. The participation rate of young black men is much lower than whites' but hardly declined in the 1970s and rose slightly in the 1980s. Although young blacks' relative wages in Table 4.7 may be overestimated, the change in the late 1980s is due almost certainly to actual increases in the wages being offered to young blacks compared with whites.

37 The total of black male college graduates earned a median $20,500 at 30 years of age in 1989, compared with $22,900 for blacks employed full time. The corresponding earnings for whites were $28,400 and $31,600.

38 In the early 1980s, 66 percent of men, 25 to 54 years old, and 33 percent of women, 25 to 54 years old, said that they were working part time because they could not find a full-time job. Current Population Reports, *Money Income of Households, Families, and Persons in the United States, 1983,* Series P-60, no. 146 (Washington, D.C.: Department of Commerce, Bureau of the Census, 1983), Table 56.

39 National Center for Educational Statistics, *The Condition of Education, 1993* (Washington, D.C.: U.S. Department of Education, 1993), p. 54.

40 Ibid., p. 56.
41 Felicity Barringer, "White–Black Income Gap Narrows in 80s, Census Shows," *New York Times,* July 25, 1992.
42 See Daniel Goleman, "Probing School Success of Asian-Americans," *New York Times,* September 11, 1990.
43 Alejandro Portes and Robert Bach, *Latin Journey* (Baltimore: Johns Hopkins University Press, 1985).

5. Is the economy to blame?

1 Robert Reich, *The Work of Nations.*
2 High-value services are defined as financial services, insurance, real estate, business, and most repair services, as well as professional services. Low-value services include bar and restaurant work, personal services, custodial services, domestic work, and so forth. There is considerable occupational variation in each of these subsector categories. Blacks, on average, tend to occupy lower work classifications in each subsector and tend to work in the lower-paying subsectors of both high- and low-value services.
3 This is undoubtedly the result of increased Latino immigration in the 1970s and 1980s. Expanding immigration, which brings in non-English speakers with relatively low levels of schooling, is a major explanation for declining Latino relative incomes in this period.
4 This is borne out by the falling relative incomes of black families living in the Midwest in the 1980s as compared with a slight improvement for black family incomes relative to whites' in the country as a whole and rather high gains in some eastern states. See Felicity Barringer, "White–Black Disparity in Income Narrowed in 80s."
5 See Appendix A for an explanation of the simulation model.
6 The total income gap increased 9 percentage points for Latinos in 1969–87 (for both the all-worker and full-time samples), only 4 percentage points of that in the 1980s (3 for full-time Latinos), and 5 percentage points for black males in 1979–87 (only 1 for full-time black males).
7 Even so, we have to be careful in attributing even part of the negative change in relative income to this one variable when other variables are changing simultaneously. Changes in minority–white male education paralleled sectoral employment changes and can also be used to explain the decline in relative minority incomes in this period.
8 See Appendix B for the configuration of the matrix.
9 When we separate out the largest single group of Latinos, those of Mexican origin (MOLs), from the total Latino sample, the figures are even more accentuated than for Latinos as a whole – after a rapid increase in the 1970s, the percentage of MOLs in higher-paying jobs declined in the 1980s from 14.4 percent of all MOLs employed to 13.6 percent. The figures for MOL men and women are as follows:

	1960	1970	1980	1986
Males				
I	11.7	9.4	14.4	13.6
II	29.4	39.5	32.6	30.6
III	58.5	50.7	53.1	55.8
Females				
I	10.0	12.5	16.1	19.3
II	36.0	44.2	39.3	38.4
III	54.0	43.3	44.6	42.4

See Carnoy, Daley, and Hinojosa, *Latinos in a Changing U.S. Economy,* Table 386.

10 Robert Reich, *Work of Nations.*

11 Hugh Daley, a Ph.D. candidate at Stanford University, developed this analysis. He classified census three-digit occupations into four categories – these two plus information repairer-maintainers and those who do not work with information – based on the historical literature regarding occupations that use information in various ways, or do not use it at all.

12 In 1989, the average annual income of a male primary producer of information employed full time was $44,000; that of a secondary user of information, $41,000; that of a repairer-maintainer, $34,000; and that of a non–information user, $25,000.

13 See Bluestone and Harrison, *The Deindustrialization of America,* and Stephen Cohen and John Zysman, *Manufacturing Matters* (New York: Basic Books, 1988).

14 The income data make business claims that increasing skills are required in restructured jobs somewhat hollow. If, on average, operatives in manufacturing needed higher skills to do their jobs in the 1980s and employers were seeking workers in short supply, why were the relative incomes of operatives increasing less than those of other occupational categories in both manufacturing and office services? The real income of white male operatives in manufacturing *fell* 8 to 10 percent in 1979–87 and that of Latinos and blacks fell 12 to 14 percent. Craft workers did only slightly better. For female operatives in manufacturing and clerical workers in office services, there was an income *increase* in the 1980s, and this may be where employers were finding shortages. But even in this case, real incomes hardly went up. White, full-time, female operatives in manufacturing earned, on average, $9,875 annually in 1979 and $15,800 in 1987, a gain that was only slightly larger than the 53 to 57 percent inflation in those eight years. White female full-time clerical workers in office-based services had somewhat higher gains, from $10,460 in 1979 to $17,500 in 1987, but in 1979 dollars, corrected for

inflation, the 1987 figure was only $11,300, an increase of 8 percent. If qualified workers for these jobs were so scarce, why didn't salaries go up more rapidly?

15 Keven Murphy and Finis Welch, "College Premiums for College Graduates: Recent Growth and Possible Explanations," *Educational Researcher,* 18, no. 4 (May 1989): 17–26.

16 Robert Reich, *The Work of Nations.*

17 Russell Rumberger, *Overeducation in the U.S. Labor Market* (New York: Praeger, 1981).

18 Michael Spence, "Job Market Signalling," *Quarterly Journal of Economics,* 87 (August 1973): 355–74.

6. *Have racism and discrimination increased?*

1 Michael Reich, *Racial Inequality.*

2 Bob Blauner, "Talking Past Each Other," *American Prospect,* no. 10 (Summer 1992): 59. See also his *Black Lives, White Lives* (Berkeley and Los Angeles: University of California Press, 1989).

3 The individual-responsibility argument provides one answer to the riddle of why attitudes explain so little. They no longer matter. The marketplace has its own natural logic that values skills according to economic performance and prices. Attitudes of white and black workers toward each other may have had some impact on wages in the past (see Becker, *The Economics of Discrimination*) but have ceased to be a factor. The problem with this argument is that it, too, fails to explain why black incomes stopped rising, especially in the face of rising black skills.

4 Jaynes and Williams (eds.), *A Common Destiny,* p. 289.

5 Ibid., p. 250.

6 See Henry M. Levin, "Ability Testing for Job Selection: Are the Economic Claims Justified?" in Bernard Gifford (ed.), *Test Policy and the Politics of Opportunity Allocation: The Workplace and the Law* (Boston: Kluwer, 1989), pp. 211–32.

7 I call the difference "wage discrimination" because, in both figures, time worked per year is taken into account. The residual therefore measures the difference in *pay rates to the different groups.*

8 There is some evidence that the estimates of the wage gap based on wage discrimination using the full-time sample of men overstate the decline of wage discrimination for blacks in the 1960s and understate the decline in 1973–9. My estimates for the all-income-earner sample (part-time and full-time workers) show a 3 percentage point decline in wage discrimination for black males in 1959–69 versus an 8 percentage point decline for the full-time sample. In 1969–73, both samples show similar declines – 3 percentage points for the full-time sample versus 4 for all earners – and in 1973–9, the full-time-sample estimate of wage discrimination did not fall, whereas the

all-earner estimate declined 4 percentage points. Since the full-time sample is more likely to be subject to selection bias, the rapid decline in black male relative labor force participation rates in the 1960s might explain this difference. But then wage discrimination should also have been higher in the all-earner sample, assuming that this larger group of working men is more similar than the full-time sample to the entire potential work force. This is not the case; wage discrimination as I measure it was higher for full-time black men until the mid-1980s, when it became equal to that of the all-earner sample. A more likely explanation for the steeper drop for full-time blacks is that the core black labor force was the earlier beneficiary of civil rights legislation, and it was not until the 1970s that black men working part time began to feel the affects of wage equalization.

9 Wage discrimination in the labor market for Latino males declined steadily from 1939 to 1969, reaching low levels by the end of that period. But with increased immigration after 1965, wage "discrimination" increased steadily until it was almost the same as that for black males by 1989. A large part of this measured discrimination probably represents immigrants' language problems, but there is also evidence that native-born Latinos also suffered greater wage discrimination in labor markets after 1969. See Carnoy, Daley, and Hinojosa, *Latinos in a Changing U.S. Labor Market.*

10 Smith and Welch, "Black Economic Progress After Myrdal."

11 The figures for 35- to 44-year-old black males were similar in the 1980s. Black males also gained on whites of the same age, especially at the college level. This suggests that the cohort that graduated from college in the late 1960s and early 1970s carried forward their gains from that time until the present.

12 They did best, relatively, at the *lowest* levels of schooling, even though it is true that, in absolute terms, those were the levels losing the most earning capability. One caveat: these figures are for all those who were working. Since black male high school dropouts (and graduates) are much more likely than whites to be unemployed, one large unmeasured effect is the unemployment rate. Yet this should have been at least partially reflected in the relative incomes of black high school dropouts. They rose despite the pressure on wages from high unemployment rates.

13 See Chapter 3 for a discussion of class and caste.

14 In a poll conducted among Hispanics, Chinese, and Filipinos in the San Francisco Bay Area by the *San Francisco Chronicle* (March 27, 1990), only 35 percent of the Hispanic respondents thought that prejudice and discrimination against their group were "a problem" (compared with 46 percent of Chinese and 31 percent of Filipinos), but 49 percent of the Hispanics thought that there was a problem with qualified members of their group rising to the top in local companies and being passed over for promotions (compared with 37 percent of the Chinese respondents and 56 percent of the Filipinos).

15 See Blauner, *Black Lives, White Lives.*

16 Blauner, "Talking Past Each Other," p. 57.

17 *San Francisco Chronicle,* March 27, 1990.

7. *Politics and black educational opportunity*

1 Robert Berne, "Equity Issues in School Finance," *Journal of Education Finance*, 14 (Fall 1988): 159–80.

2 According to David Card and Alan Krueger, southern black schools became more qualitatively equal to white schools beginning in the 1920s, with large gains in the 1940s as black teachers' salaries went up and classes got much smaller. See "Does School Quality Matter?"

3 Carnoy and Levin, *Schooling and Work in the Democratic State.*

4 The main arena where this conflict has come out in the open is the school voucher discussion. Voucher proponents have argued that education should be financed publicly but managed "privately" and in a competitive market for educational services. Most have also recognized that the poor need larger vouchers than the rich and so have argued for voucher amounts inversely correlated with income. See J. Coons and S. Sugarman, *Education by Choice: The Case for Family Control* (Berkeley and Los Angeles: University of California Press, 1978); Milton Friedman, "The Role of Government in Education," in Robert A. Solo (ed.), *Economics and the Public Interest* (New Brunswick, N.J.: Rutgers University Press, 1955), pp. 123–44; Friedman, *Capitalism and Freedom* (Chicago: University of Chicago Press, 1962); and Chubb and Moe, *Politics, Markets, and America's Schools.* See also Henry M. Levin, "The Economics of Educational Choice," *Economics of Education Review*, 10, no. 2 (1991): 137–58.

5 Kozol, *Savage Inequalities.*

6 Card and Krueger, "Does School Quality Matter?"

7 Although this measure does not pick up within-state variation, it does tell us how changing economic and social conditions among regions affected the pool of resources available to black pupils.

8 Card and Krueger claim that this process of school quality equalization had a significant impact on black wages relative to whites', especially in the South. See Card and Krueger, "School Quality and Black/White Relative Earnings."

9 California has not just gone far in equalizing funds to various districts. Even before a restriction of property tax collections imposed in 1976 (Proposition 13), the state was not increasing spending on public education as much as other states. In 1960–75, spending per average daily attendance in California went up 2.7 percent corrected for inflation, compared with 3.9 percent in the United States as a whole. In the 1980s, it rose only 2.1 percent annually, compared with the national average of 2.9 percent.

10 National Coalition of Advocates for Students (NCAS), *Barriers to Excellence: Our Children at Risk* (Boston: NCAS, Board of Inquiry Project, 1985), p. 74.

11 Kozol, *Savage Inequalities*, App. Table 4.

12 Henry M. Levin, "The Necessary and Sufficient Conditions for Achieving Educational Equity," Unpublished paper. Stanford University, School of Education, September 1992, pp. 7–8.

13 George Judson, "Hartford Educators Describe Battle with Poverty in Schools," *New York Times*, December 26, 1992.

14 Chubb and Moe, *Politics, Markets, and America's Schools.*

15 This was Governor Richard Reilly's South Carolina model. School districts got incentive payments for making structural changes that improved pupils' measured performance.

16 National Commission on Excellence in Education, *A Nation at Risk: The Imperative for Educational Reform* (Washington, D.C.: Department of Education, 1983).

17 The California data also show that most school districts spend money in about the same way regardless of their social and economic situations. Some districts spend more on administration and some less, but this is unrelated to the district's wealth or poverty. Does it make sense for districts to allocate resources so similarly when they are so different? It does when states mandate class sizes and required curricula, when teacher unions within a state negotiate salary contracts with each district that are similar, and when categorical monies for special education, bilingual education, and education for the disadvantaged are all tied to certain conditions and administrative requirements. There may not be anything wrong with such uniformity. Even private schools without state requirements are not much different from public schools except in the size of their classes – a reflection of funds available. Catholic schools often have larger classes, although not in California, where a shortage of funds has driven pupil–teacher ratios in public schools steadily upward to the 27 to 32 range in the past ten years. How high the school district sets its standard, how it manages its curriculum, and how committed its teachers are to pupil success seem to be more important than the distribution of funds across spending categories, although small school district administrations may reflect more control of the schooling process by teachers.

18 O'Day and Smith, "Systemic School Reform and Educational Opportunity."

19 See the counterreport to *A Nation at Risk* done a few years later: NCAS, *Barriers to Excellence.*

20 James Coleman, "Choice, Community, and Future Schools," in William Clune and John F. Witte (eds.), *Choice and Control in American Education*, vol. I. (London: Falmer Press, 1990), pp. ix–xxii.

21 When I focus on what affects the incomes associated with various jobs, and then on what impact this has on incomes associated with different levels of education, I implicitly reject the idea that income is attached solely to an individual's education. The incomes associated with jobs are affected by the supply of various levels of education, but we have no way of knowing the demand for education except by looking at the growth in the numbers of workers in certain jobs associated with those levels of education, as I have done. The incomes associated with certain jobs are also affected by government income policies and by who primarily holds the jobs (women, white men, minority men).

22 Murphy and Welch show that the average weekly wage premium for college education rose sharply in the 1980s after falling in the 1970s. The rise was

especially noteworthy for younger (white) workers, indicating that new entrants to the labor force in the 1980s who had completed college were doing increasingly better than high school graduates who had not gone on. See Murphy and Welch, "Wage Premiums for College Graduates: Recent Growth and Possible Explanations."

23 The measure is called the rate of return of education and corresponds to a rate of interest on an investment, where the investment in this case is the income forgone by a student when attending school. It is estimated by a regression analysis where the logarithm of income is the dependent variable and levels of education and work experience (age minus years of schooling minus 7) are the independent variables. The coefficient of each education variable estimates the rate of return of that level relative to the completion of high school, the variable left out.

24 In a labor market where the real income associated with many jobs declined (in the case of men) or grew slowly (women), possessing a negative employment signal (completion of high school or, worse, failure to complete high school) is costly to those individuals who have acquired those signals. Being a young male and having finished high school or less is more disadvantageous than being a female. Being a young Mexican-origin male with a high school education or less makes one more disadvantaged, and being a young black male with a high school education or less puts one in an increasingly worse position, income-wise, in the 1980s, even with respect to MOL workers.

25 Richard Freeman, *Black Elite* (New York: McGraw-Hill, 1976).

26 See, e.g., Wilson, *The Truly Disadvantaged,* chap. 1.

27 In addition to Tables 4.3 and 4.4, see Jaynes and Williams (eds.), *A Common Destiny,* p. 353.

28 Ibid., p. 342.

29 Ibid., Figure 7-6.

30 Ibid., p. 343.

31 Michael McPherson and Morton Owen Schapiro, "Does Student Aid Affect College Enrollment? New Evidence on a Persistent Controversy," *American Economic Review,* 81 (March 1991): 309–18.

32 Jaynes and Williams (eds.), *A Common Destiny.* pp. 343–4.

33 Ibid., p. 343.

34 Ibid., pp. 344–5.

35 The National Assessment of Educational Performance test data show a clear relationship between the level of courses taken by high school students in, say, math and their test performance. See National Center of Educational Statistics, *The Condition of Education, 1993* (Washington, D.C.: U.S. Department of Education, 1993).

8. Politics and black job opportunities: I

1 Martin Carnoy, Robert Girling, and Russell Rumberger, *Education and Public Sector Employment* (Palo Alto, Calif.: Center for Economic Studies, 1976, mimeo).

2 This type of policy is known as neocorporatism. See Phillipe Schmitter, "Still the Century of Corporatism?" in Frederick Pike and Thomas Stritch (eds.), *The New Corporatism* (Notre Dame, Ind.: University of Notre Dame Press, 1974), pp. 85–131. For Swedish wage and growth policy, see Robert Flanagan, "Efficiency and Equality in Swedish Labor Markets," in B. Bosworth and A. Rivlin (eds.), *The Swedish Economy* (Washington, D.C.: The Brookings Institution, 1989), pp. 125–74.

3 See Martin Carnoy, Derek Shearer, and Russell Rumberger, *A New Social Contract* (New York: Harper & Row, 1983).

4 See, e.g., Samuel Bowles, David Gordon, and Thomas Weiskopf, *Beyond the Wasteland* (New York: Anchor Books/Doubleday, 1983).

5 Did the Reagan-Volker shock treatment of 1981–2 have to be as drastic as it was to achieve a reduction in inflation? Many economists think that a less extreme shock would have lowered inflation without such high unemployment rates and such sharp drops in incomes.

6 It is important to remember that these are the incomes of people who had jobs – who were employed at least part time in a period when there was high employment among blacks.

7 Bluestone and Harrison, *The Deindustrialization of America;* Carnoy, Shearer, and Rumberger, *A New Social Contract.*

8 Alejandro Portes, Manuel Castells, and Lauren Benton, *The Informal Economy* (Baltimore: Johns Hopkins University Press, 1989).

9 For a summary of these practices and their patterns among different types of industries, see Susan Christopher, "Emerging Patterns of Work in the U.S.," Paper presented to the OECD Working Group on Technological Change and Human Resources, Columbia University, New York, September 1988; and William Goldsmith and Edward Blakely, *Separate Societies* (Philadelphia: Temple University Press, 1992).

10 Harrison and Bluestone, *The Great U-Turn,* p. 51. See also Paul Weiler, "Striking a New Balance: Freedom of Contract and the Prospects for Union Representation," *Harvard Law Review,* 98, no. 2 (1984): 351–420.

11 Harrison and Bluestone, *The Great U-Turn,* pp. 64–5.

12 Goldsmith and Blakely, *Separate Societies,* p. 144; Albert Hirschman, *The Rhetoric of Reaction* (Cambridge, Mass.: Harvard University Press, 1991).

13 David Card, "Using Regional Variation in Wages to Measure the Effects of the Federal Minimum Wage," *Industrial and Labor Relations Review,* 46, no. 1 (October 1992): 22–37; Card, "Do Minimum Wages Reduce Employment? A Case Study of California, 1987–89," *Industrial and Labor Relations Review,* 46, no. 1 (October 1992): 38–54.

14 Martin Carnoy, "The Labor Market in Silicon Valley and Its Implications for Education," Project Report no. 85–A8, Stanford University, Institute of Finance and Governance, May 1985.

15 Carnoy, Girling, and Rumberger, *Education and Public Employment.*

16 Ibid. I reported in Table 2.2 that the relative incomes of 25- to 34-year-old black male college graduates rose markedly in the 1960s and 1970s. The proportion of blacks in the labor force with a completed college education

who worked in the public sector was already high in 1959, but the public employment expansion of the 1960s made the percentage even higher. Further, black–white salaries in the public sector for college graduates were less discriminatory well before the later (1970s) equalization in the private sector.

17 Goldsmith and Blakely, *Separate Societies*, pp. 150–1.

18 Ibid., p. 151.

19 Ibid.

20 See Moynihan, *On Understanding Poverty.*

21 Nicholas Lemann, "The Unfinished War," *Atlantic Monthly*, January 1989, pp. 37–56.

22 Goldsmith and Blakely, *Separate Societies*, p. 155.

23 According to Alejandro Portes and Richard Bach, legal immigrants after 1965 were only one-third European compared with 50 percent the decade before. Asian immigrants had been only 2 percent of the total in 1950, but one-third in the 1970s. Portes and Bach, *Latin Journey.*

24 Recent estimates by the Department of Labor confirm that immigrants are becoming a more important factor in the filling of new jobs. According to these estimates, the number of immigrants more than doubled between 1950 and 1988, and they accounted for 11 percent of labor force growth in the 1970s and 22 percent of the increase in the 1980s. U.S. Department of Labor, Bureau of International Labor Affairs, Report no. 89-341, July 1989.

25 This is the official government position. The Department of Labor contends that immigrants do not *replace* existing workers. Ibid.

26 Carnoy, Dale, and Hinojosa, *Latinos in the Changing U.S. Economy*, p. 47.

27 Jack Miles, "Black versus Brown," *Atlantic Monthly*, October 1992, pp. 41–68.

28 Manuel Pastor, Jr., *Latinos and the Los Angeles Uprising: The Economic Context* (Claremont, Calif: Tomas Rivera Center, Claremont Graduate School, 1993), Figure 23.

29 A more detailed analysis of the riot areas shows that the labor force participation rates in South Central Los Angeles are much lower for black males than for Latinos – 58 percent compared with 80 percent (ibid). Looked at another way, black male full-time employment rates among 25- to 64-year-olds in the Los Angeles area were much lower than the Asian, white, or Latino rates: only 50 percent of blacks were full-time, full-year-employed in 1989–91 compared with 70 percent of Asian males, 65 percent of white males, and 60 percent of Latinos. But black women had among the highest full-time rates: 41 percent were full-time, full-year workers – more than the 38 percent of white women or the 30 percent of Latinas.

30 Paul Ong, "Neighborhoods, Poverty, and Race," in Eulalio Castellanos et al., *The Widening Divide: Income Inequality and Poverty in Los Angeles* (Los Angeles: The Research Group on the Los Angeles Economy, June 1989). In economic terms, blacks' "reservation wage" may be higher than the prevailing wage for jobs they could get, given their skills. The result is the same – black participation rates go down – but in the first case it is because whites do not

want to hire them, and in the second because they are not applying for low-wage jobs. In the first, rising wages would not change the outcome, but in the second, they might.

9. *Politics and black job opportunities: II*

1 See, e.g., Friedman and Friedman, *Free to Choose,* and Murray, *Losing Ground.*

2 Becker, *The Economics of Discrimination.*

3 Reich, *Racial Inequality.*

4 Jim Crow laws that kept minorities of color out of white public facilities, residential areas, and business establishments originated in the North. By 1830, slavery was virtually abolished there, and northern free blacks had obvious advantages over southern slaves. But northern blacks were segregated systematically from whites on all means of transportation, in theaters and lecture halls, in churches, and often in schools, prisons, hospitals, and cemeteries. Only 6 percent of northern blacks lived in the five states – Massachusetts, New Hampshire, Vermont, Maine, and Rhode Island – that by 1860 permitted them to vote. Before the Civil War, Abraham Lincoln himself made clear in 1858 that "I am not nor ever have been in favor of bringing about in any way the social and political equality of the white and black races . . . that I am not nor ever have been in favor of making voters or jurors of negroes, nor of qualifying them to hold office, nor to intermarry with white people, and I will say in addition to this that there is a physical difference between the black and white races which I believe will forever forbid the two races living together on terms of social and political equality." See C. Vann Woodward, *The Strange Career of Jim Crow* (New York: Oxford University Press, 1966), p. 21.

5 Northern liberals tolerated and even abetted these measures because they appeared to be rooted in political necessities – necessities bound up with business interests in the North and the South and with the largest white labor organization, the American Federation of Labor, which had excluded blacks since the 1890s.

6 Portes and Bach, *Latin Journey,* p. 47.

7 Asian-Americans' wages were systematically lower than whites', controlling for education and experience, even as late as the 1970s. Whether this was due to enclave employment (limited the extent of the market) or discrimination in the white-dominated labor market, or both, is impossible to determine. Wage discrimination did decline in the 1960s and 1970s as Asian-Americans were increasingly hired outside their economic enclaves.

8 Girardeau Spann, *Race and Positive Politics* (Washington, D.C.: Georgetown University Law Center, November 1989, mimeo).

9 For the record, there are those who believe that the decision made no difference at all. See, e.g., Gerald Rosenberg, *The Hollow Hope* (Chicago: University of Chicago Press, 1991), for an insufficiently nuanced account of this major political event.

10 Bowles and Gintis, *Democracy and Capitalism.*
11 Freeman, *Black Elite.*
12 Smith and Welch, "Black Economic Progress After Myrdal," p. 555.
13 Ibid.
14 John Donohue III and James Heckman, "Continuous Versus Episodic Change: The Impact of Affirmative Action and Civil Rights Policy on the Economic Status of Blacks," *Journal of Economic Literature,* 29 (December 1991): 1603–43.
15 Ibid. In Donohue and Heckman's words: "With the greatest relative black improvement coming in the South, which was the target of a comprehensive federal effort to dismantle segregation in schooling, voting, accommodations and employment, the inference is buttressed that federal civil rights policy was the major contributor to the discontinuous improvement in black economic status that began in 1965" (p. 1641).
16 Thomas A. DiPrete and David Grusky, "Structure and Trends in the Process of Stratification for American Men and Women," *American Journal of Sociology,* 96, no. 1 (1990): 107–43.
17 Jaynes and Williams (eds.), *A Common Destiny,* p. 319.
18 None of the relative income gains of the all-worker Latino sample appears to be explained by reduced wage discrimination. When we divide the Mexican-origin Latino sample into native- and foreign-born, we find that this also holds true for native-born MOLs, but that 50 percent of the foreign-born's gains in 1960–70 are explained by lower wage discrimination.
19 Even that part of relative income increases not explained by higher relative payoffs is explained by more than just increased minority education. It is accounted for by a combination of relative gains in years of minority education, relative shifts into higher-paying industries, and a relative increase in the time minorities got to work during the year – an indirect effect of lower unemployment rates in the 1960s.
20 See John Bishop, "The Economic Consequences of Schooling and Learning," Working Paper no. 91, Cornell University, Center for Advanced Human Resource Studies, 1992.
21 Justice Thurgood Marshall, opinion in *International Brotherhood of Teamsters v. United States,* 431 U.S. 324, 381 (1976), quoted in Eleanor Holmes Norton, "Equal Employment Law: Crisis in Interpretation – Survival Against the Odds," *Tulane Law Review,* 62, no. 4 (March 1988): 681–715, n. 34, p. 689.
22 Norton, "Equal Employment Law," p. 693.
23 Ibid., p. 694.
24 Remarks of Thurgood Marshall, associate justice, Supreme Court of the United States at the Second Circuit Judicial Conference, September 1989.
25 In those years, Republican administrations tended to go after discrimination in unions rather than businesses, but that still reflected the national sense that citizen rights should be extended to equal opportunity in the marketplace and that there were plenty of victims of such discrimination. The

business community also supported "goals and timetables" established under Nixon's 1972 executive order, once it was clear that numerical remedies were here to stay.

For business, no imposed hiring rules whatever are the best of all worlds, but if hiring rules exist, a simple, well-defined set is better than ambiguity and confusion. Eleanor Holmes Norton spells out the reasons: "Had goals been removed from Executive Order No. 11246, many states would have moved into the vacuum, creating a nightmare for companies trying to comply in multiple jurisdictions. Federal legislation mandating goals and timetables would have been introduced. Without the Executive Order requirement of goals, employers would have been vulnerable to discrimination charges. Finally, of course, minorities and women compose more than half the work force today, and white males continue to diminish as a source of skilled workers. "Equal Employment Law," p. 714.

26 Ibid., p. 703.

27 Ibid., p. 704.

28 Donohue and Heckman's work suggests that since the gains from affirmative action between 1965 and 1980 were limited to the South, labor market affirmative action may yield little future mileage. They may be right, but continued declines in wage discrimination in the 1980s suggest that although conditions in northern labor markets and northern cities may require different efforts, including significant changes in minority community responsibilities, more extensive institution building, and job programs, discrimination can continue to decline with legal support. Furthermore, the upturn in discrimination at the end of the decade suggests that undoing legal support can reverse wage discrimination.

29 Lawrence Mishel and Jared Bernstein, "Declining Wages for High School and College Graduates," Economic Policy Institute, Washington, D.C., September 1992. Since higher-educated women's wages rose and high-school-educated women's wages fell from 1987 to 1992, it is inferred that white women did better than black.

30 An additional aspect of black political confusion emerged from guilt about affirmative action. The conservative attack in the 1980s on affirmative action both in universities and in the labor market began to make some blacks uneasy about being viewed as making gains "unfairly" – not on the basis of merit. Indeed, the individual-responsibility rhetoric since the *Bakke* decision had created an atmosphere on university campuses in which many whites felt that blacks were there only because of preferential treatment. In response some blacks sense that their very achievements are suspect because they are black and successful. Further, they accuse white employers of a new kind of discrimination: not hiring highly competent blacks who are unwilling to represent black interests or the "black position" in whatever firm they are working. Such employers are apparently interested only in "black" blacks, not "white" blacks. For a description of all these issues, see Stephen Carter, *Reflections of an Affirmative Action Baby* (New York: Basic Books, 1991).

31 Marshall, September 1989, p. 4.
32 Ibid., p. 5.

10. Black economic gains and ideology: The White House factor

1 Card and Krueger, "School Quality and Black/White Relative Earnings."
2 See Figures 1a and 1b for the 1950s versus the 1960s and 1970s, and see Freeman, *Black Elite,* for the early 1960s versus the period after 1965. Donohue and Heckman, "Continuous Versus Episodic Change," also show the rise in income in the late 1960s.
3 Stephen Michaelson, "Rational Income Decisions of Blacks and Everybody Else," *Industrial and Labor Relations Review,* 23, no. 1 (October 1969): 15–28.
4 Card and Krueger, "School Quality and Black/White Relative Earnings."
5 Donohue and Heckman, "Continuous Versus Episodic Change."
6 In addition to Ickes and Eleanor Roosevelt, the black cause had a number of southern liberal supporters in the administration. They came from a tradition that had arisen with the postbellum southern bourgeoisie – a bourgeoisie that wanted to modernize the South and saw Negro education as fundamental to that goal. Clark Foreman and Edwin Embree, both of the Julius Rosenwald Fund (Rosenwald had founded Sears Roebuck), George Mitchell of the Resettlement and Farm Security Administration, Aubrey Williams of the Federal Emergency Relief Administration and later head of the National Youth Administration, and Will Alexander, head of the Farm Security Administration were just some of the southern activists who became influential in improving the racial climate during the Roosevelt years.

Although they did not necessarily agree on a strategy to improve blacks' conditions, the New Deal approach they developed was to include blacks in federal programs and, through such inclusion, to improve their class status. At another level, New Deal southerners saw black salvation in improving economic conditions in the South. Through massive federal programs, the South could be modernized, and with modernization, southern rural poor could be given the opportunity "to live decently where they are" (John B. Kirby, *Black Americans in the Roosevelt Era* [Knoxville: University of Tennessee Press, 1980], p. 55). They believed that blacks were inherently capable of performing the same tasks as white workers, citing black domination of skilled trades in the South before the Civil War. It was only because of years of segregation and racial discrimination that they had lost that capability. Recovering it meant only giving them the opportunity to do so.
7 Myrdal, *An American Dilemma,* p. 74.
8 Kirby, *Black Americans in the Roosevelt Era,* p. 22.
9 Ibid., p. 32.
10 Myrdal's study projects this same sense of optimism, and for good reasons. He believed in the welfare state, and many of his staff members and consultants on the study were white and black reformer-liberals intimately involved

in the New Deal. The idea that the American creed is based on a fundamental sense of democracy and justice has strong appeal, and he found evidence of that creed as he traveled around the country. Once they accepted that white Americans were basically just, Myrdal and the New Dealers assumed that racism was a blind spot that could be eliminated by changing the economic and social conditions of blacks and whites.

11 John Hope Franklin, *From Slavery to Freedom: A History of Negro Americans*, 5th ed. (New York: Knopf, 1980), p. 426.

12 Ibid., p. 427.

13 Ibid., pp. 438–9.

14 William Manchester, *The Glory and the Dream* (Boston: Little, Brown, 1973), p. 734.

15 Earnings for Hispanics are not available from annual Current Population Surveys for the 1950s.

16 Since the shift from agriculture to urban employment had slowed (but certainly not stopped) for blacks in the 1950s, and education equalization was positive though not large, it would have taken a significant reduction of wage discrimination or some other equalization to improve blacks' relative incomes during the decade. For black workers as a whole – men and women – this did not happen. Higher relative black education and the smaller shift out of agriculture were not enough by themselves to raise relative incomes.

17 Manchester, *Glory*, p. 935.

18 Ibid., p. 936.

19 Ibid., p. 981.

20 Title VII of the act established the Equal Employment Opportunity Commission (EEOC) to monitor compliance by the private-sector firms covered by the legislation, and a year later, President Johnson issued an executive order that prohibited discrimination by race on government contracts. From 1966 on, all private firms with a hundred or more employees and federal contractors with fifty or more employees and $50,000 or larger federal contracts were required to report their employment in each of nine broad occupational categories by race–sex group. The EEOC covered about half of all workers in the labor force. A 1972 amendment to the act extended coverage to all firms with fifteen or more employees. In the 1970s, the EEOC was also given the power to sue alleged discriminators in court.

21 Manchester, *Glory*, p. 1021.

22 Moynihan recounts this shift in his book *Family and Nation*. Unfortunately, the Moynihan version of the problem was, correctly or incorrectly, couched in terms of the disintegration of the black family and the need for a family-based income assistance policy. In the militant 1960s, this formulation had overtones unacceptable to most blacks. Yet the more likely reason Moynihan's ideas were never put into practice was the resistance of white voters to allocate funds to the reduction of black poverty. This problem is treated in more detail in Chapter 3.

23 See, e.g., Harrison and Bluestone, *The Great U-Turn*.

24 Thomas Byrne Edsall and Mary Edsall, *Chain Reaction* (New York: Norton, 1991), pp. 11, 13.
25 For Panetta's critical account of Nixon's civil rights policy, see his *Bring Us Together* (Philadelphia: Lippincott, 1971).
26 Richard Nixon, quoted in Rowland Evans, Jr., and Robert Novak, *Nixon in the White House* (New York: Random House, 1971), p. 171.
27 Ibid., p. 175.
28 Ibid., p. 224. Later, in 1970 and again in 1972, Nixon would unleash Spiro Agnew and himself against the other working-class shibboleth, antiwar, upper-middle-class youth. The law-and-order issue, as it came to be known, also entered the stock Republican social rhetoric used to lure the working class away from the Democratic Party.
29 Moynihan based these conclusions on the results of a number of studies that had emerged from program evaluations showing low returns to the very poor of education and training and on the idea that the government should have a family-based policy rather than one oriented toward individuals. He has since solidified his stance and continues to be a champion of a family-based antipoverty policy. See his *Family and Nation.*
30 Edsall and Edsall, *Chain Reaction,* p. 198.
31 Kevin Phillips, *The Politics of Rich and Poor* (New York: Random House, 1990); Harrison and Bluestone, *The Great U-Turn.*
32 Edsall and Edsall, *Chain Reaction,* p. 165.
33 David Ellwood, *Poor Support* (New York: Basic Books, 1988), p. 32.
34 Randy Albeda, Elaine McCraite, Edwin Melendez, and June Lapidus, *Mink Coats Don't Trickle Down* (Boston: Center for Popular Economics and South End Press, 1988), Figure 3.3, p. 33.
35 Edsall and Edsall, *Chain Reaction,* chap. 10.
36 Randy Albeda et al., *Mink Coats Don't Trickle Down,* p. 37.
37 This is epitomized by Charles Murray's position regarding welfare. See his *Losing Ground.*
38 Edsall and Edsall, *Chain Reaction.*

11. Is there any hope for greater equality?

1 Maya Angelou, "On the Pulse of Morning," inaugural poem. Taken from the *San Jose Mercury News,* January 21, 1993.
2 See John J. Donohue III and Peter Siegelman, "The Changing Nature of Employment Discrimination Litigation," *Stanford Law Review,* 43, no. 5 (May 1991): 983–1033. Donohue and Siegelman argue that greater benefits would come directly from having class-action failure-to-hire cases, which almost disappeared under Republican control of the Justice Department, instead of the individual discriminatory discharge cases that dominated in the 1980s and may even act to hold back employers from hiring minorities.
3 Edsall and Edsall, *Chain Reaction,* p. 282. See also Christopher Jencks, *Rethinking Social Policy: Race, Poverty, and the Underclass* (Cambridge, Mass.: Harvard University Press, 1992).

4 Edsall and Edsall, *Chain Reaction,* p. 272.
5 Martin Carnoy, "Is Privatization the Answer?" in Jane Hannaway and Martin Carnoy (eds.), *Decentralization and School Improvement* (San Francisco: Jossey-Bass, 1993), pp. 163–201.
6 Edsall and Edsall, *Chain Reaction,* p. 274.
7 See Donald Harris, "A Model of the Productivity Gap: Convergence or Divergence?" in Ross Thomson (ed.), *Learning and Technological Change* (New York: St. Martin's, 1992), pp. 100–16.
8 The shortcomings of a "supply-side" approach to training should be obvious. If there are no jobs to employ retrained workers, they will not be able to use their new training. See Peter Kilborn, "After a Town's Jobs Went South: A Program to Retrain Has Pitfalls," *New York Times,* November 6, 1993.
9 James E. Rosenbaum et al., *Youth Apprenticeship in America: Guidelines for Building an Effective System* (Washington, D.C.: William T. Grant Foundation Commission on Youth and America's Future, 1992).
10 Dieter Timmerman, "Costs and Financing Dual Training in Germany: Is There Any Lesson for Other Countries?" Paper presented at the International Symposium on the Economics of Education, Manchester, England, May 19–21, 1993.
11 See Tony Carnavale and Eric Schulz, "Return on Investment: Accounting for Training," Supplement to the *Training and Development Journal* (July 1990): S-1–S-32. They show that few companies in the United States devote significant portions of their payroll costs to training.
12 Barry Meier, "Reality and Anxiety: Lives Changed Not Just by Crime but by Fear," *New York Times,* February 18, 1993.
13 Ibid.
14 See Wilson, *The Truly Disadvantaged.* Wilson argues that the declining real incomes and employment possibilities for black men in the 1980s were a primary factor in the continued disintegration of the black family.

Index